Encore

Crucial Conversations
A Reckoning
Anger
The Magnificent Spinster
The Education of Harriet Hatfield

NONFICTION

I Knew a Phoenix
Plant Dreaming Deep
Journal of a Solitude
A World of Light
The House by the Sea
Recovering: A Journal
At Seventy: A Journal
After The Stroke: A Journal
Writings on Writing
May Sarton—A Self-Portrait
Endgame: A Journal of the Seventy-ninth year

FOR CHILDREN

Punch's Secret
A Walk Through the Woods

Gateway

Encore

A Journal of the Eightieth Year

By *May Sarton*

W · W · Norton & Company · New York · London

Copyright © 1993 by May Sarton
All rights reserved
Printed in the United States of America
First Edition

The text of this book is composed in Caledonia,
with the display set in Garamond Italic.
Composition and manufacturing by the Haddon Craftsmen, Inc.

Library of Congress Cataloging-in-Publication Data
Sarton, May, 1912–
    Encore : a journal of the eightieth year / by May Sarton.—1st ed.
        p. cm.
    1. Sarton, May, 1912– —Diaries. 2. Authors, American—20th
century—Diaries. 3. Aged women—United States—Diaries.
I. Title.
PS3537.A832Z4647 1993
  818'.5203—dc20
[B] 92–40014

ISBN 0-393-03529-8

W. W. Norton & Company, Inc., 500 Fifth Avenue, New York, N.Y. 10110
W. W. Norton & Company Ltd., 10 Coptic Street, London WC1A 1PU

1 2 3 4 5 6 7 8 9 0

For Susan Sherman

Encore

Sunday, May 5, 1991

I⊤ is the second day of my eightieth year. The journal of my seventy-ninth year will come out for my eightieth birthday, but I want to go on for a while longer discovering what is really happening to me by keeping a journal.

The great good news is that I continue to have less pain and therefore have all kinds of hopes and plans and even dream of getting back once more to England. Even if that is only a dream I did not have dreams like that during the time of the pain which was for nearly a year. One good augury for this eightieth year: one of the florists who brought flowers for my birthday came rather late—I think it was after five—and said she had seen an enormous turtle, tortoise, crossing the road. I rejoiced because this turtle was here long before I came. She is thought to be one hundred years old. Every year about this time she crosses the place to find, I presume, a nest for her eggs. We never see her during the rest of the year.

Yesterday was a day that brought me friends whom I really think of as family, who come every year, Anne Woodson and Barbara Barton. This year it was the day after my birthday, on purpose, because I knew that there would be a great deal happening on the actual day. I needed what solitude I could get if only to decide where all the flowers should go and in some cases to arrange them. By the end of the day seventeen deliveries of flowers had been made to this house—it does seem incredible—from three different florists. I must say that Forster's is by far the most imaginative. The thing I loved most, because there were lots of plants as well as flowers, is a moth orchid Martha Wheelock sent me from Hollywood. Janice brought me a videotape of Martha's wonderful Ishtar film of me, *World of Light: A Portrait of May Sarton,* which, until now, has been available only as a sixteen-millimeter movie. Nobody could see it unless they had a projector, screen, and all that. So this is a treat. It was such a perfect day, I think it may have been the best birthday I have ever had.

Anne and Barbara were out in the garden talking to Diane, the gardener, who was planting fifteen lilies for me—against the terrace wall and some against the fence. Anne and Barbara came early—such a wonderful thing—I was rather tired by then because I had been walking around, setting the table, and all that. I had been on my feet for more than three hours, which proves that I am getting better. Anyway they brought, as they always do—and oh, how I love these traditions!—a hanging fuchsia. It hangs over the border that I see from my chaise longue, that little center of life.

The whole luncheon was homemade because Janice actually made the lobster rolls. They were the most delicious I have ever had. Of course lobster is not on my diet. It is naughty but apparently it has done me no harm. Edythe had brought a superb angel cake with lemon frosting. It was so close it could be cut with a knife. Nancy brought the chocolate sauce and it turned out to be from a recipe of her mother's. All this was joyful and merry. I had a little glass of champagne—again, against the rules—but it had an enormous effect. I have not had any alcohol for a month so I became very vocal—voluble is more the word—and began to talk about Brad Daziel's preface to the book he edited, *Sarton Selected.*

Brad wrote this preface originally for something else—for Connie Hunting—and it was to deal with the letters I get. He never got down to what I wanted so the preface is beautiful but it is not what I wanted. I would like to say here, as I did after half a glass of champagne yesterday, what I did want. I

did not want letters, and there are many of them, that talk
about how wonderful my work is and praise it—they are so
welcome—I did not want letters from famous people. And
that, I had told Brad, is not the point either. What is the point?
The point for me was the letters that say "You have changed
my life," or "You helped my mother die," "You have made
my father able to read again because he got so interested, and
he had stopped reading." "My little son said"—this is going
back to praising so I should not even quote it but I cannot
resist—"my little son, nine years old, said, 'It's the best book
I've ever read.'" That was *The Fur Person*.

These letters are in a folder called "Total Work." They
very often tell a life story. It is partly the people who have
come to accept their sexual differences, been able to accept
that it is not a sin to love a woman, that like any love, it can be
good love or bad. Like any marriage it can be a good marriage
or bad. I have given courage to some of them and to many
people—this is more dubious—the ambition to write. Very
often they are middle-aged and have neither any idea of what
good writing is nor the power to criticize their own writing.
That is sad.

After the guests had left it was still early, because Anne
and Barbara got here at eleven, so I had a wonderful rest.
They did all the clearing up before they left. Then I had the
enormous joy of sauntering around the garden, looking at the
plants that were coming up. I had thought the garden was a
disaster area but found that a great deal had come up. There
have been some losses. Every year the tree peonies suffer a
little more, except for one tall, thin one protected by juniper
bushes. It is going to have two or three flowers this year. They
are white—the white, God-like tree peonies. It looks as if the
columbine has more or less gone. I may find some at a nursery
where Nancy and I are going to buy perennials on Tuesday. It
is her birthday present to me. I can't wait.

Also on that afternoon—and this was a celebration of my return to being myself—I put in four little Johnny-jump-ups that had been waiting for help. I have not been able to garden for a year, so this was a triumphant moment.

Monday, May 6

ALTHOUGH IT is now gray, and rain is coming, the day began beautifully early this morning. I have been having rather tiring mornings because they begin at three A.M. when the cat demands to go out. Today he jumped on my stomach—it hurt—before three, but I let him out. Then I came back and rested for a while. Then I let him in at six and got the tray ready for Joan, one of my helpers, who comes today. There seem to be endless things to do.

I have tuberous begonias growing under a light I bought, right next to me here in the little library, but I have to keep remembering to turn the light on and off and to water them. It becomes another chore. Of course on the weekend there was nobody here so I had to do everything, make my bed, put out the bird feeder. But the great news is that I do have more strength. I was able to take out all the dead climbing hydrangea flowers that were stuck in among the new growth. That is right beside the side door which everybody uses to come in and out of this house. All through that climbing hydrangea, which is, I guess, a good twenty feet high now, there is a beautiful small red clematis. The danger is when you pull out dead dry stuff you might break one of those delicate stems of the clematis. I think I did all right.

The big event of the day was the arrival of Tony and his wife and his little granddaughter. They came to look at the daffodils and to see me here which they have never done. We have tried a couple of times but, for one reason or another, it has not worked. I inscribed a book for Tony which said: "To Tony, whom I think of as my brother at the P.O." He is the most cheerful, helpful man imaginable. He knows everybody by name; he knows what their problems are. He has been tremendously supportive of me during my illness. He said a very nice thing; he said, "All the people who work for you are so nice and so polite."

Sometimes when I have to send someone to get the mail, they don't have the key to my box and have to ask for it. Tony is always welcoming. We talked quite a lot about it; he explained to me that he realized that the post office has to welcome its clientele because otherwise it would not have a clientele. People would drop off. Everybody loves Tony. Everybody feels the post office is a friendly place. That's a real triumph. He should get a prize from Uncle Sam!

I did not know that he and his wife had adopted their granddaughter, Kirsten Lynn Glidden, two and a half years old and a charming child, with beautiful manners and a mischievous look. She was the sort of little girl whom one immediately wants to spoil. I let her play with the puppet rabbit from F.A.O. Schwarz and she loved it. I could tell she was reluctant to leave it. But the daffodils were the lure and when Tony, his wife, and Kirsten left, they picked bunches of them. It was lovely to have them here. I hope they will come back and that I may see that little girl grow up.

Tomorrow Nancy and I are going to get the plants. The whole season is beginning. The miniature roses must go in but this morning with the gray sky the temperature cannot be over fifty. I worry about the fuchsia but it seems to be thriving. It can take a lot of cool. Of course they grow wild in Ireland where it can be quite cool at night, especially in the winter.

The daffodils are splendiferous this year. I don't know why I thought they were not going to be. Perhaps it was because it has been a slow spring. Now it is paradise and I want to say, "Stay! Don't go so soon!" So perhaps it is a good thing that it is cold. Even the rain will be welcome.

Tuesday, May 7

A wild, miserable wind and rain storm yesterday, so strong that when I went out to get the feeder I was afraid I would not be able to open the door so I could get back in—a frightening moment. And misery to see the daffodils beaten down, every thing at its height. However, we did need the rain.

Yesterday was a day of triumph and great joy because Connie Hunting sent me the essay that she used in her talk on my poetry at the celebration of my seventy-ninth birthday at Westbrook College on May second. It was so moving to me to see someone get at the center of what my poetry is all about. It has been neglected for many years. She starts out by quoting part of a poem of mine: "These are not hours of fire but years of praise, / The glass full to the brim, completely full, / But held in balance so no drop can spill."° And she says:

> The primary source of May Sarton's poetic power is the lyric impulse. Deep, authentic, never-failing, it has continued for sixty years to feed the river of her poetry, which is, above all, a poetry of praise.

°"Because What I Want Most Is Permanence," *The Land of Silence*, 1954.

The lyric impulse arises not from ordinary, everyday emotions, which play like rainbows over the surface of the pool of being, but from the wellspring of pure, or *essential,* emotion which exists in the most profound depths of our spirit. It is the vibration of these depths that makes for lyric poetry and the musicality of its expression. Orpheus's lyre is implicit in the poetry named for it.

I rested on this as on the arrival after a long journey, or like somebody who has completed a marathon and is being greeted at the end. It brought back immediately Rilke and his marvelous poem about the poet and what the poet is all about. In the version I have the translation is by Leishman. It is not the best translation, but I do not have the original so I shall make this do:

> Oh, tell us, poet, what you do?
>   —I praise.
> But those dark, deadly, devastating ways,
> how do you bear them, suffer them?
>   —I praise.
> And then the Nameless, beyond guess or gaze,
> how can you call it, conjure it?
>   —I praise.
> And whence your right, in every kind of maze,
> in every mask, to remain true?
>   —I praise.
> And that the mildest and the wildest ways
> know you like star and storm?
>   —Because I praise.°

I used to read that poem often when I was reading at colleges, but I have not gone back to it for some time.

°"For Leonie Zacharias," Muzot, 20 December 1921. *Rainer Maria Rilke; Poems 1906 to 1926.* Translated with an Introduction by J. B. Leishman. New Directions, 1957.

Thursday, May 9

AGAIN a magnificent day. I hope Nancy and I can put in the
lobelias along the little terrace border. I put in eight miniature
roses—Edythe's yearly present for my birthday, and so welcome—and they are also on the inside border of the terrace. I
did it quietly, although it had been a driven day for various
reasons and I wondered whether I had the energy. I said to
myself maybe put two of them in, but as soon as I got the tools
and water together and had on my work clothes and went out
there and lay down on the ground—that is the only way I can
plant now because I cannot stoop—suddenly time opened up
and I was completely at peace and happy.

It was not all a bad day because Connie Lloyd, Judy's
sister, now eighty-nine, Judy's nephew, Tim Warren, and his
wife, Phyllis, those three, who are like family, came to say
hello. They wanted to tell me about the Westbrook occasion
which they had greatly enjoyed. I wanted to show them the
video made in Gainesville, *Creativity in the Upward Years*.
We did laugh, Connie and I, and all of us, about the "upward
years."

Before that I knew that I would have to get some advice
from an electrician so Susan can experiment with the juicer
that Dr. Khanjani has been so anxious that I have. I am not
eager to use it and I think Susan will have to run it when she is
here for the summer. But I thought I'd better get it ready so I
called Bruce Woods. He is one of the kindest, dearest of the
men who work around here. Jim Cote, who took care of the

storm windows, was the other one whom I loved so much, but I think whoever does it now is just as friendly.

Bruce came at ten, much earlier than he had promised. The Warrens and Connie were coming at eleven. I thought I had an hour to do a thousand things; everything has piled up. I write eight or nine thank-you notes a day, but that is only a little bit of what has to be done. I am also packing books to send to friends. Nancy offered to do this but she is finishing the transcription of the dictated journal, which is more important. I must do the preface soon and choose the photographs.

Everything drives me a little too hard these days. In a funny way what drives me is the spring, the fleeting spring. Because of the enormous wind and rain we have had, a lot of the daffodils have blown down, though not as many as I had feared. But the truth is that their peak is past. We shall have them for another week and then they will be gone. It seems quite unbearable but that is what spring is—the letting go. The waiting and waiting and waiting, and then the letting go.

I wanted to go back to Wednesday because I did not do the journal. I was too busy and went to Dr. Khanjani as well. It began with a terrible thunderous heartbeat when I heard the bell of the rubbish-collecting truck at seven. It used to come at seven-thirty but I missed the announcement that it would be at seven from now on. So I dashed out of bed, threw on a wrapper, and ran out. Fortunately the man in the truck was still waiting. He had his name, Dave, on his shirt, so I thanked him warmly. He said, "I'll bring it out for you," and I showed him how to lift the garage door. He has offered to get the rubbish there so we won't have to drag it out. This is an event which soon will include the recycling bin.

After that, the day jogged along too fast. I went to Dr. Khanjani and that always makes for hurry, but I thought about the kindness of Dave and the kindness of Bruce and realized that York is a very munificent town judging by the people who work here: the carpenters, the rubbish collectors. How kind they are! And also the UPS people, who offer to place something heavy for me in a different room if that is what I want, and do it so cheerfully.

Now I must have a bath, I must get dressed, and I must make my bed because Eleanor, who cleans for me, comes today. Eleanor's day and the weekend are the times I have to make my bed. It is costly in energy.

Friday, May 10

YESTERDAY WAS not a good day. I saw Dr. Khanjani at eleven-thirty and before that Nancy and I had put in four flats of lobelias. That was what, I guess, was too much for me. In the afternoon I felt exhausted. I had my hair done and came back but couldn't rest.

Now, this morning, another disaster. I put the thermostat up to a little over seventy at five because the air was quite chilly and I was not feeling well. I felt rather nauseated and queer. The heat went right up to eighty so when I came down at six it seemed terribly hot, and I wondered if I had a fever. I put the thermostat down to sixty but the heat didn't die down so I finally turned it off at the source, the button at the head of the cellar stairs. Then I called Goodwin Oil and they will come this afternoon.

So once more I don't get my rest. What really finished me off yesterday was that I suddenly realized they had forecast rain and I had better pick flowers for Susan's room or they might be all beaten down or I might not be able to pick them.

There is no way to take the pressure off right now. I have to try to be wise and do a little at a time and not let it get to me that there are perhaps a hundred letters I should answer right away.

Saturday, May 11

SUSAN AND CYBÈLE, her little poodle, are here and the house is alive again. Pierrot is very excited. He spends a great deal of time watching the door behind which Cybèle is. But at the moment perfect peace.

Susan and I did quite a big piece of gardening, putting in the perennials including a charming dwarf aster—a wonderful purple/blue—and some Shasta daisies, and one globe thistle because they all died this winter. I thought I had lost the astilbe, but it is doing very well. Susan put in a beautiful white columbine that was part of what Nancy and I had bought— her birthday present to me. Now I have a second birthday present—someone who will plant it.

Yesterday was a tiring day but also a very satisfactory one. Karen Koslowski, who is so kind, came and took me on a shopping project to get in the things that I needed for the weekend. The holistic diet is demanding as far as shopping is concerned. So I got apricots and stewed them up in the afternoon, broccoli that I cooked for Susan and me to have, and flounder, and wonderful halibut which had just come in. We waited while they cut it for us.

It is going to be a *real* treat tonight with an artichoke! They were on sale when Nancy and I stopped by the Golden Harvest the other day when we were getting the plants. They

"Susan looks beautiful"

do look lovely. So this will be quite a feast. I also baked apples yesterday. The energy is there but I am knocked down by the pain. It was bad yesterday.

Nevertheless, a year ago I was not able to garden at all. So to be able to put my hands in the earth to dig is life giving, though I am weak; It is almost as if the earth were nourishing me at the moment. I could feel it as if it were food.

Susan looks beautiful. We are going to try the vegetable juicer which that wonderful electrician, Bruce Woods, set up for me the other day.

There is a certain amount of pressure about the journal getting done. Yesterday I read and corrected twenty pages— it is now three hundred thirty pages. Tomorrow I shall try to do another twenty so that I will be caught up to Nancy's transcription. But there is still the enormously important selection of the photographs. I am looking forward to that. I think I must call Eric and find out what the deadline is.

"Oh you kitten! What a tail!"

I was talking to the cat then because he has got a burr on his tail. He is lying beside me with a magnificent bunch of daffodils and narcissi in front of me on a little table—*and* lilies of the valley from Susan's garden beside them.

Connie Lloyd was so funny when she and the Warrens came to see the video of me. She wanted so much to see the cat, and I knew he was up here. He sleeps most of the day in a straight chair in my bedroom or on my bed. When she came down I asked her if she had seen him. She said, "Well, I could not believe there was a living animal, there are so many stuffed ones, but then he opened his eyes and there was the living animal!" He jumped down right away. I do have an almost life-sized lamb, and a smaller one, a magnificent duck, a gosling, and a donkey besides my living Pierrot. So it is quite a zoo, as Connie said.

This has been an absolutely perfect weekend with Susan. Perfect weather, the daffodils at their last great glory.

Susan and I lived in perfect accord and peace for the two days—enjoying life to the full. It was partly because I *am*

feeling better. Then Susan always manages to do some wonderful deed in the house—clearing out a cupboard this time
which had bottles and glasses in it, all mixed up. Now there is
order and peace. This order and peace is inspiring me to try to
tidy up my own clothing. Because I have lost so much weight
there is an enormous amount that has to be collected and
sorted out to give away. And now, because I feel better, I
cannot simply think about this, but must begin to do things, to
be active.

Monday, May 13

THE GREAT EVENT of the last two days, besides Susan's presence here, was a marvelous quotation by one of the nuns at
the Carmelite monastery in Indianapolis. Sister Betty was in
retreat when I stayed there so I did not meet her but she had
the kindness to copy out, from a book by Piero Ferrucci called
Inevitable Grace, something which goes right to the state of
myself, my health and my life, in a marvelous way. The beginning of the quotation from *Inevitable Grace* is "Empathy,
however, is no solitary event. On the contrary, it is that which
permits artists to feel and express the most concealed needs,
pains and dreams of a whole society. The aim of the poet, says
Pablo Neruda, is to embody hope for the people, to be one leaf
in the great tree of humanity." Then Ferrucci quotes from
Neruda: " 'My reward is the momentous occasion when, from
the depths of a coal mine, a man came up out of the tunnel
into the full sunlight and the fiery nitrate field as if rising out
of hell, his face disfigured by his work, his eyes inflamed by
the dust and, stretching his rough hand out to me, a hand
whose callouses and lines traced the map of the pampas. He

said to me, his eyes shining, "I have known you for a long time, my brother!" That is the laurel crown of my poetry, that opening in the bleak pampas from which a worker emerges, who has been told often by the wind in the night and the stars of Chile: you are not alone, there is a poet whose thoughts are with you in your suffering.' " And back to Ferrucci: "Empathy then is an expansion of consciousness. Through this faculty we are able to become one with trees and ants and elephants, birds, rivers and seas, children and old people, men and women, suffering and joyful people, rainbows and galaxies. Thus we become able to breathe and live in other beings or to find them within ourselves, as in a living microcosm in the most unlikely face, in the strangest of situations, in the remotest places, we discover ourselves and once we reach this point there need never again be the feeling that we are strangers in a strange land." It is a good Sunday sermon, isn't it?

Tuesday, May 14

IT IS almost incredible to have another magnificent May day. We are being rewarded for all the bad weather we had in April. And now in the great sequence the ornamental cherries are out on the terrace and right where I see them from my chaise longue here. The marsh marigolds have gone. As one goes, another comes. You have to keep running to keep up with the spring!

Yesterday I had the joy of watering with the hose. In the morning I felt anxious, there had been so much wind and it has been very hot at the same time. So some of the plants, the

perennials that Susan and I planted, needed water. I watered
the little roses by hand. The pleasure of turning on the hose
was pleasure late in the afternoon yesterday, after an otherwise jagged, difficult day in which I got too tired. But things
are popping in the garden, and I did manage to do a rough
preface for the seventy-nine journal.

An enormous number of fan letters still come in; this
morning there were three, interestingly enough, from women
of very different ages: one sixteen-year-old young woman
who says, like me, she has always liked older people; one from
a woman in her fifties; and another from a woman in her
seventies. It is thrilling to feel this span and that the work has
been sustaining to such different kinds of people. That is a
reason for rejoicing, but my desk remains a kind of misery. It
is in such disorder. I did manage to pack a few of the new
books to send off and to write maybe four or five notes and
that was the day.

Yesterday I had two doctors to see, Dr. Petrovich and Dr.
Khanjani. Dr. P. was pleased with me and said he had not
seen such a smile for a long time—such a smile of mine, I
mean. So that was good. Then Dr. K. rejoiced because I was
weighed at Dr. P.'s and I had gained three pounds! This is
good news. But the X-ray of the spine that they took last week
did show a shadow which might not be good news and I may
have to have a CAT scan. That overshadowed the day at the
end.

I went to bed tired and then Pierrot, who really enraged
me, did not come in at twelve (I think I had gone down three
times to call him). Then I took my sleeping pill and did not
wake up until half past two when he came in, telling me in no
uncertain terms that he had waited much too long. He gave a
growly, miserable meow which he repeated for a long time.
Then he leapt on the bed and was tremendously affectionate,

pushing his nose against my face and purring very loudly. He is now listening carefully to everything I say and has just rolled over on the straight chair where he likes to sleep in the morning.

Thursday, May 16

I SAW Dr. Khanjani at nine-thirty this morning—the earliest appointment I've had. In some ways it is a good time, although next week it will be Monday and Thursday at three. I am leading two lives and that may be why I have a sense of rather too great pressure right now. The day seems to fly out of my grasp like a bird that I cannot catch. I came back after getting some carrots because Nadine, one of my two helpers, can use the juicer and make me carrot juice tomorrow. That errand and having my hair done took until eleven. I was tired and wanted my lunch but I made myself go upstairs and try to find photographs for the journal. That is the big job right now—to get it done. When I called Eric Swenson yesterday he said that if he had photographs by the fifteenth of June, it would be possible to bring the book out by my birthday. It is a lot of work. I did not find—I looked for almost an hour—the photograph I had hoped to find of Pierrot sitting on the wall like a mage as he does so often and which I would like to have appear rather early on.

Yesterday was more or less consumed by Jan Daniels. She is seventy-five, which I had not realized, so it was quite a thing to come all the way from California to see me for one hour. It turned out to be two hours and I was completely

exhausted at the end, but I like her. She is a marvelously good
potter. I think the reason I accepted her coming—I simply do
not have the strength for visitors—is because she started
being a potter at fifty-nine. She has been happily married to
the same man for something like forty years. She has three
grown-up children whom she loves. She lives in Los Altos,
California, where she makes her magnificent pots. She is convinced they help people in much the same way that they tell
me my work helps them; it gives them comfort. I can see how
a very round, ample pot can give one comfort.

Jan Daniels' pots are open-ended, rather raggedly open-
ended on purpose, but the texture is something very much like
Maria's, the famous Pueblo potter. Jan Daniels only buffs her
pots. They are not in any way altered from the original substance of which they are made. She does not use a wheel. It is
all done by hand.

She was most appreciative of the house; I suppose, in a
way, seeing me here, you learn a great deal about me without
even talking. When I said I was tired when she arrived because I had already worked hard at my desk, she said, "I'll
talk." I could not help saying, "But listening is difficult and
tiring too; in fact, listening is much more tiring than talking
for most people."

I watered with the hose yesterday for an hour or more. I
watered by hand the white columbine that Susan had planted
for me which is not where the hose can reach. The lobelias are
looking plucky and full of themselves—a wonderfully bright
blue. Everything comes and goes so fast I have to catch my
breath. Now the lilacs are here and, in a day or two, the iris
will arrive.

Royce Roth sent me an admirable short novel that I have
greatly enjoyed. It is called *Amongst Women*, by John
McGahern, an Irish writer with a very Irish face who has
written several novels. He has a wonderful style: a grim tale

about family life, an Irish family in a small country town dominated by a domineering father, who, at the same time, is a
powerful character and strangely lovable by the end, although adamant and narrow. A rewarding book. Some of the
descriptions—of getting in the hay, for instance, tremendously hard work for three or four days—are magnificent.

Friday, May 17

I CANNOT believe how time is rushing away from me! It is as if
I were on one of those rafts on the Colorado River, bouncing
from rock to rock. This morning I did manage to write a few
notes and get ready a long list because Karen K. is coming to
take me on a shopping expedition in a few minutes.

Now I have begun to read another novel which is going to
be, I hope, an adventure. It is a best-seller called *Possession*
and I shall be talking about it, as time goes on.

I am having a hard time with my digestion. Dr. Khanjani
believes this is par for the course: you get worse before you
get better. But it is difficult and it was a hard night last night
because of the cat. He did not come in until half past one and
then wanted to go out at three. I minded the one-thirty going
down because I was blind with sleep.

I had an interesting dream between nine-thirty and
eleven when I went down to get Pierrot and he did not come.
The dream was about Katharine Davis, oddly enough, who
appears in the preface of the new *Sarton Selected*. In the
dream-meeting with her and her friend, who was not her real
friend but an imaginary dream-friend, I pretended not to be
May Sarton. We had an interesting talk. At the end I said,

"Do you know who I am?" She said, "Yes," and walked away, obviously crying. It was so vivid that, for once, I remembered it very clearly when I woke up.

Yesterday, lacking tulips all eaten by the deer, I, for the first time in weeks, ordered flowers—pink and lavender tulips—and they are good to have in the house because the daffodils are completely gone. The whole world of daffodils is not there and it is a terrible loss. This spring has been such a rewarding one, one day after another, as the great sequences follow each other, the lilacs now. They have suffered on this place although everywhere else they are flourishing. I think it was the icy winds in December that wounded my lilacs, which are old here anyway.

Sunday, May 19

THIS IS a peak-of-May day. I have never seen a more beautiful one. It is cool, the ocean is brilliant blue, and all the leaves are shining. There is a little breeze to keep the insects down.

Maggie, my friend from Hallowell, has been her wonderful self, finding everything possible that needs to be done—and doing it with great alacrity. She is giving fifty copies of my book to raise money for Hospice. She brought them, carrying them in paper bags—ten at a time. This morning I signed them. She passed me one, opened at the right place, and I signed it as I do when Bill Ewert is here with the Christmas poem. We did that in about an hour. Quite a triumph! I find that if I do not concentrate absolutely I make mistakes. Each one is signed with my name and "York, May 1991."

Before that I had read thirty pages of the journal, which still needs correcting. There is a lot to do before June fourteenth to get it off. The question of the photographs is also on my mind all the time with an occasional good idea of what I could use. Very often I spend an hour searching and don't find the photographs that I remember.

Earlier than that I had readied my breakfast tray so that when Maggie got up she could make my breakfast and bring it to me. I can bring up a tray now but I fear I'll fall backwards on the stairs, so it is a treat to have somebody bring it up. I had my breakfast peacefully and then did reading in the journal. Meanwhile Maggie had her breakfast and was reading quietly when I decided at about nine that it was time I got up. She helped me make my bed and then made her own. Then she asked me what she might do after I had signed the books. I thought of a flat of basil that I had bought the other day; we found a place where that might go, and she put it in. I also noticed how terribly the weed that invades the phlox has spread. It has leaves much like those of an aster, and is hard to discover among all the other plants. She must have done a good half hour's work in one place, and it looks ever so much better. Pierrot has completely taken over and practically destroyed a small cozy armchair that faces the television where guests who come to see me usually sit as I lie on my chaise longue. The cat has clawed his way in and clawed out the stuffing of this chair and it looked like hell! A few days ago I wondered if it would be possible to use some of that slick paper that is used so much now for parcels, with a gummy surface on one side—whether that could not be gummed to the badly scratched places on the chair.

Maggie was doing this when I went downstairs to see Janice, who had come to pick up all the books for a sort of Sarton celebration she is organizing to raise money for Hospice in June. I went down, and there was Mary Ann, who seems always to send flowers when I need them most—often roses. These were that wonderful, very pale apricot rose that is new on the market but is among the most beautiful I have ever seen. It also has a delicate scent. Mary Ann, who works so hard, looked so very pale that I worried about her.

The morning has been filled with stunning acts of friendship. What a lucky old woman I am!

Earlier in the morning Margaret and Barbara brought the Sunday *Times* as they have offered to do every Sunday. It is an enormous help as it means I do not have to interrupt the morning when I usually write letters. Last week they brought tulips from Barbara's garden. Oh how they have lasted! They are still here—tall, purple and pink. Today Margaret walked in with an armful of white lilac, with bright pink roses strewn among it—staggeringly beautiful on this staggeringly beautiful day.

The only out is that I have had a bad attack of pain ever since Maggie's visit. I did manage to cook a good dinner of swordfish, broccoli, and short-grain brown rice. Dr. Khanjani has suggested that short grain would be better for me than long grain. I am glad to say that Maggie brought with her the makings of a mint julep so that she could have that since I myself cannot drink. I am so glad she did, it made it seem homey and delightful as it always is when she's here.

Thursday, May 23

WE ARE HAVING a magnificent May. Since last week the weather has been dazzling: clear skies, everything shining, and all the sequences following each other in splendor. The only trouble is that everything goes as it comes. The peonies are not out yet, but they will be very soon. And then what? The azaleas are to come.

Meanwhile I am having a hard time with all my usual troubles, therefore I feel tired in this period when I have to work exceptionally hard. Even if I were well it would be hard because the journal of my seventy-ninth year must be off to Norton by June fourteenth. The struggle now is, more than anything, the photographs, but also the correcting of the manuscript, which is quite a big job because naturally what is dictated does not have the form it would have if I were able to write it. It does not have the style I wish it had.

There have been events in the last two days. On Tuesday Dorothy's son, Dan Wallace, came. Dorothy, my contemporary, was a student of mine in the Radcliffe Seminars. We became friends. She is a remarkable, warm, giving woman who has just built herself a magnificent swimming pool that looks like a great Palladian room. She swims every morning because she has had bad arthritis. She has made herself well by swimming.

Anyway here is Danny, with his wife and two little boys. Dan is teaching in a public school in Wolfeboro, Maine. They spend their weekends on an island which I suspect they own. He is well-off but has chosen to lead a giving life as a teacher. He was here for an hour, with his red beard and those penetrating eyes. He taught me a great deal and was quite aware of doing it. At the very end, after having asked me a lot of questions about my physical condition, he asked me whether I would let him "lay on" hands. I have never had this experience before, but after all, at a time when I am not well I may as well try everything. So I said, "Of course, Dan, go right ahead." There I was, lying on my chaise longue, and for about fifteen minutes, maybe more, Dan laid his hands and pressed very gently on my bowels and I did feel warmth flowing through me. Later things went better, so I think he may have helped.

He must be an extraordinary person because an English vicar near Oxford where Dan studied theology for a year— about ten years ago—who had become his friend, invited him to give the Good Friday sermon. The Good Friday sermon apparently is three hours long. Dan chose to do the seven segments on the seven last words of the crucified Christ. What interested me most about this was that he had decided that he would not prepare a text but only a form. This, I think, was wise. I know it myself in my poetry readings, that if I overprepared the readings were never as good as when I let the flow be spontaneous; in other words, let the subconscious have its innings. So, day before yesterday, Dan left with a good hug. I confess that although I enjoyed every moment of it I was tired at the end.

Yesterday a huge event: Rene Morgan dropped in on her way from Albuquerque to the Cape where she summers. Her kind niece and nephew-in-law drove her here from Marblehead. They went off to lunch and left us to have a good talk and to eat delicious lobster rolls. This is not something on my diet but it seems to have gone down very well. Even better:

apricot frozen yogurt on which I placed some sun-dried apricots in their juice that some savvy person had sent me for my birthday. It was delicious.

I am tired of my same supper every night. It is always white fish (sole, flounder, or haddock) with rice and a vegetable. Never mind, I do feel better. I am able to do the book and everything that has to be done in the house. It has been bad luck that two of my minions have not showed up this week. When I have to make the bed and carry a tray up and down stairs it takes a little of that precious energy from work later on. Now I must get at the book before I say another word.

Saturday, May 25

AFTER A magnificent week of cool, bright air, suddenly a *swamp* of heavy, damp, hot air with a southwest wind has descended upon us. It was eighty degrees when Susan arrived here last night at eight o'clock. It took her seven hours to drive from New York because it is the holiday weekend.

I am proud of all I did yesterday because it demanded physical energy which I do not have at my command these days. After I got up, I finished reading the manuscript of the journal, which means that we are on schedule. It gives us two weeks in which to get the photographs together. That is a complicated job, but at least the main work is done. Nancy still has to collate the Xeroxed copy with the original because I made my corrections on the Xerox copy and changed quite a few things. I am still undecided as to the quality of this journal but at least it is off my mind now.

Unfortunately I only got it done just before Karen K. was

coming to take me shopping and it had begun to be hot. But we did it in just a little over an hour because Karen is so efficient and quick and, of course, carries everything in for me—a tremendous help. We went to the hardware store—one I have never been to—hoping they would have things for the desk, but not at all, only hardware and seeds and tools. So that was a waste of time.

Then we went to the Meadowbrook Mall and I was able to get the desk things I needed. We did a vast shopping for food and ended up at the fish market where I spent twenty-four dollars on fish for Susan and me over the weekend and two lobster rolls because I had invited Edythe for lunch.

Now that Edythe has moved to an apartment she suddenly has time. During the past year, when she was emptying her house and selling it, I had not seen her nearly as often. It is precious to see her at least once a week and catch up on everything. She is such a beneficent, untiring person and also does wonderful things like sewing for me, shortening the pants I have just bought, for instance. We had a dessert of vanilla frozen yogurt and those sun-dried apricots. One thing I love about Edythe is that she enjoys a good dessert just as much as I do. The lobster rolls were delicious, with a generous amount of lobster.

I felt the day had been well-started, and I did try to rest but it was terribly hot and I kept getting up, remembering that I should do this or that. I finally got up for good at three-thirty and began the cooking to get ready for Susan's dinner. Unfortunately she was so hot and tired when she got in that she never did eat it, but I made new short brown rice and put some broccoli on, unfortunately interrupted by the telephone, so that it was a little overdone. Then I had my supper—a delicious fillet of sole.

That was only the beginning because while I was cooking I was hauling hoses around: first the side that I see from my chaise longue which was terribly dry, then the front terrace which also was terribly dry with some plants lying down, and finally the side of the fence which has not been watered at all. So far we have been lucky this spring but now we need rain, and there does not seem to be any in sight. Thank goodness Diane got the hoses up for me so I can water. But I had to go down below the terrace five times to get the hose sprayer fixed at the right angle so it would go over the wall into the little border in front and also to the whole border below. Going down five times, and turning the water off and on, was exhausting.

But I did go up, as I try to do every day at about half past five, to open my bed and get everything tidied up and ready in my bedroom so I feel I have a good servant when I go to bed.

Susan—I don't know how she does it—looked beautiful when she walked in. This morning when I went down I saw a great bunch of white peonies that she had brought. I didn't see them yesterday because last evening a swarm of flying ants made the side door—our usual entrance—unusable. Susan had to drag everything in by the front door which is now embellished, in a ravishing way, by wisteria in full bloom. The lilacs are on the way out. It is sad to see them go, but a single white tree peony came out, by the grace of God. Before dark I picked it to float where we can see it today.

"Clearing the desk"

Memorial Day, May 27

WE ARE having typical New England weather of swings from one thing to another. When Susan arrived here Friday evening the temperature was eighty, the air muggy and hot. It was like that on Saturday also. Then Sunday it suddenly became very cold. It was fifty-one when I let the cat in at six!

I have been depressed during this weekend because I feel so ill. But I have made some heroic efforts. One has been, in three days, to clear off the top of my desk which was literally a foot high with unanswered letters. This does seem incredible unless one knows that an average of ten letters come each day. I make an effort to answer what has to be answered that day. The other nine or seven or six get pushed aside for later. Of course there are many more in the month of May because of my birthday. There were literally hundreds. Many of these are from people I hear from only once a year with whom I want to keep in touch. It has been a difficult weekend all round but it will be marvelous to get the desk cleared. I'm going to go up as soon as I get dressed this morning and finish the job.

Susan is going out to get Nolvadex—I ran out. It is the medicine that is supposed to dry up the liquid in the lining of the lung and it does seem to be working, although it is wildly expensive.

Meanwhile, outdoors everything in the garden goes on at a great pace. The new delight is the stars-of-Bethlehem. They do star the perennial bed below the terrace. Iris is out but there is not a great deal of it. I must order some more. What else is out? Peonies are about to blossom. The white, tree peony is out. There were four magnificent blossoms this year. From up here I see it across the lawn—a great wonder there in the garden.

I was interested to see an interview with A.S. Byatt. Her strange novel, *Possession,* was sent me by Maggie Lewis. I find it pedantic, and I do not consider it literature as Maggie does. I was interested to read that Byatt seems not to be a *gemütlich* person. She is the sister of Margaret Drabble.

The cat is now on my lap and doesn't like my dictating. Is that a tick? It might be. There, there. Wait a minute!

Wednesday, May 29

THIS WEEK is simply flying away because of the holiday. It is
an absolutely pure, beautiful day with the ocean tranquil like
a mirror, satin blue, and the green of the field so brilliant that
it shines. Together they make a kind of magic. Now the grassy
path that is kept cut from my house right down to the sea is
also visible as the grass grows longer. The azaleas are coming
out, the yellow de Rothschilds, which are like a waterfall, a
wonderful gold, and have a delicious scent. They are glorious
this year. Both the white ones to the right of the house are
flowering well. It seems to have been a good year for azaleas
and rhododendrons. They are just about to flower. The tree
peonies have done very well too. It is amazing how much has
survived and in fact how much the plants must have enjoyed
this severe winter without snow. The pink rugosa rose which I
thought was dead has revived. The only strange thing is that it
is a very pale pink. I suppose it must need some form of fertili-
zer to bring back that rich, brilliant pink that it used to be.

I was near despair yesterday because of never being without pain again. When the phone rang twice in the morning I
found myself crying from frustration because I am trying to
organize the photographs for the journal. What happens
every morning is that when Nancy brings the mail at half past
eight there are always two or three things that demand answers and I feel crushed by the weight of what is on my back
every day before I can do anything. When I am alone and

have to get the mail myself, I get it later and in some ways this works better.

I have been thinking about old age and how much I enjoy the freedom of it. By that I mean the freedom to be absurd, the freedom to forget things because everyone expects you to forget, the freedom to be eccentric, if that is what you feel like, or, on the other hand, the freedom to be quite rigid and to say, "But this is the way I do things."

Pat, my visiting nurse friend, kindly came and changed the little bandage on the hole where that strange black substance was when we went to the emergency room at the hospital. It was comforting to have her do it because of course she knows and it is rather hard for me to see just where it is on the breastbone.

I am now deep into Margot Peters' *Unquiet Soul*, a biography of Charlotte Brontë. I must admit that because I have been so depressed, this book is not the best one for me to be reading right now. Charlotte Brontë's life was one of tragic frustration for so long. It is an excellent biography and I am enjoying it and look forward to going to bed to another onslaught of the terrible life it was in the nineteenth century to be a governess and, in some cases, still is. The fantastic lack of pay, no holidays, and the limbo in which a governess existed. That is, she was not one of the servants so she could not enjoy their company at meals, but neither was she a member of the family, who treated her snobbishly. She had to keep herself to herself and deal with often naughty children whose parents always defended the child against the governess. That, at least, was Charlotte Brontë's experience.

Saturday, June 1

JUST IMAGINE! June already, but another of these rather dour, chilly, overcast mornings. We have had one after another, and it is depressing. There is no incentive to go out and pick flowers. But the azaleas have never done better.

This weekend I have no guests, no one to look after me. I decided I wanted two weekends before Susan comes when I would be a completely free agent. I see very well how it works both ways. The dear people who come to help me, Joan, Nadine, Eleanor Perkins, have helped stabilize my depressed moods. These last two weeks have been hard from the point of view of pain. The very fact that someone is coming makes me pull myself together, get up, get the tray ready, and then I have the luxury of going back to bed and having my breakfast brought to me. But on the other hand, this morning I was grateful not to have to hurry to get up, to have to get ready for anyone. It is now nearly half past eight and I am still in bed although I have had my breakfast and carried it up. The cat came in at a reasonable hour—I think it was at about eleven last night—so I had a fairly good night's sleep for a change. Of course he goes wild when there is a full moon as there was two nights ago.

I think I am about a half an inch better. Dr. Khanjani is convincing when she insists that two months has not been long enough to undo the work of twenty years or more and get rid of all the accumulated poison. So I must just "bear and grin it" as my father said when he was in terrible pain with an attack of gallstones. I was called at two in the morning by his wonderful maid who lived in; I dashed over, and there he was in bed in excruciating pain. Even then—and I did admire him—he could joke, and said, "I must just bear and grin it!"

Fans are so kind and think of me so generously, but yesterday, late in the day, around five, after my rather grueling session with Dr. Khanjani, UPS delivered over twenty pounds of Bing cherries from a California fan who has been most generous before. But it is not kind to send such a weight to somebody as frail as I am—this *ton* of heavenly cherries sits right at the door and now I have to call five or ten people and tell them to come and take some because I am allowed only stewed fruit and no sugar; I have to forgo the pleasure of these magnificent cherries. This is a day when I have a lot to do, as I must get the mail and do some errands, and, hopefully, write a few notes.

Tuesday, June 4

WE HAD a good rain all night. Of course I had watered in the afternoon, dragging the hoses around. Today I do not have to worry. I had planned to water all around the side of the fence. I can see from my window that the double yellow tree peony is out. It is a little bit later than the white and the wonderful pinkish orange and gray which is the most original and beautiful of them all, except the white, God-like one.

Although I had things to do upstairs, am not feeling well, and there is not much to pick now, yesterday I did go out for about a half hour of pure bliss. I find I have energy in the garden that I cannot summon for anything else. I tied up some of the daffodil leaves which had been sprawling and getting in the way of other plants trying to come through. I staked two white peonies that would have been beaten down by the rain last night if I had not done it. The peonies are not doing well. I think I must plant some new ones and certainly more iris. I have ordered an iris catalog and that will be fun, especially if I can get the intermediate-height irises which are much more useful in the perennial border than the tall ones. I not only did a little gardening, I made a bunch—not a total success, but it was great fun—with some of the strange allium that are covered with prickly points. They are lavender and greenish, not a solid mound like the giant ones that are magnificent this year. These smaller ones have very original designs, so to speak, and with a dark purple iris which has just come out, and some double purple perennial geraniums, made an interesting bunch which I loved making.

Pierrot came in earlier last night so I was able to get quite a long sleep. But the trouble is that I am anxious and badgered by having to get the manuscript off to Norton so soon.

Yesterday I made a stupid mistake. I had thought that my appointment with Dr. Khanjani was at ten-thirty. When I got there she was away and her car was away. But thank goodness she came and very kindly gave me a treatment. The only trouble is I missed the whole morning's work and now I have to go again Thursday at ten-thirty. Tomorrow I have a permanent wave. It is a ridiculously busy life considering that I do nothing, nothing whatever.

As for the journal, I have many doubts about it but we shall have to see how Eric Swenson at Norton and Tim Seldes, my agent, feel. When it is off my hands it will be much easier to do this journal and it will be much easier to live my life, because it was like a third leg all the time, having to work at that journal as well. A lot of letters that I want to answer are still waiting.

Nadine told me today that she had been reading *At Seventy* to her patient who died yesterday. The reading had meant a great deal, so that when she fell asleep, the patient would say, "Just let me hold the book." This, I must admit, touched me deeply.

Wednesday, June 5

WE ARE having cold, rainy, dismal weather although the rain was needed. I think the garden is happy although tossed around by a cruel northeast wind.

I remember now, because I have been correcting the journal, that last spring was much worse. Last May it rained almost every day and was very cold. So we have been lucky on the whole.

Yesterday, at about eleven in the morning, Eloise Armen, who has been managing and taking care of Eva LeGallienne's life for the last twenty years or more, called me to say that LeGallienne had died in the night—a gentle death. She had called the dear night nurse because she thought she wanted to go to the bathroom but then decided she didn't. I think from what Eloise said that back in her bed she simply drifted off and never woke up again. A beautifully gentle death for that great woman. She had been not quite "all there" for years. She was ninety-two, but for a long time still made the rounds of the bird feeders, still fed about nine raccoons every night with all kinds of goodies, and, the last time I was there, two skunks!

For six years of my life, from the time I joined the Civic Repertory Theatre as an apprentice when I was eighteen until my own little company failed in the middle of the depression, Eva LeGallienne was the most powerful influence in my life. She taught me an enormous amount and was the magnetic pivot of everything I thought and did. She was an extraordinary woman. In the years of the Civic Repertory when I was an apprentice, which meant that I did walk-ons and acted in student plays—later I was head of the Apprentice Group—I spent almost every evening from a little before eight until the curtain went up in LeGallienne's dressing room. We talked about books and life in general. She was a marvelous friend. From the beginning she guessed, I think, that I was a writer rather than an actress, although I was made a member of the First Studio, a group selected from the Apprentice Group to go on with the company. I also saw her in Westport after the Civic Repertory failed and through all the years until very recently when she was not seeing people because she did not recognize them.

She was a great gardener and we loved to talk about that. I remember I gave her a Queen of Denmark pale pink rose that turned into a great enormous bush that climbed up half the house in Weston where she lived. Then she made a wild garden of a great part of her place, which has been willed to the town as a sanctuary. I wonder what will happen to the house itself and all the memories there: the marvelous library which she had amassed through all her roles? For instance, there are a great number of books on Queen Elizabeth, a great number of books on Ibsen, on Chekhov, and biographies of the actresses she most admired, Eleanora Duse and Sarah Bernhardt.

It was in many ways an extraordinarily fulfilled life. She had dreamed, when she was a child in Paris and spoke perfect French, of doing all the roles that she adored seeing Sarah Bernhardt perform. As a matter of fact she did play most of

them, including *Camille,* which was a great success at the
Civic, and *L'Aiglon,* which she did on Broadway and I think
missed out because of its being a translation. It really cannot
be translated into English. It is too melodramatic, too theatri-
cal. Of course she looked wonderful as that glamorous young
man. She even played Hamlet, as Sarah Bernhardt did. I wish
I could have seen it. She did that at the Dennis Playhouse on
the Cape. Of the roles that I think of her as greatest in, the
first is Masha in *The Three Sisters,* a role where there are
very few words but she is on stage most of the time, suffering,
thinking, and being aware. To project thought was one of the
ways by which Eva LeGallienne was able to communicate on
stage. I have never seen an actress who did it so supremely
well. In Ibsen's *The Master Builder* she held a pause for almost a minute. This is unheard of in the theater. It was in the
second act, I think, when the master builder has just treated a
rival, a young architect, very badly. LeGallienne was silent
for an extremely long time before she said, "That was a very
ugly thing to do."

I had the great good luck, the terror, and the fun of being
her understudy for a week both in *The Cherry Orchard* as
Varya and in *Alice in Wonderland* as the White Queen. Nothing could be more exciting than a role in which you get a laugh
at the end of every sentence. The White Queen has extremely
good lines, including the famous "Jam yesterday, and jam
tomorrow, but never jam today!" It was a great event for
me—that roar of laughter coming at me and also getting
through the role of Varya in *The Cherry Orchard* with only
one brief rehearsal. I had been the understudy but it never
occurred to me that LeGallienne would ever be ill. So it came
as a great surprise. I was in the country—a two-hour drive
from New York—relearning the lines and trying to remember
exactly what she did. So terror played its part. Alla Nazimova

The White Queen, Eva LeGallienne

was playing Madame Ranevsky. At the end she said, "You did very well, dear, but you looked too happy." I thought that was wonderful!

Then LeGallienne—although she did not approve of my founding a company at my young age, knowing that I was not ready—supported me in every way that she could. The reason I founded the Apprentice Theatre when the Civic Repertory Theatre failed was not as arrogant as it might seem. I did it to try to keep a few of the apprentices together. It was the middle of the depression and they would have had little luck on Broadway. I decided to give rehearsal performances, had big black boxes built that could be moved around as scenery, and chose ten modern European plays which had not been seen over here. Those in French were translated by me. Eleanor Flexner and Kappo Phelan were directors. I had seen the danger at the Civic of the one woman who ran everything and was never herself directed. The New School for Social Research lent their tiny theater and we were announced as a course in modern European theater. Because we had no scenery and wore no makeup or costumes, the critics were impressed and we got some good notices. Brooks Atkinson, for one, was friendly.

Eva LeGallienne was most supportive. There are wonderful letters from her to me in the Berg Collection. I consider her as one of the greatest friends I have ever had and certainly one of the great influences. I wonder why she was never a muse. I did not write poems for Eva LeGallienne and I think that was because we were very much alike. So she told me more than once to explain to us both why we were never lovers!

The tragedy was that after LeGallienne was fifty, after the Civic Repertory Theatre closed, and she and Margaret Webster founded the National Repertory Theatre, she never got back what she had had as the founder and director of the

Civic and as the very great actress that she had been there.
Parts did not materialize and in the last years there were very
few. So from the time she was fifty or sixty until she was in her
eighties she was not used. To see this extraordinary talent
wasted was cruel. But there she proved what a great woman
she was for she was never idle; she gardened, she wrote
books, she translated Ibsen and Chekhov, she saw her friends,
and altogether had a rich life—including the friendship of
many raccoons.

Thursday, June 6

AFTER GLOOMY, rainy, cold weather for forty-eight hours, the
sun is out. Although it was only forty-five this morning, it is
going to be a beautiful day.

I have been thinking a great deal about Eva LeGallienne
ever since I heard that she had died two days ago. What an
extraordinary friendship ours was! Here I was, eighteen years
old, an absolute innocent, just graduated from high school,
and I found myself an apprentice there in that marvelous
theater, watching rehearsals, able to see what a great director
Eva LeGallienne was. Also she did all the lighting. She was
Renaissance woman, spending a whole afternoon, sometimes
longer, working with the great electrician we had at the Civic.
Sometimes the lighting was extremely important. For instance, her *Romeo and Juliet,* for which she had designed
semi-abstract sets, required very special lighting. This she
was able to achieve.

But what was so amazing was her taking me in as a friend.
I think it was for various reasons. One is, of course, that her

father was the poet Richard LeGallienne who, when she was a child, married a novelist, and all the literati of nineteenth-century England at that time came to the house. So the fact that I was a poet made her feel at home with me more than the fact that we were both European in background. LeGallienne began her life in Paris, because when her mother, who was Danish, separated from Richard LeGallienne, she took Eva and her sister Hesper to Paris where Eva studied drama and where she perfected her French. Sometimes, as I grew to know her better over the years, we talked in French, especially over the telephone. I miss her voice.

She was and remained a nineteenth-century person, extremely conservative. The only battles we fought intellectually were over politics. She hated Roosevelt! Partly this was so because she disapproved of the WPA. She disapproved of art being mixed with charity, and this with some justice. She had hoped to get money from the WPA for her Civic Repertory, but she would have had to employ unemployed actors. She felt that art must be based, and choices must be based, only on talent, not on need. Of course what she did not realize was how many good actors were out of work.

She was nineteenth century in her morals, in her ideas. For instance, she was furiously against psychoanalysis. When I told her that I was getting some therapy about a very unhappy love affair I was engaged in, she came to my room in the middle of the night (I was staying over the weekend there in Weston), knelt down on the floor by my bed, and launched into a tirade against my doing this, saying it was cowardice. Of course many people did not know what was involved in a good therapist–patient relationship, and mine at the time with Volta Hall was very good.

LeGallienne had a marvelous sense of humor. We laughed a lot when we talked together. She was incredibly brave, taking an enormous amount of defeat as the years went on, after the Civic had to close. But she was so inventive about her life, and so filled with life, that she always found things she wanted passionately to do and did them even outside the theater.

Monday, June 10

THIS EXTRAORDINARY WEATHER goes on. I have not been able to talk into this machine much lately because I have been in so much pain—again with that feeling of desperation. I do not know what to do with myself. But yesterday and today things are a little better. Today I had a normal movement which is such a grace that I really have to thank God!

Yesterday Jean Alice called from the Carmelite monastery. How splendid to hear her voice. In talking with her again I realize how much in touch they are, those religious orders, with what is going on in the world, how deeply they pay attention.

The journal of the seventy-ninth year is almost ready to go and it will be a relief when it is out of my hands.

I was amused by a rather characteristic day of mine as I thought about it. What fun it is to have money to spend! I signed the contract with a Japanese company that is doing a translation of *Mrs. Stevens Hears the Mermaids Singing* and will pay me fifteen hundred dollars through my English agent who handles all that. So with fifteen hundred dollars on the way I sent Pat Keen, my English actress friend who is having a dry spell as far as work goes, two hundred pounds. I felt so happy to be able to do it. Happiness flooded in.

. . . as it flooded in when I put the hose on and watered the clematis which is just beginning to open. That too is a transcendent joy.

Thursday, June 13

WE ARE having strange, cloudy weather but it is cooler today and the sun is out now. Until today every time I have wanted to pick flowers there has been a thunderstorm, but *finally* I've got a lovely bunch for Susan's bedroom with one of the white peonies, single, with such a wonderful pompon of stamens; two tradescantia, lavender ones (the tradescantia survived the winter wonderfully, better than it has ever done); and some of the wild geraniums that I ordered in a deep blue. Such a great color! And now the Oriental poppies are coming out, that precious salmon pink. But the garden is very wild and needs work.

There are wonderful things about living in Maine. Nancy came in yesterday and said, "When I got up this morning there was a big moose in the woods below the house!" And that evening I saw fireflies for the first time this year. Oh how magical it is! That was because the air was so humid. All these points of light are incredible. Of course Pierrot would not come in until two!

Today we get the journal off to Eric Swenson with the photographs and that is a boon. I am hoping to get my desk cleared and start a new life now that it is off my mind. Part of the new life, of course, will be having Susan here, having someone to do an errand.

Friday, June 14

HAPPINESS HAS COME like a bird now Susan is here. I see everything freshly through her so sensitive eyes as well as my own. It all comes alive. A burden laid down. The kind of happy freedom from things that have to be done first, for a change. Living the day comes first, with managing merely to survive and do what has to be done no longer necessary. My cup runneth over.

Saturday, June 15

NOW WE are back in our dear routine, Susan sitting by my bed while I have my breakfast, and we talk then and plan the day.

Yesterday was a triumph because although I was in a great deal of pain I did manage to garden. I planted six tuberous begonias that Joan Jansen gave me. That was a good piece of gardening: preparing the place, weeding it, digging, and I lying down to do it, much to the amusement of the painters who have only one more day, on Monday, before this huge job of painting the outside trim on forty windows is done.

When I got up from my nap I saw that the Chinese ring I have worn for twenty-five years or more had slipped off my finger, my hands are so thin now. It was an awful shock. It is an old Chinese ring and it has become part of my identity. But Susan and the painters went right out to try and find it, moving heaven and earth to do so. One of them did find it. Amazing grace! I was staggered with pleasure to have it back. Now I have twisted it in such a way that it cannot slip off. But I must remember when I garden to take it off my hand.

I think some of the toxic waste inside me must be coming out, but the result is an awful lot of pain. I talked to Lee Blair this morning. She has had so much pain from a bad knee. She helped me because she agrees that the thing with pain is that you must go ahead and do what you want to do even if it hurts. That is how I managed to garden yesterday. Of course the satisfaction, then, outweighs the pain. Today I am hoping to put in three miserable-looking iris that I ordered. That means pulling out a lot of the centaurea, which is lovely in June with its blue flowers but will really take over the garden if left to do it.

Friday, June 21

THE SECOND very hot day. Yesterday was ninety and one of the hottest days I have ever experienced here. Today there is a little breeze and the air is clear. We are promised a cooler and brighter weekend. I have not felt like dictating for days. I guess it began on Monday when I was so ill I did not even go to the doctor, the first time in three months that I have not kept an appointment with her. I think it may be that I had a twenty-four-hour virus because the pain was not quite the same as my usual digestive problems. So I got through the day and Dr. Khanjani was very understanding. She told me yesterday when I saw her that all of this may very well be just part of the gradual clearing out of the lymph glands and the poisons. She explained the tremendous explosions of gas that I suffer now as part of it and considers it good, not bad. Whenever I see her she does cheer me up.

It has been quite an eventful week. But the chief event is having Susan here. It is hard to explain what a difference it makes, not only to have someone who makes wonderful meals and clears up after them, but much more than that, to have someone here who sees the place and all the beauties, every flower, with such excitement and appreciation so that *I* see it all again as if I had never seen it before. This morning she said, "The astilbe is coming out!" She notices each thing that is happening. It is lovely having her little dog, Cybèle, here again. So it is a very happy home life at the moment.

Meanwhile there have been quite a few guests. Joy Greene came on Tuesday for an hour. She walked in and was overwhelmed by the beauty of the place, of the room where I sit. Spontaneously she said, "It's so beautiful!", which means a lot because Joy has such good taste. I have the fear always that things have got too cluttered. People give me things and there are little collections, for instance, of netsuke in the library and in the plant window room there is a collection of those Battersea boxes I'm so fond of. It does make for some clutter but I try to keep it down to a minimum.

Out of every window one sees beauty. Susan, who has not been here at this time before I think, was in love with the winter scene when the branches of the trees are so visible and there are no leaves; now it is all green, flourishing, and screening—green screens everywhere. The garden is a jungle.

Joy and I always, inevitably, go back to the past we share, now a good seventy years old. We spoke about Shady Hill, which is still a marvelous school. One of her friends thought they would send their child to the Lexington public school but when it came down to the nub they could not resist Shady Hill and so the child is going there. When people asked me when I was a child where I went to school I always said, "Shady Hill. It is the best school in the world!"

Joy is looking wonderful. It was great fun because Susan helped me find a bed-and-breakfast for her. I cannot put people up now, I get so exhausted. I wanted to pay for her B&B. We found an old Victorian house which looked right out on the harbor, but the rooms seemed to be rather cold in atmosphere despite the magnificent view. So I made a bunch of flowers for Susan to take over, but fortunately, someone wanted that room for five days, so Joy was kindly upgraded to a hundred-and-sixty-dollar-a-night room which had a hot bath, a Jacuzzi, a bidet, and a special kind of shower which massages your neck. She said she had the most wonderful night she's ever had, trying out all these things. It was a sunny hour we spent together. She came back the next day which was Wednesday and I showed her the video from Florida, *Creativity in the Upward Years,* and I could feel that she was moved by it.

Then in the afternoon came Doris Beatty and Jerry, her husband, who go back to my first visit to Berkeley where I was a guest in their house. They are on a trip for Elderhostel and are about to go to St. Johnsbury, Vermont, for a week. Doris is a wonderful person, so giving in every way. She brought a ravishing bunch of flowers, with blue iris and some deep purply pink small ones, and lavender freesia, and a couple of Shasta daisies. An exquisite bunch. She brought a box of superb candies which, although I am not supposed to eat them, I am going to steal one about once a week! These are famous candies from San Francisco. The first time I stayed with Doris a friend had left a box of them for me and they were open in my room. At that time Doris had an enchanting English sheepdog called Maggie. We went downstairs to see the garden, I think, for maybe fifteen minutes. When we came back the entire, big box of chocolates had disappeared into Maggie, who was looking very pleased with herself and did not throw them up, much to my surprise.

Unfortunately I found it difficult to suggest to Jerry that he go for a walk to let us have a little time together because it was so gloomy outside, sort of drizzly rain. Jerry is an extremely charming man, so we had a good talk, but it would have been better had we had a half hour alone. We did come upstairs so Doris could have a glimpse of Pierrot.

The big news—and it really is great news—is that Tim Seldes called me late yesterday afternoon to say that he thinks the journal is splendid. He called when he was only halfway through so it was a real compliment. He could not wait to tell me. He agrees that it will need some editing and that I should not have to do that. And that the preface, where I felt I should explain exactly what's wrong with me, might be cut altogether. But his enthusiasm was heartwarming, because I have had terrible doubts. And also because his colleague, that charming woman Miriam Altshuler, had called me on Wednesday or Thursday to say she had just read it and thought it was special, but she spoke unenthusiastically. So I was terribly depressed after her call. Now all is well. I have the incentive to put something on the tape today.

Thursday, June 27

It is a blessed time here. Peaceful days, cool and bright, as the sequential joys of the garden continue. Now it is the Japanese iris. They are so much like orchids, and they come later than the usual iris so it is always like a kind of iris reprise when they show themselves. I have ordered six more, together with three violet monarda, from Wayside Gardens. I have ordered lots of bulbs, but this time I have resisted tulips since they are always eaten, if not below ground during the winter, then as soon as they bud by the deer. I have ordered lots of allium, some more of the big ones, and the new one about eighteen inches high that is blue and should look glorious. The Kousa is a long magnificent white waterfall at the back of the house. That has been one of the two or three great successes of this spring.

Susan and I have a good rhythm now, meeting as we do and parting, with various reunions along the way, while we each work at our various tasks. I usually go out to the terrace to see what has flowered overnight and pick a few flowers, in my pajamas, early in the morning. Then I go back to bed and wait for Joan or Nadine to bring my breakfast. What luxury! I call these two delightful women who work for me my minions. I love the word which must derive from the French *mignon:* darling. For they are darlings. They bring a wonderful start to the day of ordering and caring. It's a real help, spiritually as well as physically.

Susan and I come together again at lunchtime. She makes

the most wonderful soups using all kinds of herbs. Usually I
have a half avocado and stewed fruit as well. I read the newspaper then, and sometimes keep the mail until lunchtime. It is
hard to do that because I am curious! Then I have my nap—
two hours. One has to remember I have often been up since
five and sometimes since four. Last night Pierrot wanted to go
out at half past one, come in at four, go out again at six. It is
lucky that I go to sleep in the intervals quite easily.

After my nap we have a reunion with—it used to be tea
and cinnamon toast, which I can't have anymore—now it is a
peanut buttered piece of toast and some fruit juice. Sometimes we look at a video. Yesterday it was the first hour of *My
Fair Lady*. What a delight! The music alone is so nostalgic and
it is a splendid production. Audrey Hepburn is amazing, so
real, tremendously effective and beautiful in the role. And
Rex Harrison, perfect; this was a role made for him, although
I had forgotten how mean the character is.

After that I go upstairs again and get my bedroom ready
for the night and perhaps lie down for fifteen minutes. Then
we have supper—these days at half past six—and I go up at a
little after seven, talk to Maggie Vaughan on the telephone
every evening for a few minutes, then read for an hour or two.
At about ten I go down to get the cat in and to take my Sea
Klenz.

Friday, June 28

A HEAT WAVE! It will be a hundred today, seventy percent humidity, very uncomfortable. I do not remember it ever going to one hundred here. Yesterday we did not have even a small sea breeze—deadening air. But today we are promised a high south wind in the afternoon and perhaps thunderstorms.

What care I for this discomfort when it looks as though the new laxative is breaking the vise I've been in? A true vicious cycle. It has given me four days now free of that constant anxiety and pain. I hardly dare say so for fear it will be another false hope.

Susan suffers more from the heat than I do. It makes me want to do something active, curiously enough. At six, after feeding Pierrot and letting him out, I braved the mosquitoes and picked an adorable small bunch of three different roses— climbers—all here before I came. New Dawn has been a joy always and, although cut back severely last year because it was about to topple the fence, it is as bountiful as ever now. There is also a bright pink single rose over the gate entrance, lovely and scented, but it does not last when picked. Finally, a single, very bright pink, golden-eyed wild rose. So I have a fugue of roses in the cozy room where the plant window dominates. The pleasure of picking a few flowers and finding the right vase for them is incomparable.

Yesterday I managed to write to Char, my Wisconsin friend, always moved by how terribly physically demanding her life as a milk farmer's wife is. They do it together, she and her husband and her two little children. Milk prices are down. It seems as though some small farmers never get a break. Char is a great woman, liberal politically, and very much involved in things the world round. She went to Nicaragua with a group of farmers' wives and came back gung-ho for the revolution. Her group brings out a newsletter which keeps me in touch with what is going on. At the time she went there were the terrible cruelties of the Contras.

I am near the end of Glenway Westcott's journals. On the whole, a disappointing book. He is honest, but the first part is so absorbed in homosexual sex it becomes a little boring. Only as he grows older and begins to put something before a penis does it get interesting. Of course he and Monroe Wheeler, the president of the Museum of Modern Art in New York, knew everybody in the art and the literary world. Glenway was president of the Institute of Arts and Letters for many years and helped a great many young writers. A very good man, in a way, and yet he did not—as he often says in his journals—fulfill his promise. It became harder and harder for him to finish a novel, partly because he had had great success with his early novels, and they are masterpieces, especially *The Pilgrim Hawk* and his early books. What strikes me as I read is that although you may know every famous person in the world, your life may still not be very interesting. That is what comes through in his journals. Though I delighted in certain elite enthusiasms that he and Monroe shared, such as theirs for Maggie Teyte, the singer of the wonderful Fauré and Duparc music for French poets, and Janet Flanner and Djuna Barnes. So much of it brings back a whole period, and *that* I am enjoying.

Saturday, June 29

Iт is not as terribly hot as it was yesterday, not as humid, and there is a little breeze.

I am feeling depressed because I see that the garden is dying—this garden into which I have put twenty years' work, not to mention lots of money. It is terrible to see a garden dying. My mother's garden died a year or two after she died. It is one more thing that makes me feel I should not have lived so long. I have not been able to garden for two years, and Diane is an excellent gardener but has not been able to give me enough time. She put in the seeds and then she did not come back for a month. Nothing has flowered. The annual bed is full of weeds, and everything needs pruning. To go out over and over again and see work that desperately needs to be done and not have the energy to tackle it is devastating. It is a grim day. I wish for the first time there were some way of leaving here forever. Then I would not have to watch the garden die.

Susan has brought the mail. I am happy to hear that Barbara Mills Solomon is doing a biography of Ada Comstock Notestein. Ada Comstock was such a great president of Radcliffe College that I was moved to find a letter I had written to thank Ada for a letter about *The Small Room*. Barbara Solomon sent it to me. I think I must copy a paragraph of what I said about her as a president because I feel it so deeply.

As I grow older and also see more and more of colleges in one way and another, I come more and more to appreciate you. In fact, I'm afraid you have become a touchstone, and that is hard on almost *all* other presidents! In some extraordinary way you never ceased to be yourself, as open as sunlight—one never felt the self-consciousness or the guardedness that power of this kind so often induces in those who wield it, and perhaps especially in *women* in administrative positions, alas. I feel privileged to have witnessed greatness in a college President (it must be even more rare than greatness in the arts!). But, lest you think, I am in any way referring to Radcliffe *now*, let me quickly add that I rejoice in Mrs. Bunting and all she is setting in motion. She seems a very fine choice indeed.

I do feel depressed in spite of this nice "find" in the mail because I am again in trouble with my digestion. I thought I had found a way to solve this problem. I am in a lot of pain today and was yesterday. I do not see the way out.

Monday, July 1

I CANNOT believe June has gone. Yesterday was a great celebratory day, my first outing, my first leaving of this house for more than a half an hour or so for over a year. Susan and I set out for North Parsonsfield to visit Anne and Barbara. It is just on the edge of New Hampshire and as one climbs up the mountain road there is a certain point where you see the whole Presidential Range and even Mount Washington, although that was not clear yesterday, then dip down into North Parsonsfield and their farm. I haven't been there for so long that of course there were big changes: the best, a framing of

Anne Woodson, Barbara Barton, and May Sarton at Deer Run Farm

the barn and the great field beyond, which Anne keeps cut, by a low fence, a rectangle, cut—well I don't know how to say it—half a rectangle enclosing a little bed of flowers. Already there is a clematis growing—and wonderful flax; such blue! Glorious! It shows off what I think is the most beautiful of Barbara's many creations: the sculptured heron. This is the heron that the maple fell on and looked as if it could not be saved but it has been wonderfully repaired and looks beautiful now.

The barn is a national treasure in my view. It is huge, and always so unbelievably neat, with wood stacked for the winter, and the small area where the hens have their domain. Anne laughs and calls it the nursing home because they cannot bear to put these few remaining hens down. I think there are five or six; they lay perhaps two or three eggs a week. So she is giving up hens as produce now. I am very glad of it.

We went on our slow walk around the garden, seeing everything that has happened. The herb garden was taking up a beautiful space of lawn and now it has been moved to the side and does look very much better. The greatest treat at Deer Run Farm is the birds. When we sat down to our lobsters we were constantly exclaiming at the birds: two pairs of rose-breasted grosbeaks, we only saw one of the males; indigo buntings, which I had never seen; two bluebird nests which have already produced families. We did not see a bluebird but we heard about them. Oh yes, baby nuthatches. So amusing, the little things. And a hummingbird—a very mean one, Anne says, who chases off any other male hummingbird.

I even had a tiny drink—half an ounce of liquor. It was exciting. The lobsters, which were soft-shelled, were marvelous. As always we talked about everything under the sun, about our mutual friends, about the past, so much of which I've shared with them since they moved into this paradise—a paradise of their creation. It was a rather uninteresting house, with an overgrown garden, and now it is a charming estate, with many, many treasures. Everywhere there are sculptures by Barbara and everywhere there are very knowledgeable and satisfying groups of plants, planned and planted and cared for by Anne, who is a genius of a gardener.

The time, as it always does with them, went quickly, and it was five by the time we got back. Cybèle had been left here. We decided that was wiser than imposing her on a household where there are always birds flying about in the house. It was cool; we could not have left her so long if it had been one of those terribly hot days.

It seems that we are going to have two cool days and then, again, a spell of heat. Susan leaves today for a week at home where she can work on the computer, on her book using unpublished materials of mine. I am anxious to know that it is done. I shall miss her. She is leaving me all kinds of wonderful soup, and I have invited people every day, people whom I haven't seen lately. I seem to be getting better—a little better anyway—every day.

Tuesday, July 2

ANOTHER WONDERFULLY COOL, brilliant day!

I am shaken by a lot of things that have happened. I have been in a tailspin over the garden, knowing that I could not live here and watch it die, and having learned that Diane is simply not to be counted on. She made a choice a year ago at least to work for Mary-Leigh Smart and Beverly as well as me. There was not time to do the job she had promised she would do for me. So the garden has been literally dying. To watch a garden die is very much like watching a child die—a child on whom you spent enormous amounts of love and money for twenty years. As well as hundreds of hours of happy work, it has cost me over thirty thousand dollars. I must admit I was as close to suicide as I have ever been last week. But my luck has held and Diane brought me friends of hers who did one huge day's work for me for a hundred and twenty dollars. Yesterday they landscaped the whole perennial garden. Pat Robinson runs the firm, which only gardens, doesn't try to do anything else. Pat has an assistant and has promised to come once a week for five hours for one hundred dollars a week. It sounds like a lot, but it also sounds like very little considering what needs to be done. That is all I can afford. Little by little, things will get in hand again, and that is great news.

I was in the middle of talking with Pat when the phone rang. It was Maggie, dear Maggie, in tears because she was being sent to the hospital at once because of the cat bite she suffered two or three days ago. She was to have come here today with an early Fourth of July feast of salmon and fresh peas from her garden. She was heartbroken that she couldn't come and I am heartbroken that I won't be seeing her. It is a perfect day for such a visit and all the news is good except that and the news of Eleanor Blair. But a cat bite is a serious thing. I just hope and pray they will get hold of it. She is now being given fluid antibiotics, is in bed of course, and the arm is infected with a red line, she says, up her arm. She has a fever of a hundred. I am afraid she won't get home for a few days. Fortunately her daughter, who lives in Beverly, can come, and there will be friends as well as family.

In some ways far worse is Eleanor Blair's plight. She is now ninety-seven, legally blind as well as extremely deaf. She does manage to hear something on the telephone with one of those amplifiers. She had two confrontations in the last week or so and apparently had a mild heart attack after each one. Fortunately a God-sent Wellesley girl is there as a tenant who has become very fond of Eleanor. Eleanor is a darling woman—at ninety-seven always cheerful, always full of optimism and good cheer. The nurses in the hospital, I hear, already are fond of her. I had a long talk on the phone with Catherine, the Wellesley girl. She won't hear of doing anything but help Eleanor, even giving up her summer job. She is determined to get Eleanor home from the hospital, and she is the one Eleanor called. It is complicated because Eleanor is beginning to lose her mental balance, is determined not to stay in the hospital, understandably enough, and to go home to be with her cat Mitzi.

The doctor, according to Catherine at least, is wrong in that he won't tell Eleanor how ill she is. Her heart is very weak. He tells her that she's fine and can go right ahead and go home. What he doesn't realize is that she is blind, deaf, and has no help. She has to dress and bathe herself, has to get her meals. I think it is criminal of this doctor to send her home without finding out whether she can manage. Catherine says very wisely that you can't give her a nurse from outside, a stranger. She won't have a stranger in her house because any stranger disturbs the order of things. She knows exactly where each object is and if someone changes its place, she is lost.

So it is a difficult situation. I must say I went to bed last night in a traumatized state because of the perilousness of life on all sides, knowing that at any moment something frightful may happen. Although I do have a gardener, last week has taken its toll, because I was very near despair and also it is hard to forgive Diane. I did forgive her and told her we were friends, but she did leave me in the lurch—a very sick old woman—and it isn't right. Now I have her last bill for two hundred fifty-eight dollars, without a word of thanks or anything else.

Wednesday, July 3

IT IS still cool. I am proud to be able to say that I did a little gardening and got the tuberous begonias in that I have been nursing under lights in the little library. The only trouble was that the phone rang twice and I stupidly tried to reach it in time. In one case I did but by then I was terribly out of breath. Afterwards I felt it had been a big mistake to do it. However, I was out there for an hour and I am hoping to do more today.

The big event today is that Marcie Hershman is coming, just for a little talk and to celebrate the fact that her remarkable book is coming out in the fall, with, I hear now, what I wrote about it with such difficulty on the jacket. For once I managed to do what seemed at the time like the impossible.

Luckily Nancy told me that the new *Shady Hill News,* which comes out, I think, only once a year, was full of things that I should be interested to see, including a wonderful photograph of Anne Thorp, whom I celebrated as *The Magnificent Spinster;* and a very amusing photograph of my class for which they wanted some missing names, some of which I can provide, I think. As I looked through the news of other classes and saw what Shady Hill has turned out to be, how many of its students become public servants of one kind or another, how many are concerned actively with the environment, with social services, I was dazzled by what this school is and can do.

One of the most moving things in this issue is two obituaries: one of a student who died at twenty-six, greatly beloved, and one of a teacher in the craft classes who was him-

self a great craftsman, named John Eliassen. This is an obit of
Eliassen by the Reverend Bruce Bayne, who I presume may
be a graduate. I think I must read it all:

> John is an angel for us. He has been, and he is. We must
> be very cautious and careful that we do not squander
> John's gift. We are all angels to each other, as John has
> taught us, and we must discern the angel in us and the
> angel in the other. We must be careful to be the angels
> God means for us to be, and we must allow another to be
> an angel for us. That is what we learn from John. His gift
> was particularly to allow us to be who we are. He was a
> friend without placing his own agenda over ours, leaving
> us free. Being who we are—angels—is not easy, but nei-
> ther is it hard. It is what John means we must do.
>
> Right after John died, another telephoned me, an
> angel for me. I told her what I was going through.
> "Here's what you need," said she. "It comes as a gift
> from the fourth century, from St. John Chrysostom."
> Here it is, a gift for each of us:
>
> > He whom we love and lose,
> > Is no longer where he was before,
> > He is now wherever we are.

I read that and the tears just sprang from my eyes. I thought
of Eva LeGallienne, of course, who has been with me all these
days since her death, and, of course, of my parents who are
never not with me. They are where I am.

Thursday, the Fourth of July

I HAVE on a red shirt—a red patriotic shirt—to celebrate. I am having a lobster with Edythe in a little while. It is a beautiful, clear, cool day with a few high clouds, but not a perfectly blue ocean this time.

I have been in a state of happiness. Very rarely in the past year have I been happy, because of illness. But after the trauma of thinking I had to watch the garden die, the relief of finding a wonderful gardener who will take over is so great that it is like suddenly being levitated above the ground—to the extent that I have buzzing in my head the idea for a short novella. I do not suppose it will ever get written, but I have not had a creative urge like that for months.

Yesterday Marcie Hershman came. We had agreed that we would not try to eat in case I wasn't feeling well, that we would just sit and talk. But I felt very well. I am doing better than I would have thought possible a month ago. So I said, "Let's go out, to the new Foster's, where I see they have steamed clams. That I can manage." So we went out. We were the first people there at half past eleven. I ordered clams and Marcie ordered a lobster roll—only to find out that they had run out of clams last night! It really was a blow, but then I ordered the lobster roll, too, did not eat any of the bread, and had—*mirabile dictu*—a half a glass of Chardonnay. All of this seems to have worked pretty well in the digestive system.

I have gone back to David Cecil. At first I was a little

disappointed in the book *David Cecil: A Portrait by His Friends,* which I had ordered from England months ago. He was a wizard conversationalist, ebullient, erudite, wildly enthusiastic, and imaginative. That is, over and over again, what his friends write about him. But now that I have gone deeper into the book, I see that he was an extraordinarily beautiful person—charming and welcoming to everyone. I would like to quote now from one of the portraits, by Teresa Whistler, former wife of Lawrence Whistler. She was taught by David Cecil and afterwards worked as his secretary. She says:

> His commonsense eighteenth-century side made an equally strong impression on me. It did not at all conflict with his uncommon sensibility. He had shrewd, on the spot judgement about human nature. Good sense with good manners and the practice of contentment made up in his view a large part of wisdom. All his cultivation— the light touch, love of beauty (especially romantic beauty), the wide reading, strong sense of history and grasp of affairs (belonging to his family inheritance)—all this rested on something more profound which we did not much discuss then, but later we did, as the bond between us deepened: a spiritual foundation which was unusually sunlit. He agreed with Johnson—"the only end of writing is to enable the reader better to enjoy life or better to endure it." Literature was to him news—of a homeland he never doubted—and spoke to the soul.

It was a tremendous joy to see Marcie whose book *Tales of the Master Race* is to my mind a work of genius. It is her first published novel and has earned her a good advance. I am glad to report that they will use part of my blurb on the jacket. Marcie's book tells us what went on in German cities under Hitler, as, for instance, guillotines in the cellars of various chosen executioners. It is a horrifying story. I hope very much that it will be read as there seems to be a growing group of extreme rightists who wish to prove that the Holocaust never happened.

Marcie was in splendid form, looking very well, and on her way to Israel next month with her friend. She says that the lesbian group she lives among—in Brookline where she lives—includes many who are planning to adopt a child or to have one. Just below her in the apartment she rents in her house is a lesbian couple who have a little Brazilian girl whom they got when she was five months old and who is now a year and a half old and a perfect joy, according to Marcie.

Sunday, July 14

TWO VERY DIFFERENT, wonderful days: July twelfth and thirteenth. On the twelfth, by great good luck, it was a cool day, not very bright, but cool and there were no mosquitoes for the first time this summer. So Susan suggested, and it was a very good idea, that she bring out the cushions for the chaise longue and the chairs and that we offer Bruce and Deborah Straw, who were coming, champagne on the terrace. We had some marvelous champagne biscuits that Susan had found and we had a delightful time, with the cat wandering around looking lordly, and good talk about everything. Bruce and Deborah have come into my life in the last couple of years and I am happy to have them as friends. They live in Burlington, Vermont. Deborah is a writer and teacher; she is particularly interested in teaching the old. She even had a woman of ninety in one of her classes. She has her students keep journals. She must be a great teacher—so much so that when she

CREDIT: BRUCE CONKLIN

May, Cybèle, Susan

and Bruce gave a party for me some years ago when I first met them in Burlington, one of Deborah's students was there—a woman in her sixties I would guess—who suddenly turned to me and said, "You should give up writing altogether and just teach." I was upset—she didn't know my work of course—but I realized then it was because she had had such a great teacher that she felt teaching was *the* most important thing that anyone could do. So that was nice.

Bruce has recently bought a hand press and is doing some wonderful work, notably an unpublished essay of Henry James on Burlington. It is a beautiful job.

They came with flowers, short-grain rice, and an invention of Bruce's. I had begged him, because he does invent things and is kind of a natural-born engineer, to see if he could find some way of keeping the squirrels away from the bird feeder. This he succeeded in doing to some extent, although occasionally a squirrel manages to go under the chicken wire that he surrounded the bird feeder with. We'll see what happens. His doing that for me makes me think of all the people who help me with things. How lucky I am!

When I talked to Doris Beatty in Berkeley, California, yesterday she said she had found a hot water bottle that heats itself—I think you have to rub it—if the lights go out. Isn't that a wonderful present? When the lights went out the other day for an hour, in the middle of my nap, I was miffed that I could not have my hot water bottle.

Yesterday—in some ways a gloomy day—it began to rain heavily in the middle of the afternoon, and rained all evening and all night. Today is a little brighter. The rain was good because we needed it so badly.

Yesterday was a fine, homey day which both Susan and I enjoyed, although she did a huge shopping that took most of the morning. It was only somewhat dimmed by my having bad pain again. I expect this will happen now and then. But on the whole I am much better. I wake up looking forward to the day.

We watched, in the afternoon, a wonderful old movie on Juárez, the great founder of Mexico as we know it. What joy it is to see this kind of treat with Susan, for I would never do it alone. It was very well written and is a fascinating study and exploration of two very different men, each in his way appealing: one, of course, very great, Juárez himself; the other, the emperor Maximilian of Hapsburg, a good man, but, unfortunately, totally ignorant of what he was getting into, cheated by a fake plebiscite, to think that he was wanted by the people. It was interesting also to see an early Bette Davis, looking so young and pretty, in rather a small role as Maximilian's wife.

Susan cooked us a celebratory supper, of rice done somehow with herbs and onions. It was wonderful. And haddock, very fresh and tasty, and her marvelous carrots, very thin and in curls, just delicious. So here I am, a lucky old woman, rejoicing in her life on this great earth.

Tuesday, July 16

ANOTHER WONDERFUL clear day, although they say that the humidity will be creeping up. But right now we have beautiful, champagne air. Nadine has done a wonderful job of cutting the grass on the terrace, made carrot juice for me, made the bed, and is off. So all is peaceful while Susan works in her room, Nancy works upstairs, and I am about to go up there to read part of Susan's book, which is so exciting. It really is going to be a wonderful book, I think.

I am behind because I did not dictate yesterday and that was too bad because on Sunday we had a splendid day. We had been invited by Margaret Whalen and Barbara to go over there. They have a beautiful house which they have renovated themselves, on a rocky ledge in Cape Neddick, looking over toward Short Sands. They are beneficent, darling people. Susan enjoyed it tremendously and so did I. They have an old dog, sixteen years old—so well behaved. Each teaches, in different schools, Margaret the first and second grades in Exeter; Barbara the fifth grade in Durham. They are doing an experiment in Durham which is being watched all over the country. They are bringing into a class of especially brilliant children five or six retarded, or in some way crippled, children. Barbara has already decided on a plan to get the less advanced children to work on a project about the Monarch butterfly. She is talking about getting big enough bottles, so every child can have a bottle. There are, I think, six of these children with problems. She takes them on all kinds of expeditions. She and Margaret are the most giving teachers I have ever heard of. These are public schools of course. They even used to have the children come after school, a few of them, sometimes for supper. That seems to be going way beyond the call of duty! Now of course they are older. Margaret talks of retiring next year. She will be sixty then. Barbara is eight years younger and says she loves the children and does not plan to retire for a while.

We had a beautiful time. They asked me what I could eat, so we had something I can eat, which is steamed clams, although Dr. Khanjani says "no." But she also says, "It is your own risk. Don't blame me!" I have had no trouble with steamed clams. I feel it is about the healthiest food there is: full of iodine, very soft, easy to digest. So today I am having lunch with Edythe and we will go to Foster's little restaurant where I hope they'll have them.

I am immersed in *Possession*. It is an extraordinary work, and yet one which I find extremely unlovable and rather pretentious. But one realizes that an enormous amount of learning has been tamed and a lot of first-rate imaginative work has been done. So it is something to admire, but never to reread. That is a test for me of whether a book is really good or not.

I am now very busy getting ready to go to the Cape for my yearly visit with Rene Morgan. This time it will be like moving a household because of all the medicines and all the things like chlorophyll and aloe vera that I take every day and have to have with me—for example, Sea Klenz, which is a great big jar. But we shall manage. Maggie will drive me down.

Now I must go up to my desk, rejoicing, and dying to see what choices Susan has made from my early, unpublished letters, journals, and so on for her book. It is quite exciting.

Wednesday, July 17

WE ARE in for some very hot weather, but until now the air has been surprisingly clear. Wonderful in the garden these days are the lilies—the lilies and that blue hydrangea, that incredible blue, I should say, that I ordered from Winterthur and which is a wild success. There is something about the flat bloom of this hydrangea—instead of being a mound they are flat, which gives them great character and charm. Now the phlox is out, at least what was not eaten by deer.

Yesterday morning I had the extraordinary experience of reading fifty pages of Susan's book which she has been assembling and thinking about for five years—using all unpublished material of mine, mostly from my archive at the Berg Collection at the New York Public Library. It is called *Among the Usual Days*. It really gave me a tremendous lift and made me rejoice and feel that all that work that she did was not in vain—as I sometimes have wondered whether I was simply not worth all this. But I am. It is a remarkable series of statements by a person who goes on growing to the end, and who is a poet. This comes through all the time. Susan has a very good eye for what is important—and for what is important in different ways, because it gives an idea of what I'm thinking, it puts the reader right down where I am—in a certain house, for example, Elizabeth Bowen's *Bowen's Court*; Basil de Selincourt's at Kingham near Oxford; or La Roselle at Satigny with Meta. Of course, as I read, all these faces come up through the text. It is like a great feast of friends and the many lives I have lived. I am eager to go up and start on the second part.

Monday, July 22

AT LAST the heat wave has broken. It has been the hottest I can remember, even on the Cape, to which I go tomorrow to stay with Rene. To wake this morning and be a little chilly was a marvelous moment.

I have a lot to talk about today because recently it has been impossible to work because in addition to the heat, I again have had an enormous amount of pain. I am tired of it and do not know how to handle it. If it is the toxic material at last coming away, the pain is a different pain from ordinary digestive pain. Unfortunately the pain killer Tylenol plus codeine does not seem to work. Yesterday morning, for instance, the cramps lasted for two hours when I could not even get up. I could not have a bath. I just had to wait. And then last night again for two hours. Now, at nearly half past seven in the morning, I have been struggling with it since five.

There have been good things in these two days. On Friday, in the awful heat, Barbara Solomon, who is writing a biography of Ada Comstock, came with her daughter to interview me about the letters—these wonderful letters that with her prodding I discovered Ada Comstock had written to me about various books—especially *Faithful Are the Wounds*, which of course brought back all the bitterness of Harry Levin's reaction. He was sure that my character Professor Goldberg was a portrait of him. Actually I based the character on an instructor I saw only once at an English faculty meeting. I was teaching freshman English at Harvard at that time. Harry refused to believe me and has ever since been an enemy in a very real sense, that he has done me harm and has certainly tried to do so. This is sad.

Barbara Solomon is a charming woman. She came in a lovely straw hat with a red ribbon which had been the hat of her fiftieth Radcliffe reunion last year. She had run the Radcliffe Seminars before I gave them for two years, and she has done a great deal for Radcliffe in many ways. I think she will be an excellent biographer, and I am longing to see the biography because certainly Ada Comstock was a great woman—a great president of Radcliffe when it was difficult to be president of Radcliffe, the stepchild of Harvard. I do not know whether people still remember, but when my father taught the history of science at Harvard he had to give two lectures on the same day because, instead of the Radcliffe girls being invited to come into the Harvard lecture halls, the professors were asked to give a second lecture at Radcliffe.

I greatly enjoyed our talk. It brought back so much that has happened, and one rather interesting story which I think it is time to tell. In the last year of my theater company—the Associated Actors Theatre, Inc.—I had the idea that Radcliffe might be interested in paying us five thousand dollars to base in Cambridge. Five thousand would have kept my company together for a year. We would have rented a house in Cambridge and worked from there. I sold Ada Comstock on the idea that students would be able to watch rehearsals, would even be in some of the plays, and of course would see the finished productions, which were often modern European plays that had not been seen in America.

Ada Comstock had agreed to this proposal, and it would have saved the company and our dream. I was very happy about it, and she was enthusiastic. But unfortunately a friend of mine, Mrs. Henry Copley Greene, Rosalind Greene, whose daughter had had a bad experience with a love affair with a woman—and Rosalind was savage on the subject of homosexuality—took it on herself, without even telling me, to go to Ada Comstock, having persuaded Katharine Taylor, the head of the Shady Hill school, to go with her, and told Comstock that there were homosexuals in my company. At that time I had not come out, but it was true that one of my directors was a lesbian. I immediately called Ada Comstock, of course, and asked her to see us, which she did very graciously. She was put in an impossible position by this. She could not have been more tolerant in all she said, or nicer and kinder. But she did say, "The trouble is now I know this fact. If it came to the attention of the trustees I am afraid it would be a bad business. So I'm going to have to go back on this agreement with you that I was so looking forward to keeping." That was a savage blow, and I found it hard to forgive Katharine Taylor, whom I had, until then, adored. But somehow I cannot keep resentment and forgave Rosalind and Katharine long ago. But the harm was done, and our last chance of surviving was gone.

That was one day. The second day was even better. Marilyn Kallet, the poet and good friend who is editing a book of essays about my poetry, came to see me. She has been teaching in Tennessee. I am so happy about her visit. She looked absolutely beautiful. She has a little girl, six years old. We went out to Foster's for lunch and had a lobster. What a celebration! And a good talk about everything. She said that she hadn't been sure she wanted a child, but now she is in love with Heather, her little girl, now six. Marilyn told me that she was homesick. She has been teaching at Hofstra for two weeks and rented a car to come up and see me on her way home. She must be in the air now on her way to Tennessee.

When we came back from lunch she taped a short interview with me, with some questions she particularly wanted answered about the muse. This is not an easy question to answer because it is so intangible. The muse was not always a lover by any means. In fact I think the most productive muses, productive in the sense of being the ones for whom I wrote the best poems, were not lovers—Edith Kennedy and Louise Bogan are two examples. Even women who had dazzled my heart did not become muses. For instance, Eva LeGallienne, who was glamour personified and whom I adored; I think I may have written only one poem for her in all those years.

There is now the hard news that tomorrow when Maggie drives me to the Cape it is going to be humid and hot again. But at least today and tonight will be better, and I should be able to get the packing done. Yesterday I couldn't do anything. I realize when I have this pain how much I enjoy the little things like packing a suitcase or arranging flowers. If I cannot do them it is very frustrating.

The most important thing I have to say today has to do with watching the video Stephen Robitaille made in Gainesville with the unfortunate title of *Creativity in the Upward Years*. The phrase "upward years" makes me laugh. But Marilyn was very much moved by it and I have discovered that I can enjoy seeing it indefinitely. As I watched it now for perhaps the sixth time, I thought, I must be very narcissistic to enjoy watching myself over and over again. Of course there is the marvelous Mozart music, beautifully synchronized with my reading. That is a joy, but the reason I can watch the video forever is that here is this old thing, me, doing quite a good job under certain difficulties like bad lighting and having almost lost her voice. I watch this old lady with enormous interest and some admiration, but I do not feel related to her. She is simply not me as I recognize myself. So it makes a rather strange play in which I am watching someone who is not the May Sarton I am inside myself.

Wednesday, July 31

I HAVE been away on the Cape for my annual holiday at Rene Morgan's in Harwich. Rene's house is a little jewel, set down among those Japanese-looking pine trees that are so characteristic of the Cape. In the ten years or so that she has had the house, bushes and trees have grown up around it and it looks as if it has been there forever—a gray-shingled Cape Cod house like so many others. It has a nice screened-off, outdoor patio where we could not sit very often because it was either frightfully hot or cold, not a good week from the point of view of weather, but a very good week from the point of view of friendship.

Unfortunately I had a hard time with my old digestive problem so I was in a great deal of pain. Still, there were good moments and times. Rene is one of the most benign people who ever lived in her capacity to do whatever a friend needs, to respond to any demand. So she was wonderful at bringing me hot water bottles when I needed them most, and at leaving me alone when that was what I needed. I had a wonderful week. I have no regrets about it. And it was great fun to have Maggie drive me there and drive me home. On the way and on the way back we had a picnic, each time in quite a lovely picnic place at a table. As usual, perfectly delicious food was provided by Maggie: crabmeat sandwiches on the way, and

on the way back it was cream cheese and parsley with a delicious white wine which I had a little of, and cooked peaches
with vermouth—all perfectly delicious. The vermouth tasted
a little like ginger.

The great event of the week was a visit by Laurence and
Eda LeShan, and a great, wonderful talk about everything
under the sun. Eda has had a mild stroke and she, I know, was
shocked at seeing me because she has not seen me for two
years, two years during which I lost fifty pounds. I have not
seen her since her stroke, so we each had something to face.
We did enjoy it so much. I always enjoy them. Our spirits
meet in a thousand ways, from politics to coping with old age
or the cost of living. They are such great human beings.

I had brought a bottle of Mumm's that Mary-Leigh had
given me for my birthday, but unfortunately we couldn't have
it because neither of them can have liquor. I should not have it
either, but I find a half glass of champagne is not a bad thing.

While I was away Susan and Nancy held the fort. It was
not easy because they had to deal with the painters, who are
now painting the inside of all those forty windows in this
house. Such beneficent men, but I know it was chaos and hell,
the smell of paint all the time, and people milling around all
day. Luckily the dear women who work for me came, two of
the four days they would normally come, and helped tidy up,
wash curtains and clean. Meanwhile I was spared all this
nightmare of clutter and I am grateful. Now it is wonderful to
be home again.

Friday, August 2

It is going to be another hot day, but so far fairly dry. When I came back from the Cape I walked into a house filled with the most amazing bunches of flowers, including a great many tiger lilies. It turned out that imaginative Susan had gone out on the roads and simply found wild places and picked wild-flowers. These lilies were really wild. There were many other things whose names I don't even know, but the bunches were spectacular. The charming part of the story is that when she was plundering an open field right on Route 1, a man came out and said, "Go ahead, pick them! You have the right tools"—she had some clippers with her—"and by all means, yes, take the lilies!" Somehow there was something so endearing and so much of what is best about York, the kindness of people, in his doing this.

In the garden itself what is best now is the balloon flower—platycodon—a marvelously exciting deep blue in the middle of all the magenta phlox and the white Shasta daisies. The garden looks spectacular at the moment.

Today I go to see Dr. Gilroy, whom I haven't seen, it appears, for five months. The main thing is that he has a very good weighing machine so I shall find out whether I have gained anything.

I am immersed in a French book that my cousin Solange sent at my request. It is called *Une Soupe aux Herbes Sauvages,* a soup made with wild herbs—what a marvelous title! The book itself is extremely interesting but also depressing

because it tells in great detail how hard life was for the peas-
ants in Provence in the years before World War II. A terribly
hard life, and narrow. This woman, who came out of that
environment and became a schoolteacher, is not narrow at all.
One wonders how genius like this springs out of such extreme
lack of sophistication. One of her sisters died in childbirth
because she would not allow the doctor or the midwife who
were present to look under her nightgown. The baby was
born dead and they did not even know when the water broke.
Then she died of puerperal fever. This is a brutal story. It was,
for once, a marriage for love. Mostly, in the countryside there,
marriages were made for land. If your son will marry my
daughter he'll bring with him such and such a field, and my
daughter will bring that little area of woodland. So many
hearts were broken by these arranged marriages, but this
poor woman was happily married and then taken in such a
brutal way.

Sunday, August 4

A SOMBER DAY it is—very chilly and gray. But of course it is
much more viable than a hot day would be. I look forward to
getting something done today for a change.

Yesterday, my mother's birthday, was a perfectly beautiful day, with a calm, sapphire ocean beyond the golden field
that is now in its supreme beauty. The field will be cut, of
course, within a week or so and go back to stubble, but now it
is glorious. I am glad to say that Susan has got a photograph of
it because it is one of the irresistible sights of Wild Knoll in
August.

We celebrated my mother's birthday by giving each other a present. I gave Susan a little cup and saucer from Mother's collection. I am ignorant about the English china she collected. It is something she loved and it has been on her desk downstairs ever since I came here. I think it will look lovely in Susan's beautiful apartment.

Susan gave me an adorable little Limoges box with a cat sitting on it. We opened a bottle of Mumm's. I drank two glasses with no apparent bad results so far. It was delicious. We ate some of those marvelous Italian *biscottes* made for champagne. They are very good indeed—not too sweet and yet not too sharp.

Both Susan and I had mistaken *Singin' in the Rain* for *An American in Paris;* both of course have Gene Kelly as the star. *Singin' in the Rain* is without doubt the worst movie I have ever seen! There wasn't a single funny or clever line. We had Kelly dancing, but it was a 1920s musical about the coming of talking pictures. Of course we all remember "Garbo talks!" The plot here concerns the star of a silent movie which they changed into a talking movie and, of course, the female star had a dreadful, screaming voice and they had to get somebody else to play her part. So we turned it off after half an hour; there was nothing else to do. But we had plenty to talk about.

We had a delicious supper of flounder and Susan's wonderful carrots and stewed peaches with a little ginger on a slice of orange pound cake for dessert—a sumptuous meal.

There was only one contretemps in the middle of the night because Pierrot demanded to be let out at half past one, which is his usual time these days. So I let him out. Then I fell fast asleep almost at once and dreamed that he was meowing to go out, so I got up, hazy with sleep, and trotted downstairs thinking he would follow me. Of course he was already out. I had forgotten. No Pierrot. So I hung around, wondered if he was in the cellar, finally went back to bed and realized that it had all been a dream.

Last night I did not have any extraordinary dreams like the ones I have been having lately. I was spared the nightmares.

Now everything is on edge, getting ready for this Monday which is going to be a humdinger of a day. It is the day on which Neila Seshachari from the State University of Ogden, Utah, comes to interview me. There has been a rather ticklish correspondence over the interview. I am not looking forward to it. Not only that, but Pat is coming early in the morning, and meanwhile a box of iris has arrived—tiny little slivers of iris. I am disappointed. Pat must try to put them in. Of course Nadine will be here. The interview is at eleven. I see Dr. Khanjani at one-thirty. I have suggested to Neila that she come back at four and see the video. She brought books for me to sign although she knows I am ill. She does not seem to be imaginative about the needs of other people.

Finally I shall find myself alone here—Susan having left for New York for a week. I shall make my little supper and, I am sure, miss her very much.

Tuesday, August 6

YESTERDAY WAS a day I had dreaded for days and it was a very full day—perhaps typical of my life now which seems to be rather driven, although I get so little done.

Pat Robinson, who gardens for me, came at eight. She usually comes in the early afternoon. What's wonderful is that she can do the things I've wanted to do for so long and not had the energy to do, among them to take the lily-of-the-valley out of the terrace garden. It was God-given that she came because a big order of iris came two days ago, and I wanted them to have places. She took out all the lily-of-the-valley, which Susan was very eager to have for her garden in New York.

At eleven Neila Seshachari came to interview me for the *Webber Review*. I had dreaded the interview because I felt that her questions did not lead me to good answers. She is a charming woman, a Hindu, married to a Tamil, a lovely-looking woman who, I could hardly believe, has a son of over thirty. Strangely enough, for the interview, I had gotten myself into a storm of nerves. I felt dizzy and rather queer as though I were talking through a haze, so I don't think I did as well as I should have. Themes were introduced and never resolved. For instance, I was anxious to talk about what the United States had done for my father and me. She had questioned why I felt alienated in the United States. Actually it was more than I felt more at home in Europe. But the fact is that if I had grown up as a Belgian poet, I would have had a very hard time. Belgium is a country divided between two languages, Flemish and French. Also I'm sure that English is the best language for poetry, combining as it does the earthy Anglo-Saxon syllables and the Latin clarity of the Norman. Just off hand: a crystal earth. It does not make sense but the combination of earth and crystal is what I mean. I wanted to say that. Also, for my father, whose great dream was the writing of the history of science, it was a godsend to be forced out of Belgium as a refugee from the German armies in '14 because there are no foundations in Europe, so far as I know, like the Carnegie Foundation which took my father on, paid him a small salary for the next forty years or until he died, and made it possible for him to do his heroic work in peace. Although we were never well off, this security, and the fact that he did not have to teach full time, was an enormous blessing.

After the interview with Neila, Susan brought me lunch before she drove off to New York. So kind of her because it was then about half past twelve and I was due at Dr. Khanjani's at one-thirty. I made it, and she was extremely happy that I am having, suddenly, an incredibly good time with my digestion.

I came back and Neila, whom I'd invited to come back at four as she had books for me to sign, brought lovely red roses. We played the video of the interview. It is useful, particularly the part where I talk about old age. I answered some of the questions she asked me better on the video. It is a precious addition to my archive.

The great event is a book, and that is Eudora Welty's correspondence with the literary agent Diarmuid Russell, who came into her life at the right moment, when she was writing short stories but not selling except to very highbrow magazines like *Southern Review*. Diarmuid immediately recognized genius. For the rest of his life—he died in 1973—and for all of her career, Diarmuid was there as a wonderful critic, friend, and fighter for Eudora Welty. I just hug myself to think what might have happened if she hadn't found this kind of agent, because Diarmuid believed in quality. He believed that quality, in the end, would pay. So I must say once more that I was also incredibly lucky to have him as my agent. I was not writing short stories when I first went to him, but novels. I had published a couple of novels as I remember. I sent him a little short sketch that I did for fun, called "The Old Fashioned Snow." He sold it to *Colliers* for six hundred dollars! This was more money than I had ever seen, and I was staggered by it. With that inspiration I went on and, in the end, sold thirty or so stories to the slicks through Diarmuid, and also some pieces of autobiography to the *New Yorker* where

Diarmuid introduced me. His introduction carried weight.

He was a brisk, business-like, tough man, the son of the poet A.E., with a great sense of literature and what it's all about, and an enormous respect for writers. He could make mistakes, however. He advised me not to publish *Mrs. Stevens* . . . Fortunately I said, "Well, Diarmuid, let's just try Norton. If they turn it down, I'll give it up." Of course Norton took it, the only stipulation being that I not use a pseudonym, as I had been tempted to do because it was a daring book dealing with the homosexual woman poet back in the 1960s. My present agent, Tim Seldes, resembles Diarmuid in his honesty, his toughness, and his sensitivity. I am lucky to have an agent who cares about the kind of, in some ways, unsuccessful writer I am.

Thursday, August 8

ANOTHER OF these marvelous, brilliant, cool days, with the ocean its autumn color and everything standing up straight, and happy in the coolness.

Yesterday I finally threw away the enormous bunches of wildflowers that Susan had gathered. They were glorious, but suddenly I had had it and wanted the flowers to represent my vision of life rather than hers. So I went to Foster's. I had not been to the florist for weeks. I was beside myself with all the beauty there. This is the beginning of the autumn flowers, so there were wonderful asters, chrysanthemums, marvelous carnations, five dollars a dozen. Those I did not get because I wanted a big lily. I got some asters with a big white lily and some single yellow chrysanthemums, very beautiful, that I have not seen before—I think they are flown in from Holland—and one huge lavender Shasta daisy which I would love to have in my garden. I succumbed finally to a white gloxinia plant. The plant window needs white these days. There is a little too much of the orangey-pink geraniums and hibiscus and this lifts it all up.

I came back very excited and arranged the flowers and then waited around for Roger and Ann Sweet and two of their children, Lydica and Chris, to come at eleven for a reunion. They used to come to Maine every summer and so I saw them every year. It is a family of six children. Stopping by here was an event for them and an event for me as I watched them grow up. Now they are all doing extraordinary things. Chris is working in Princeton, New Jersey, on something to do with computer chips. Ann, his mother, told me, "Of course he'll set you up with a computer which will take your dictation and arrange it all. Just think of that!" Well, it terrifies me. Lydica has been one of the children who love my work. She was crazy about *Harriet Hatfield* much to my pleasure.

They are a most remarkable family. They have a summer place in Sullivan, right next door to Nelson where I lived for many years, so they bring me news of the neighbors, which is always precious. They have now made a pond which they are stocking with trout and bass and a fish with a strange name which apparently scours the bottom and keeps it clean—horn pout, that's it—what a name for a fish! Ann has a wonderful garden. Maybe next year I can get Susan to drive me there because it is about the same distance as going to Huldah's—a little over two hours. I would love her to see Nelson.

After the Sweets left I went to see Dr. Khanjani who is very pleased with me and tells me there is a little flesh over my ribs now, as I learned at Dr. Gilroy's. So in a spurt of enthusiasm I weighed myself only to find it back at ninety-five exactly.

Today there is no one helping me which, in a way, is a relief. Eleanor called to say she would come on Saturday. She has to take her husband to the veterans' hospital today. I got up at six, got the tray ready for my breakfast, made my breakfast, and carried it upstairs. I could not have done it six months ago. I could not have lifted the tray and especially I could not have taken it down the stairs. After having my breakfast I looked briefly at the television news, which said that Terry Anderson might have been released, but did not accompany the English reporter who was released. It does seem an agony of suspense for Terry's sister, who has fought so long and hard on his behalf. Apparently the reporter was chained to the wall much of the time, blindfolded, and in solitary confinement for five years.

Pierrot is now lying full length on the bed beside me and will help me read the mail. The house seems very silent without Susan and Cybèle. On the other hand silence is precious.

Friday, August 9

LUCKILY we are going to get some rain. There was a kind of pale rosy sunrise this morning. It has been a long time since I've seen the sun rise, and I loved it. But then before breakfast I immersed myself in a copy of the *New Statesman*—a lot of them had accumulated while I was on the Cape—and read a devastating report on what we really did in Iraq. I realized especially when reading an article by John Pilger that underneath this summer there has been all the time a deep, buried depression in me. The depression has to do with the war in Iraq and what we did. We bear such a heavy load of guilt which most Americans are absolutely blind to. What are we doing to help rebuild Iraq? Pilger says:

> The full cost of Iraq's "defiance" of the earlier dead-line was summarised in a report published last month by the Medical Educational Trust in London. The American-led attack caused the deaths of up to a quarter of a million people. Child mortality in Iraq has doubled: 170,000 under-fives are expected to die in the coming year—an estimate described as "conservative." (UNICEF says five million children could die in the region.) In addition, 1.8 million people have been forced from their homes, and Iraq's electricity, water, sewage, communications, health, agriculture and industrial infrastructure have been "substantially destroyed," producing "conditions for famine and epidemics." In the wider world, the American action has caused the equivalent of a natural disaster in 40 low- and middle-income countries, where the economic cost is calculated at $18 billion. Add to this the continuing ecological disaster and the stimulus to the international arms trade.
>
> Bush set in train this mayhem knowing—as many of us now know—that Saddam Hussein was likely to withdraw his forces from Kuwait; his emissaries and signals were either ignored or misread.

It's so terrible to think that Bush is a national hero and that somehow or other nobody in America thinks about this or takes responsibility for it. So it is a huge festering cancer of irresponsibility and stark sadism at the center of our civilization—if it can now be called that. We go on having parades and congratulating ourselves that we lost only a little under three hundred people (it now appears they were lost mostly to friendly fire). So no wonder the Iraqi people hate us. By all this we are building up Saddam Hussein. He is the martyred one. The fact that he is still alive and that he is the one magnet for loyalty means simply that we have left him, as it is, stronger than ever. In all this, Bush comes through as so superficial, so nationalistic in the most infantile sense, that it makes me shudder and begins this day, as it has so many others, under a heavy, heavy cloud. I am ashamed to be a citizen of these United States.

Saturday, August 10

YESTERDAY Peter Pease came to take me out to lunch. It was a glorious, cool, bright day, unfortunately followed by an absolutely wild, terrifying night of hard rain and wind. I felt lonely. It was almost like a hurricane. Now it is still raining and I have had to do a big shopping and I am tired. But I want to talk about Peter because he is such a rare friend. I do not have a great many male friends. Peter, I think, has been coming here for about five years—came first because he liked my work. We hit it off right away because he is a romantic. He is a successful lawyer, has his own firm, is divorced with two children whom he adores and whom he sees a lot. I think if I were forty—he is forty now—and had not married I would try awfully hard to get him to marry me. The reason he is so rare is because he *is* a romantic—not a fashionable trait these days. But mostly he is rare because he loves women. He is more than interested in women; they fascinate him. He wants to know all about them. He reminds me very much in this way of myself when I was a young woman who was attracted to women and the tremendous excitement of discovering a new person. This was during those years in England when I was, as I have said elsewhere, in love with everyone and everyone was in love with me—partly because my theater having failed, I was suddenly released at twenty-five into a normal young woman's life. I suppose, in some ways, Peter is released into the life of a bachelor now.

We talked about everything. He is sensitive to the state of the world. One of the subjects we talked about was—how shall I say it?—the obligation to be happy and to enjoy, as he does so much, the world around one: the people, the plants, the flowers, the weather—and yet to be as aware as possible of the suffering and terror of the world we live in, of the children who are starving, and of how to keep a balance between one's private life, which one wants to be as happy and nourishing to others as possible, and an awareness of tragedy beyond the bounds of the personal which must never be out of our minds altogether.

It happened that yesterday I really was in a state of depression about our treatment of Iraq and about the war in general. So seeing Peter was really a blessing. He usually brings me a present. Once it was a wonderful Zuni bear made of dark red rock. This time it was a small poem which he had written himself and which touched me very much.

It is true that European men are more apt to like women. For the American male a woman is too often simply a sex object. You know: how can I get her to bed? With no preliminary finding-out about each other, people go to bed. No wonder there are so many divorces. I feel that Peter is a male who makes love. He doesn't *take* a woman.

Back to Peter's poem:

> I have
> no hearth,

                    but this.
                    A heart at rest,
                    a kiss.

I read it as we were driving to the restaurant. I found it touching from this forty-year-old successful lawyer who is such a
romantic at heart! I said at once, "Peter, if you can say 'a
heart at rest' you are a wise man." It is true. It is rare—a heart
at rest. Most days now mine is.

Sunday, August 11

I HAVE HAD a tremendous adventure toward which I have
been moving very slowly for months, and that is that at five-
thirty I called London and talked to Juliette Huxley at last.
She sounded just like herself and seemed very glad to hear
from me, but she kept saying "Where are you?" so I am afraid
she hoped I was in London—as now I begin to think I may be
one day again. It really was thrilling to hear her voice and to
be in touch again. It sets the seal on my being well at last.

Yesterday Joan Jansen and her husband came, he tactfully
leaving us alone, and I took her out to lunch. His family is
from Antwerp so we are fellow Flemings. He is a great sailor
and has a twenty-seven-foot sloop, she told me. Joan is a most
remarkable woman who is now in the middle of her doctoral
thesis on the attitude of the Roman Catholic church to abor-
tion. She is a birthright Catholic, but disillusioned by the present pope and by what is happening now. She is a grandmother with a darling little grandson. The hard thing, and it is
true of many people these days, is that her mother lives with

them. She is ninety-two, somewhat paranoid, and extremely difficult. Joan is the kindest person in the world, but this is very, very hard. She has been married almost thirty-one years, and now she and her husband are never alone. So that coming up here—unfortunately through a colossal rainstorm—was a kind of escape. We had not seen each other for a very long time.

She brought magnificent flowers—Aurelian lilies, that wonderful crimson and white, and lavender asters. They are glorious! I think I'll have to bring them up to my bedroom to enjoy them. After all, I spend quite a lot of time in my bedroom.

Tuesday, August 13

ANOTHER BEAUTIFUL DAY. I am immersed in the book of Eudora Welty–Diarmuid Russell letters. This is a most extraordinary document and we must be grateful to Eudora Welty for publishing it. It also makes one nostalgic. Where are the literary agents today who are as pure as Diarmuid was? Of course, he inherited that purity from his father, the poet A.E., who would never have thought money was the most important thing about writing. One of the interesting revelations is the tremendous effort that those remarkable stories of Eudora Welty's took. When she finished the story "Livvie," she wrote Diarmuid:

> I am glad you thought the new story all of a piece. It was a supreme effort, really, that I made to have it so, but I thought the odds were against me, and felt worn out and

depressed afterwards. If there was any way to get the
envelope back out of the slot in the post-office after mailing, like with a long hook and a string—you would never
get a story, though I will race down in the middle of the
night, I'm so anxious to put it in. [April 23, 1942]

This is another insight on Welty. I was so happy to see that
she loved the *Très Riches Heures*. She is now working on the
series of stories on the Natchez Trace.

I suppose the subconscious mind as well as the conscious
can take a great liking to some time and a place in history
and see it in everything—but why? Isn't it mysterious? I
have never known much about the thirteenth century in
France, though I like it very well—enough to have cut
out and framed some of the "Très Riches Heures" a few
years back to hang over my bookcase, and on penetrating
through the superciliousness of Henry Adams in this
book [*Mont Saint-Michel and Chartres*] I find the things
I do most greatly admire, in the directness, simplicity of
belief, gaiety, strength, aspiration, purity, exuberancy,
etc. of that time reflected in all he relates, but I have not
got this *passion* for it that lies underneath. I feel depressed, though not scared to go to sleep at night or anything. Maybe you noticed that in my new story ["Livvie"] the Natchez Trace turned into a moat for a minute.
I was writing fast, in the center of my concentration, and
put that down, and just left it in. How can I speak of this
to anyone—they would think I am crazy, and maybe you
do, and maybe I am. It all may be just spring fever. Then
longen folk to goon on pilgrimages. There may be somebody in the world now thinking so hard on the 13th century that in my openness of dream and vacancy of mind I
caught it. I guess it will pass—although now I am determined to read and ponder all I am able on the time, and
force the connection through and see what is so marvel-

ous to me. I have to, when I can't doubt it—I had to say this to someone. [April 23, 1942]

There is one more passage that is so characteristic I cannot resist it. She is talking about the story "At the Landing."

I feel like trying to find some old silent niche this morning, that I must have had somewhere around, just to be still, for that's all I can be about my own evolving ideas, if I ever have any. There was something starting off in my head that I wanted to try in N.Y. if I can come away. Everybody is different, but for me ideas must go far off into excursions of their own, once they start, like somebody that walks along a little road in some country and samples the various berries and breaks off a stick to climb over the wild places with and drinks out of the brooks that come, and on & on, and you have to wait till they come back before you know what they found, but you had better be there when they get home. I think you might whistle to them, but not talk about them. [July 13(?), 1942]

Thursday, August 15

JEAN DOMINIQUE'S BIRTHDAY. I woke up thinking about her because we had been looking for photographs yesterday for Susan's book. I found many of that wonderful face. Of course no photograph could show the extraordinary eyes. She wore dark glasses most of the time so that sometimes when she took them off for a minute it was like a blaze of light. They were large and very intense, gray, as I remember, very much the

Jean Dominique (Marie Closset)

color of my mother's eyes. When one thinks of pure love and how rarely it is experienced in any life, I think that she and I did exchange, over a long period of years, a pure love because we felt we were twin souls. We never said this, but it was true. She was, of course, much older than I. Once she laughed and said with great pride, "I've loved as many times as you have!" That was wonderful. She was a romantic but also deeply rooted in reality, with a passionate sense of life which was visible in her study—the walls lined with Impressionist paintings, mostly by friends like Theo van Rysselberghe; always flowers. Her desk was in the middle of the study, which was very tidy as I remember it. She taught various courses in art as well as literature so there might be some materials for that strewn about. There was a stiff little bench, covered, in the window at the back of the room where we sat together often. Sometimes in the last years she would lean against my shoulder and fall asleep.

The *New Yorker* is carrying the last section of John Cheever's journals—much more endearing than the first group, a year or so ago, turned out to be. In these years he is dying of bone cancer. Somehow or other his cynicism and his black moods are shot through with a kind of humor and acceptance which is rather unexpected and very moving. He also goes to AA and has stopped drinking and, of course, this makes a huge difference in the whole atmosphere of the journals. I was struck by one passage because it so much resembles me and I am sure many other older people as they begin to lose their memory. It is terribly frustrating, of course. Suddenly I can't remember the name of my best friend. Cheever says:

> In talking I forget what it is that I was talking about. I am very reluctant to say that I have forgotten what I was talking about, but that is the case. The stratifications of memory that are revealed at this time of life can be bewildering. I presently find my way back into my own conversation, but I am embarrassed to have admitted for, I think, the first time that cliché of old age: "And now I have forgotten what I meant to say."

The line I love is "I presently find my way back into my own conversation"!

Yesterday was a great day because I saw, as I do about once a year, Susan Garrett, the one whose name I just forgot! She went to school to learn to be an administrator and became the administrator of our York Hospital here. Such a battle! Most of all the amount of male chauvinism. She never talks about it but I am sure it was there. She had to contend with the board. She has written a book about it in which she has had to make composite people. She cannot talk about the real ones. I am dying to read it. At the hospital the whole atmosphere was wonderful when she was head. How dear she was. I was there several times during that period and I remember once she brought me a red rose. It was exciting to be brought a red rose by the administrator of the hospital!

Susan is now sixty. It is hard to believe; she doesn't look that old. She has always been, I think, an extraordinarily wise woman. I suppose if you are married to a genius like George Garrett, you grow wisdom as a protection. The one comment she made that I could perfectly recognize was that because of George they see a great many writers. He is the most generous of writers in his backing of younger writers, and he teaches a lot. The result is that their house is full of writers, and writers are always complaining. Almost no writer is ever happy! That is why this book of letters between Diarmuid Russell and Eudora Welty is so precious because all through it flows their friendship and the richness of their relationship. Literally rare. We laughed a little about writers. I was able to say, "How wonderful it is to be having lunch with one who has nothing to complain about!"

It is a time of extraordinary serendipity for me because I am well. I say that and it ought to be written in capital letters: I AM WELL! and have been for about eight days. There is some pain, there are some uncomfortable times, but the difference is simply colossal! Waking up in the morning and looking forward to the day! I seem to be a little steadier on my legs. Dr. Petrovich, whom I saw two days ago, told me that I must not worry about not gaining weight—I am still at only ninety-five—because it is better for my heart that I be thin.

I found out that, through a misunderstanding, my check from Norton, advanced on the new journal, was not sent for two months. Now it is on the way.

Saturday, August 17

YESTERDAY WAS quite a day—an assemblage of all my life in
some ways. Susan and I spent more than an hour on the
photographs for *Among the Usual Days*. This means digging
up all kinds of things from when I was a child. There is one
darling one of me in my English granny's arms when I was
three months old, leaning over to touch a flower in the garden.
Then there are typical camp pictures of me when I was getting my Junior Red Cross, lying on the deck in a swimsuit and
cap. And so many others, because there are also all the
friends, the places, the houses of friends where I have stayed.
It is endless, also very rich, and brings so much back. At the
end of an hour I was almost *engloutie*, would be the French
word, drowned, as if by grasses under water—those grasses in
still ponds that can pull you down.

Phyllis Chiemingo came and I was so happy to be able to
take her out to lunch. Phyllis has been a great lover of the
work for many years and collects Sarton with the passion that
I collected Japanese netsuke. In spite of all her searches
through bookstores she is still missing three books. The early
ones are very hard to find. What she has done for me I cannot
describe. She is a great sender of flowers. More than once,
when I have been depressed, in the middle of the winter,
alone, sick, a fantastic bunch of flowers has arrived just to tide
me over the hump, like lifting me up on a great wave of joy.
We had a chick lobster and a good talk.

I had a short rest because at four Claire Douglas was

coming. The name was vaguely familiar but I had not put it together in my memory. Typically, I had forgotten why she wanted to see me. She arrived with a half bottle of Mumm's, a cake, and some herb tea, such dear presents. I had been feeling a little cross because I was tired, but all this immediately set the machinery going again. I looked at her and said, "I have seen you somewhere before!" She laughed and said, "Why should you remember that I was in your Radcliffe Seminar on the writing of poetry?" It was extraordinary that I had forgotten her.

Claire is writing a book on the woman who was the mistress of both Jung and Harry Murray, the psychiatrist who was the head of the Harvard Psychological Laboratory. What interested her, which is fascinating to me, of course, was what makes a muse? This woman she is writing about was a muse for these two great men. Claire is fascinated by the subject. I said that a muse should not be too giving, the muse should be the *princesse lointaine*, I suppose, is the phrase. We had a good talk about everything. She knew my work. After all, I had been her teacher. The most moving thing about that hour—and it was very moving—was that she said that when she was at Radcliffe she was very miserable, and nobody, none of her professors, was kind or interested, except George Sarton, my father, and May Sarton, me. She said she had gone to my father because she was working on a paper on Omar Khayyám, not the poet but his other self who was a scientist, something I didn't know. My father, who was at that point in the middle of the Middle Ages in his work, was interested and made her feel important. She said he talked to her mind and did not patronize her. I was so happy to see my father in the guise of a man who really cared and, if I may say, cared about women students whom the Harvard professors were apt to scorn. Altogether it was quite a day. I went to bed tired and in a good deal of pain.

I have nearly finished reading an extraordinary novel, *Light Years*, by James Salter. Is it a first novel? I am not sure, but his is an extraordinary style—a Mandarin style—a style which makes you want to stop and copy things out all the time. It is a depressing novel which is, I think, about the inevitable failure of the search for happiness. A married couple with two delightful daughters devote their lives to giving the children an ideal nurturing. Of course it does not work, but there are astonishing bravura passages. I am grateful to Bruce, who gave it to me.

Tuesday, August 20

IT HAS BEEN a wild two or three days since I have talked into this machine. I am in a kind of whirlwind because there is too much going on and I have not the strength to cope with it. It is hard to describe how full the days are. On top of everything else we had a hurricane! We had been warned of it and it landed yesterday. Wild wind and rain, in some places eight inches an hour. We did not have quite as much as that, thank goodness. The lights went out at three-fifteen and they have been out since then. It is now three-fifteen, twenty-four hours later, and it appears there are twelve thousand people without lights, so I am afraid we are in for it. Without electricity we have no water. It is particularly difficult for me not to be able to flush the toilet, and I miss the hot water bottle terribly. But a few years ago Huldah gave me an alcohol stove that you can heat water on, so this morning I was able to heat up some soup.

Yesterday was a fantastic example of what my life is like

these days, what pours in from the outside, as if my whole life were constantly pouring through my mind because of the letters that come. Recently, for instance, I have been asked to remember everything I could about Nazimova. I knew her almost not at all. I was in the Civic Repertory Company when she played Madame Ranevsky in *The Cherry Orchard*. I understudied Eva LeGallienne in the role of Varya; I played it for a week when LeGallienne was ill. The people I've known, who are often so much more famous than I, are dying, so I am asked for remembrances, or for letters, or whatever it may be. Today, for instance, I was asked by Marilyn Kallet, who is editing a book of essays by younger poets on my poetry, when she and I first met. It was in Rochester, New York. I have no memory of such things. I was lecturing and reading poems a great deal then. So I suddenly realized I could call Peg Umberger who was there and she would remember. I did so and she did—late July 1980. It was an effort of imagination. It took time—a small part of the day. Another thing Marilyn wanted was my translation of Valéry's *Palme*. Louise Bogan had sent it on to Jackson Matthews who was then working on the poems of Valéry for the Bollingen Foundation. He thought Louise had written this translation and he was looking for a new translator for the poems. So they then hired me and Louise to work together. It was quite an experience. We worked for a long time on the translations at fifty dollars for each poem. But in the end they decided that the only thing to do was to make prose translations with poems scattered about among them. My translation has never been published. Marilyn also wants photographs for her book.

I wrote Margot Peters, who is doing a biography of me. This was all yesterday mind you. I telephoned Mrs. Dwight in Bar Harbor. She wants to see the garden and write something about it. A lot of time went into correspondence.

I am working every morning with Susan on the photographs for her book. Looking at the photographs has been like living my whole life again. My mother and father and I each kept everything. The result is a very rich store.

Wednesday, August 21

WE WOKE up still without light or heat, and driving rain! The most gloomy morning you could possibly imagine! Susan did somehow manage to heat some bottled water on the alcohol stove and brought me my breakfast. But we really were dismal; because it was so grim we finally had to laugh about it. Why couldn't there be sun? It sounded from what we heard as though the power would not be back until tomorrow—and possibly not until Saturday.

So I decided we must do something, and I invited Nancy and Susan to come with me to Foster's for a lobster. At least we would have a hot meal and some fun. It was a merry lunch. When we came home—glory be!—the lights were on! The first thing I noticed was the hum of the refrigerator. Then, of course, the glorious possibility of putting on the furnace. It was fifty-eight outside, strangely enough, but I had felt cold for thirty-six hours. I could not get warm. I put on all the winter blankets and already had on two sweaters. I am still shivering, even now.

Now, at four, a person I have never seen—a fan—is coming. I must have a short rest—I have already rested a little—to prepare for her.

The great news is that Norton is going to reissue the *Collected Poems* at last and include the three books of verse that have been published since it came out. This is wonderful!

Tuesday, August 27

I HAVE NOT done much dictating lately because there has been a whirlwind of things that had to be done, primarily to finish going over the copy-editing of the journal which will come out on my eightieth birthday. Nancy mailed it yesterday—a tremendous relief. This time there was not an awful lot to be dealt with. One of the chief problems was how to spell *miaow*. I finally gave in and let them have their way, which was *meow*, though I think *m-i-a-o-w* sounds much more like a cat; it is more onomatopoetic. But you cannot fight about everything. Eric Swenson, my editor, did a very careful editing and made it much easier for us than it would have been had he not been very much on the job. So that is one big thing off my mind. It means that yesterday I managed to write a couple of notes. I found a letter written in June, a charming letter from an eighty-three-year-old former bookseller who has always read my work and said some awfully nice things. So I was delighted that I had the poem Bill Ewert printed for me for my seventy-ninth birthday to send her.

That reminds me that one of the good things that has happened lately is that on Saturday Mary and Bill Ewert came for our traditional glass of champagne while we discussed the Christmas poem which Bill has to have in August because he wants to ask Mary Azarian, who has done such beautiful work for us, to illustrate this new one. She will need time, and it has to be done well ahead.

I am happy about the poem, and so were the Ewerts. We

had a cheerful, happy talk. Bill is high up in the administration of the New Hampshire schools and one of the most modest, though ebullient, men I have ever known. For the first time he talked a little about his job and what they do. In some ways the New Hampshire schools are wonderfully good, and we heard quite a lot about them. Mary and Bill's two sons are now almost out of the nest. The younger one, nineteen years old, goes to college this year but will live at home, so he is half in and half out of the nest.

Susan's departure looms. She will be leaving on Tuesday. I have to remind myself that being alone, the total silence has a great resonance for me. I shall miss her dreadfully, but I shall find other parts of myself that can be nourished. Perhaps I shall start listening to music again. In any case I hope very much to get to work on a short novella which has been in my mind but has been somewhat lost in the middle of all that has been going on.

It looked for a while as if I had no legal right to let Susan read my letters to Louise Bogan, of which I had transcripts from the Amherst Library Special Collection in her archive. It seemed unbelievable, but there was an original letter that said I must not show them. But then wonderful Nancy found a second letter apologizing for the rather old-fashioned bureaucratic tone of the first letter by a man who has since left. Now I am told I can give them to everybody to read and the only thing necessary is that Ruth Limmer, who is the official trustee of the archive and of Louise Bogan's estate, give her permission. It seems very odd that one has to get her permission to use parts of letters that I have written, but that is the strange legal position that we are in.

Friday, August 30

I CANNOT BELIEVE that August is gone. We are having fright-fully hot weather.

I have missed two very important days which I will now talk about. Tuesday little Sarton, my namesake, came with her mother, Dorothy Molnar. They brought delicious vegetable soup Dorothy had made, bread, and a magnificent rhubarb pie. But the main thing was to be together and have a quiet, sustained talk. Sarton is now eleven and about to enter the sixth grade. I can hardly believe it! She is a darling child, unselfconscious, open, natural, and very concentrated. She sat down to look at some books I had put out for her in case there was a time when she became bored with so much conversation, and she was absolutely concentrated as she sat on the floor looking at them. She is used to being with adults, but she is also used to being with children and loves playing. When I asked her what she hoped to be, whether she knew already, she said she wanted to be a doctor. I found that heartening.

Dorothy looked beautiful. She had a very hard time after Sarton was born because Stephen, her husband, had decided to go to law school to change his profession from a social worker, which is what Dorothy is, because he might make a better salary which they were going to need with little Sarton to bring up and put through college. From Sarton's third to sixth years, while Stephen was in law school, Dorothy was commuting daily fifty miles to her social work. So little Sarton

CREDIT: SUSAN SHERMAN

Little Sarton reading

was shunted around. A different person drove her to school every day, and she had a woman who took care of her, more or less, but Sarton said that the woman didn't do anything, that is to say, I guess, she didn't play with her or read aloud to her. She was just there. For Dorothy I think this was a traumatic time, but she survived. What is as important, she and Stephen managed to give Sarton a good life. Out of this, amongst other things, has come a charming book which Stephen and Dorothy wrote together, called *Who Will Pick Me Up If I Fall?* It is about not knowing what day it is because every day a different person comes to pick the child up. It is a very amusing book, and they had the luck to find a genius to illustrate it.

The next day, which was Wednesday, was going to be very hot. But we set out in Susan's Toyota, which has air conditioning luckily, for Center Sandwich to see Huldah Sharp, her daughter Leslie, and perhaps her granddaughter, Christina. Huldah had a terrible operation recently to try to alleviate the intense pain in her neck. She looked marvelously well and beautiful although she has had a hard time. She, most unfortunately, has become stone deaf so one can only communicate with one of those magic pads where you can write something and then erase it. The trouble is she asks a question like "How is our mutual friend Lee Blair?" Lee Blair is having an extremely hard time but I cannot describe it in one word on the magic screen, so I have to say, "She's fine." I did write Huldah a long letter yesterday—which is one reason I did not put anything on the cassette—because I wanted to answer some of these questions at length. And that I did.

It was lovely to be with her, sitting together on the sofa, surrounded as always by her dogs. Leslie made us delicious chicken sandwiches. Huldah had made a great spinach soup and the cake I love best—the one she used to make for me. I do not know the name of it. It's a very dense cake—I don't know how to say it—the opposite of an angel cake, more like a pound cake. It has nuts in it and must have an icing of brown sugar melted with butter. Anyway, it is absolutely delicious.

Then, as a great surprise, the granddaughter Christina

arrived as we were finishing lunch. She is half Greek—her father is Greek—and she is a beautiful girl with a Mediterranean look, very dark eyes and dark hair, tall and graceful, and full of life. Her passion is the theater. She is doing the props and sometimes stage-managing for the local summer theater there, a very good one which does excellent plays.

It was hot but luckily there was a little breeze. I had been afraid for Huldah's sake that it would be an unbearable day.

Those have been two important days in my life—two very different parts of it. I have known little Sarton since she was about four. They have come here every year. One year I lent them the house while I went to Rene Morgan's on the Cape. So they feel at home. Sarton loved Tamas, my beloved Shetland collie. This time she had the joy of seeing Susan's dog Cybèle, who is a fluffy white, tiny poodle. Sarton's face was really a sight to be seen when she looked at this extraordinary dog who is like a special plush dog come alive, with very dark eyes. Susan told Sarton—I had not known this before—that when she first got Cybèle, who followed a dog also called Cybèle whom Susan had adored and who had died, it was hard for her to take on a new dog but she knew she must do it. So when she first got Cybèle it was not easy. She had grave doubts and cried a great deal, until one of her friends saw the dog and said, "She looks just like May Sarton!" Well, after that, of course, there was a great way to introduce her! I have looked at Cybèle since and have felt very drawn to her, although I think she is much prettier than I ever was!

In a little while Karen K. is coming to take me to do the shopping. I am going to try to get half bottles of champagne. I find I can drink a glass of champagne with no bad aftereffects. The trouble is that a whole bottle is much too much for Susan and me. Then I shall go to a wonderful vegetable place and see what we can find.

Dorothy Jones, a friend of mine who lives in New Jersey, is coming to take me out to lunch.

Susan's departure gets nearer, and I must say that I feel awful pangs, but after she goes I'll get into a new routine and all will be well.

Labor Day, September 2

SUDDENLY IT is autumn! The light, the air, everything has changed to a cool brilliance. The ocean is dark, autumn blue. The air sparkles. It is almost unbelievable because Saturday morning had the heaviest, most humid air I think I have ever felt here. You could not breathe; it was frightening. But in a couple of hours the wind had changed, the blessed Canadian air had poured in, and we were happy and exhilarated by it.

Yesterday was a perfect day to have a lobster at Margaret Whalen and Barbara's. They have an incredibly beautiful place in Cape Neddick which looks out over the bay. It really might be somewhere on the Mediterranean. I was trying to think why, and I think it is probably the trees. There are small trees in the foreground with a sloping lawn that goes down to amber-colored, wave-gentled ledges. Then the water, which is so clear you can see right down to the depths. Margaret and Barbara swim every day at high tide. It does seem perfect heaven. We sat on their outdoor patio, porch really, and looked out and drank champagne. We felt we were the luckiest people in the world, Susan and I, to be with such dear friends in such a marvelous place.

I have been meaning to laugh at something again which made me happy the other day. I've been somewhat overwhelmed by the extraordinary kindness that comes to me from all sides. The other day when we came back there was an enormous bunch of flowers, for example, from an unknown fan. People like Pat Chasse go out of their way to offer to do things for me and then actually do them. I was thinking that to be worthy of all this I would have to become a saint, which I said to Karen. She laughed and said, "We don't want you to be a saint. We want you to stay just as you are." With all the warts. She didn't say "with all the warts," that's what I added in my mind. She said, "You'd be much too meek and mild as a saint." So I guess I do not have to be one.

That phrase, which is, of course, also Mr. Rogers', meant more than I can say when he wrote me a fan letter some years ago before I appeared on *Mr. Rogers' Neighborhood*. He wrote me a short but very moving letter about my work which ended, "I like you just the way you are!", which was his leitmotif at that time and perhaps still is. I was feeling depressed about myself and feeling no good. So that "I like you just the way you are" did me a world of good.

I do not think it is a happy Labor Day for labor. In fact, it is an unhappy day for labor, which is in the doghouse, even with working people. One cannot forget that labor itself became corrupt; the leaders became corrupt and, in many cases, went to jail; and many who were corrupt did not go to jail.

Thursday, September 5

How MANY DAYS since I have talked to this machine, this alter ego of mine? Susan left on Tuesday and I do not believe I put anything on the cassette that day. But I was extremely aware of the silence, the silence was palpable: no Cybèle barking to let me know that Pierrot wanted to get in; no nearly silent footsteps on the stairs, giving a little creak now and then. Although at first it's always hard, and I feel as if I were alone in the world, the silence is tremendously moving and exciting. I had so hoped to get back to creative work, to begin to think seriously about a short novel I have in mind, but my desk has never been more appalling in its demands.

Yesterday I spent almost the whole morning writing a blurb for the first volume of Marguérite Yourcenar's autobiography. It is a complex work, like everything she has written—difficult reading in a way, and next to impossible to blurb. What she has done is original for she starts with her own birth, but from there we go backward hundreds of years, beginning in the fourteenth century, into her family history. Her mother's family came from the country near Liège and she has wonderful chapters, especially in the Victorian age, of their different *châteaux* and exactly what life was like in them—a formidably selfish, routine life. But she has chosen some exceptional people among them to write about in depth. It is a remarkable book.

Besides that, I had on my mind yesterday the need to answer a letter from a Professor Little whom Marilyn Kallet has asked to do a chapter on my poetry for her book of poets. It would deal with what it is like to have been so unrecognized, whether I feel it has done me harm or good. I had to think about that. I feel more and more sure that I escaped a lot of trouble by not being famous at all until very late in my life and having had nothing whatever to do with the literary establishment. That was the decision I made when I went to Nelson: that I would not go to them. They had ignored and treated me badly—but someday they would come to me. Someday is now, and they are coming to me. On the seventeenth and eighteenth Margot Peters, who wants to do a biography, is coming to see me. We shall talk about that, although I'm not sure that I can face having a biography written while I am alive. I believe so strongly that everything should be told, but I had always thought of that as—yes, after I am dead.

For some reason while I was writing to Professor Little, I suddenly remembered the remarkable translations of my poems into French that Germaine Lafeuille did years ago. She was a retired professor of French from Wellesley College and had hoped to get them published in France. I was disappointed, as I know she was, when that didn't work out. They are beautiful translations, although sometimes I remember feeling that they were a little too smooth, which is the inherent danger in the mellifluous French tongue. Sometimes I wanted something of the Anglo-Saxon rough sound—earth, birth.

I did not have a good rest because, as almost always happens when Eleanor Perkins is here cleaning and using the vacuum, Pierrot had totally disappeared when I came back from lunch with Edythe. I called and called. I even went out and lifted the door of the garage as he sometimes gets imprisoned there. No sign of him, no meow. I went up and down the stairs I don't know how many times. Finally, after the phone had rung once, I went down again and turned the light on in the cellar and called. He came out, very reserved, not interested even in food. He had been frightened by the UPS man. He is now out and I know that he is safe. When I cannot find him, then I know how much I love him and how the silence here would be unbearable if he were not with me.

Sunday, September 8

THE WEATHER is beautiful these days. Everything glows in the autumn coolth against the brilliant blue of the ocean. Unfortunately I am in pain again. It is discouraging because I thought I was over the hump, but I am not. Especially now, when I have so many appointments and see so many people every day, it is not easy.

A real event happened yesterday. Rod Kessler came with his wife, Sarah, and their three-month-old baby, Martin. Martin is an absolute joy and at one point I was able to hold him in my arms. Sarah said, "You do it very well. Some people don't know how to talk to a baby." Martin smiled, and he is so likable and responsive at three months that it is easy to hug him. They have a teenaged Swedish *au pair* girl who had just arrived that week and apparently she is afraid of the baby, which is too bad. But I am sure she will become fond of him. Then she will be able to hug him and know what to do.

Rod was looking marvelous. He was born to be a father and now he must be well into his thirties, perhaps forties. Sarah, who is divorced, has another little boy who is eight or nine. So it is a real family. The whole visit seemed to me benign beyond words. I would have purred the entire time, had I been a cat!

Rod took some photographs. I am afraid my hair looked particularly bad as I have a permanent next Tuesday. He goes about it so quietly and unpretentiously that I think in some ways he is the best photographer I have ever had, though Bruce Conklin did do a marvelous job and is coming on the twentieth to try again. With so many small books about me coming out from the university presses there will be a demand for a good photograph.

At four o'clock Maggie arrived. She hasn't been here for months, it seems to me. Her arrival is always an event and a joy-bringer. She brought mushrooms she had picked on the golf course at North Haven, and we had them for lunch today. We had a very superior Sunday lunch which was first mussels, cooked with a little onion and white wine; then these elegant mushrooms on toast; and finally a little peach yogurt. Last night we had sole which she greatly enjoyed. I'd gotten it in and made some rice. We had tiny beets from her garden.

In spite of considerable pain last evening we did have a

CREDIT: ROD KESSLER

May with Martin Abrams Kessler

good talk. We always do. It is a real exchange of lives, and as our lives are very different, it is an exciting exchange. I love to hear about the farm and also about her extensive family. At North Haven these last few weeks she has had grandchildren there almost the whole time. The grandchildren now are ready to go to college, are already in college, or are in the last years of high school and so are very grown-up and great fun. When she goes out to a cocktail party she lets them cook and they produce enormous amounts of highly seasoned Mexican food.

Monday, September 9

ANOTHER PERFECT, early autumn day.

Between four and six these days I'm in great pain, which flattens me out for the rest of the day.

I have now finally come to terms with my ignorance about our treatment of the American Indians. I suppose when I was young my mind was more directed towards Europe and my friends there, and, of course, the wars—the wars of those times. But I have finally come to understand that I have to realize what we Caucasians did. It's so shameful that one can hardly bear to read about it. I am now reading Matthiessen's marvelous book *In the Spirit of Crazy Horse*, which was banned, or kept from being sold, for seven years while litigation went on because he was being sued by the Bureau of Indian Affairs—he and the publishers—and also by an individual. Now it is finally back and one can buy it in paper.

The fact is that the Indians never broke a single treaty we made with them and we, if you can believe it, have broken *every* treaty. We have not only broken treaties but we have done things so brutal that they make one's hair stand on end, such as killing all the bison so that the Lakotas would starve to death. In so doing we made the bison into an almost extinct species. This is brutality comparable to Stalinism in Russia or, for that matter, the Holocaust in Germany. There is a kind of resemblance there because at the root of all this was complete contempt for the Indian culture and life. We felt they were simply savages, that they were contemptible. We had no respect even for their crafts—disgraceful when you think of the marvelous potters, for instance, in the pueblos. Their pots were made by scum, not even fit to be fed.

Many Indians starved to death; many children. The reservations were the worst land that could be found. When the barren land turned out to have gold in it, that land was taken away.

This is very hard reading, but I think every American should have to look at it and face it. It is much worse, in some ways, than anything to do with blacks because the Indians were *here*. It was their country, and we tried to destroy them. We nearly succeeded. What is moving now is the renascence and the numbers of Indians who are trying to recover something of what has been lost.

Tuesday, September 10

WHEN I was fourteen my mother and I spent a year in Europe, staying with Céline Limbosch, outside Brussels. My father had a room in the Divinity School at Harvard, where he was finishing the first enormous volume of his *Introduction to the*

History of Science. It turned out to be a very hard year, for both my mother and me. I have never known altogether why for her, but I felt uprooted at first. The bitter, cold, damp winter was not good for me. We had a long walk to school and the school was terrifying. It was Jean Dominique's Institut Belge de Culture Française, but she taught only the older students. I had Marie Gaspar, her great friend, a character, but a rigid teacher. I had come from the Shady Hill school where learning by heart would have been scorned; there we were expected to use our own words to prove that we had really taken in what we were talking about, whereas Marie Gaspar required learning the entire textbook by heart.

The reason I'm bringing this up today is that the Limbosch children and other children I met teased me for being an American. I was very proud of it and used to go about singing "America the Beautiful" loudly. They teased me because they said that Americans had murdered the Indians and that it was cruel and terrible. Nobody had told me anything about this. We had come, of course, as refugees. My father very quickly became Americanized. He was supported by the Carnegie Foundation and was so grateful to have the Widener Library for his studies that I never heard anything against the United States from him. So the Limbosch teasing about Indian massacres filled me with rage. I think all my life I have put off having to know what we did to the Indians. Now at last I'm coming to see how bad it was and must come to terms with it.

Thursday, September 12

A GLORIOUS cool morning. I think it was under sixty, but brilliant. I am so happy because I can wear my autumn clothes now and change into some different colors. I have some teal blue things—a color I have not worn before.

I woke to bad pain. I am terrified of going out to do shopping with Karen K., though she is so kind she would let me sit in the car if I thought I could not walk around.

Yesterday at about four, the man from Henry's Garage Doors came to try to fix the garage door so that if I ever again got locked in there—as I did recently—I could push a button inside and lift it. He was a very nice man and at first teased me by saying, "Why didn't you just put the car in reverse and ram it through the door?" He was a man perhaps in his sixties, bald, extremely kindly. In about ten minutes he had fixed it. So I said, "Well, luckily I have my checkbook downstairs and what do I owe you?" He said, "Oh, I was just on my way home. Forget it. There's no charge." I had been boasting about being a writer. I am afraid I'm apt to do that with workmen. I think it is partly because I want them to feel that I am a worker, not just a rich woman. Anyway I said I would give him a book. I went through a lot of heart-searching to try to decide which one I had that I could spare to give away. I finally decided on the paperback of *The Magnificent Spinster.* He may not like it at all but at least it is signed and he knows that I appreciate what he did.

Another wonderful thing happened yesterday. It was such

a munificent day all around. Dear Eloise Armen, after I had said I would love to have a paper cutter or something LeGallienne had used every day, sent me a beautiful long wooden box, painted with a kind of fleur-de-lis pattern, which was always on the table beside LeGallienne's bed. With it was a small magnifying glass, which will be wonderful for reading telephone books, and a long beautiful silver envelope opener. I carried the box up and down, trying it in various places, and finally decided to put it on the round table by my chaise and keep all the clutter there in it. By clutter I mean pens and all that kind of thing. It looks so grand there and in a strange way goes with the curious bronze leopard head that Juliette Huxley gave me and which an African chief had given her and Julian. It was so large and solid that it didn't go with anything else. Now this box, which is not elegant but sturdy, is just right.

On Tuesday Eric Swenson, my editor at Norton for twenty years, came for a glass of champagne and we had a good long talk. It is only about the second time in that long span of our relationship that we have had a chance to talk in person. I was seldom in New York. It has been, however, an extremely fruitful and wonderful author–editor relationship, mostly because he believed in me to the extent that he could persuade Norton—of which he was vice-chairman for many years and is now semi-retired—to publish my poems. Norton has published everything I've written since they took *The Small Room,* which had been turned down by two or three publishers before they saw it. I remember one publisher wanted it to be rewritten and the love affair brought up more. The book begins with the chief character starting her first year of teaching, having broken off with her fiancé. That was because I wanted her to be concentrated on the whole process of education. I find that a lot of people now go back to it and like it.

Eric looks wonderful at seventy-two. He even did the Bermuda race with his yacht last year. This year apparently there was no race; it is only every other year. He will be off to Italy with his wife in October for two weeks. He shines with good-will, humor, love. It was a wonderful two hours. I only felt tired at the very end. He is pleased that I'm keeping a second journal. He also spoke warmly about Susan's book about me and that did me good.

In the mail yesterday came Doris Grumbach's memoir of her seventieth year. It's a very well-written and thoughtful book by a depressed person. Apparently she did not want to be seventy, so the whole picture is different from mine. I wanted to be seventy. I find hers extremely good reading, so I cannot bear to stop. I am reading it much too fast and I think I shall have to read it again. I know that I must not swallow it whole. There is something about a journal, I think, that does this to readers. So many readers tell me that they cannot put my journals down.

Friday, September 13

A SUPERB autumn day.

Sunday, September 15

A GRAY, AUTUMNAL day, but the whole house is warm and feels alive again because Susan is here for the weekend. I am not feeling well but her presence lights things up. And then it is lovely to have a delicious meal cooked for me! We had swordfish last night and white sweet potatoes which I am fond of, and Susan's special French carrots—light, delicate, and slightly caramelized.

For two or three days I have been meaning to set down some praises of Jean Palmer, whom I have not seen for almost two years because I've been too ill and had to keep putting her off. On Wednesday she came, as usual bearing all kinds of goodies that she had made: ginger cookies, which are delicious, and a meat loaf, which, alas, I had to give to Nancy because meat is not on my diet, and two little jars of jelly which she had just made. A new kind of cookie is a welcome gift in this house.

Jean Palmer is an exhilarating friend to be with. She is now sixty-six and I think I am not wrong in believing that she is happier than she has ever been. She divorced many years ago, brought up two children on very little money, but now is fairly well off. She bought a little house which reminds me very much of my house in Nelson. It is a Cape Cod house to which she now has added a closed-in porch for those winter months. Jean is happy because she is constantly busy creating. Because of her arthritis she has designed a garden which is raised so she does not have to kneel. Her chief joy is in writing children's poems and she has had one small book published. You can see in her bright blue eyes and their sparkle how much she enjoys the idea of children now that her own have all grown. Her inspiration is being with them again as she invents her verses for them.

We had a good talk about everything. Since I find it hard to talk with anybody who believes that Bush is a good president, it is lucky that Jean does not.

Otherwise I have been immersed in the Indian story which is so painful it is hard for me to read at all. I shall take a deep breath and give myself a rest with Ann Tyler's new book.

Yesterday, among several events, came a letter from Nancy Mairs, enclosing her description of their recent trip to England. She won a prize and with the money decided to take her parents and her husband, who has not been well at all, rent a house in the Cotswolds, and explore from there. Nancy has multiple sclerosis and is in a wheelchair, so this kind of adventure takes courage. It made me nostalgic to read about the Cotswolds and those wonderful villages, Upper Slaughter and Lower Slaughter, Chipping Camden, and so on, because I used to stay in the Cotswolds at Kingham with Basil de Sélincourt and his wife in one of those lovely golden stone houses. But it also made me homesick for England itself. Nancy says they fell in love with England all over again. One of the most interesting things I found in her short notes is the number of good meals they managed to have at a reasonable cost. England has become very expensive now. I read about these meals hungrily since most of what they had is not on my diet, especially a cream tea! I was happy to be in touch with Nancy again after a long interval during which we have not corresponded.

Yesterday's mail was overwhelming: so many lives poured into mine, a little like having too many strong drinks when this happens. There was one letter that moved me very much. It was from a man who was responsible for arranging my reading at the Smithsonian some years ago. We went out to dinner with some other members of his office and shortly before the end, while we were still having dessert, he excused himself and said that he had to go and give a shot of morphine to a friend of his dying of AIDS. That was the image that set off my poem "AIDS" which came out in *The Silence Now* and has been used, I am glad to say, a great deal at money-raising dinners and so on. I sent him the poem as soon as it was written but I never heard from him and I was surprised; I wondered whether I had made a mistake. Perhaps it was opened at the office by somebody who did not know he was gay or some other disaster accompanied its arrival. So now, five or six years later, I get a letter from Marcus Overton saying how much the poem meant.

It reminds me of another occasion when a very delayed response became doubly precious. That was when Volta Hall died. He was among the three or four therapists whom I have seen during a long life. He was the one who helped me most. We were right in the middle of a crucial discussion of my relationship to my mother. One day when I got home at Fourteen Wright Street, Judy opened the door and looked so stricken that I said, "Judy, what's happened? Has Tom Jones died?" That was our cat. She said, "No, but Volta Hall has had a heart attack and died." I suppose this is one of the most terrifying blows life has to offer: when your psychiatrist disappears. Within the next two days I wrote an elegy for Volta Hall which is in the *Collected Poems* and in which the repeated line is, "Now the long lucid listening is done." I sent this to his widow with a bunch of violets. There was no reply. I thought perhaps there is an unwritten rule that the wife of a psychiatrist does not make contact with a patient even after he himself has died. So I thought no more about it. About ten years later I had a note from her asking if she could come to see me. She came and told me that I would never know what that poem had meant, that she could give it to her children so they could see what her husband and their father had been for so many patients and what he was in himself. She also came—and this touched me deeply—to ask my blessing on her remarriage, as though I was speaking, in a way, for Volta. "Of course," I said, "that's what he would want."

You never know, when you send out a bird with an olive branch in its beak, whether it will come back or not.

Thursday, September 19

OVER THE LAST several days I have been loathe to do this dictating for some reason, partly because my calendar has been too full, the desk overcharged with letters I should answer, and there have been some personal problems which I cannot discuss in the journal. People always think I tell everything in the journals but it is far from the truth. This time I have had quite a shock.

Good things have happened since I last talked. One of them was the arrival, two days ago, of Margot Peters who had written me to say that she would like to do my biography. She has written a remarkable one of Charlotte Brontë, which I didn't know when she wrote to me, but I did know that she had done several biographies and I was very eager to see what this one would be like. It was with some apprehension and some excitement that I waited two days ago for her to appear at four o'clock, on one of the hottest days we have ever suffered here. I made some iced tea and suddenly remembered that my mother used to put ginger ale in it. It did give it a little tang, with a piece of that wonderful mint in it that was here in the garden when I came—apparently a rather rare kind.

I liked Margot Peters at once, although I threw her completely by asking, "What was the reason for your wanting to do my biography?" She said that it was almost too direct a question and I could see that she was silenced by it. But later on she told me several reasons that pleased me very much. One of them was that she realized that I have had a tough time and not had the recognition that I deserve. Another was an agreement about a writer whom we both do not like, Anaïs Nin.

Little by little, I believe honesty pays off. Nin was dishonest from the beginning, as she never confesses to her readers that she is married to a rich man.

Margot came back yesterday morning and we had another good talk. Last night she had dinner with Carol Heilbrun in New York. I am eagerly waiting to see what Carol's impression has been.

The good news is that Margot is willing to wait until after I die to publish. She would be immersed in the book, she thinks, for about five years. Of course by then I hope I shall be dead! If I am not, she said she would simply lay it aside. I did not realize that this is done fairly often. Agnes DeMille's biography of Martha Graham was held back several years until Graham died.

Saturday, September 21

I AM LIVING through some sort of transition, disoriented by my ill health. I have a great deal of pain now; but, more than that, I am unable to cope. When Margot was here, after about an hour of talk, I felt suddenly dizzy and ill. This has happened several times lately; whenever I talk with someone for an hour or even less, I feel faint. I wonder whether it may be that the cancer in the lining of the left lung is spreading to the lung itself. Even the oxygen at night does not help a great deal. Of course we have had some stifling weather; last week we had one of the worst days ever because the humidity was so great. One really could not breathe. I am ridiculously sensitive to changes of weather. My mood goes up and down with the sun and the rain, and I am a little frightened by how extremely frail I feel. Behind this is my fear of how I can handle my life when Nancy is gone. I say to myself, it is a challenge. Judy Harrison will be a tremendous help; I think she really will. I must call her and make a date for her to come and go over things with Nancy during the month of October.

Margot Peters sent marvelous flowers the day after she left. They gave me a tremendous lift.

Yesterday when I came back from lunch at Edythe's new apartment, there was Pat gardening for me. She was planting the Japanese iris that I had ordered and which, unfortunately, came last week, and four violet bee balm which have done well. I was, in a way, delighted when Pat confessed that she too had been taken in by the Michigan bulb contest, which means that about every week or more often you get tons of papers you have to fill out because they say you are now eligible for this or that amount of money, and meanwhile it would be a good idea if you bought this or that. It is a racket! What one resents most is how time-consuming it is.

It was wonderful to see Edythe so happy in her apartment. It is elegant and just big enough. The furniture from the house—which was a big house—fits in here and shows up in a new way, so that I thought many things were new, but it was simply that they looked so well in this new surrounding. It has a little balcony so Edythe's love of gardening has a small outlet. Now the balcony is decorated with chrysanthemums and miniature roses. Everything is near at hand. Edythe kindly kept her Sheltie in the car because Jamie loves people but is rather a jumpy dog and not very well trained. Edythe came down with us and let Jamie out and I had a chance to see her. I have not seen her for a long time. She is a charming dog and brought back poignant memories of Tamas, although she is much thinner, thinner boned and smaller, but she has that wonderful Sheltie face, so loving. It's marvelous to see that after a whole year's work—getting the old house sold, then emptying it, lifting and carrying—all this leads to perfection. It gave me joy to see Edythe in her charming nest.

Thursday, September 26

THIS IS the second dismal day. It rained—poured—as it must have in the Great Flood when the ark had to be built. In some places, four inches fell. Pierrot was terribly frustrated. He kept going and meowing at the door, looking out and seeing that it was impossible, and coming back. Last night he finally got me up at three, sure he wanted to go out but then didn't, finally went out at five and then didn't come in. I was so afraid that something had happened. I suddenly realized again that if anything happened to Pierrot I would be in a bad way. He is out in the hall now, meowing! He does not know what he wants.

The biography of Rose Macaulay, *Rose Macaulay, a Writer's Life,* by Jane Emery, is a lifesaver right now. I ordered it from England and I knew when it came that this is a book I must read slowly because I will be so sorry when it is over! Luckily it is a large tome, an extremely discursive biography, but that is good. Rose Macaulay was an extraordinary woman with whom I feel an affinity. She always had wanted to be a boy; she wanted to go into the navy. It was only when she was about eighteen that her parents were firm in telling her that she had to become a young lady and could not be a boy. She had the great luck, however, of spending her childhood in a tiny town in Italy, south of Genoa, with her five brothers and sisters and her parents. They led a completely free, wild life—a kind of child's dream—going on tremendous swims far out, climbing mountains, climbing trees, especially to read there. I could associate with all that because it is what I used to do. They invented all kinds of games. They were taught at home by their parents.

This childhood remained forever after as Rose Macaulay's dream world—as did Anne Thorp's childhood for her. She was one of five also, although they were all girls. She tells wonderfully of the bonding among the children. Rose Macaulay has written better than anyone about the child's view of the world and the child's view of parents. Her mother—a truth I was rather loathe to accept—was a tempestuous woman who had favorites who changed all the time. She neglected and snubbed her next-to-youngest child because her adored youngest died. So little Eleanor Macaulay was a pariah in her own family and never became a part of the clan. This is so cruel. It goes to show, again, that family life is not all a warm glow as it is thought to be, especially by those who, like me, do not come from a large family.

The author, Jane Emery, I know nothing about. What she loves to do is make contrasts between what is going on in the child's mind and what Rose Macaulay writes finally about the same thing. Of course I did know—and this will come later— that Macaulay, who was always considered a brilliant and witty spinster, actually had a long love affair with a married man and thus fooled everyone. She was extremely secretive about her private life.

Nancy is not here today and not yesterday either because she had to have a tooth out. As these were particularly dismal days, I was frightened driving back from the hairdresser in the rain. In fact I ran into a rock because I could not see, the windows inside the car were so fogged over. Fortunately the rock did no damage. It was coming down like cats and dogs.

In a way I guess it is good for me to have to go out. The only trouble is it takes the energy that I need at my desk. I have to get used to this because soon Nancy will not be here. It does seem a rather perilous time and I shall be anxious to see how the lung X-ray I am having today comes out. In a way it would be a relief to know that something was really wrong because I feel so weak these days, so trembly it is quite ridiculous.

Tuesday, October 1

THE AIR is suddenly chilly. I never feel warm. The leaves are beginning to turn so there are brilliant spots of color as one drives along. That is a great joy.

I am having a hard time, the hardest in perhaps six months of pain and problems with my intestinal tract. Unfortunately the cat has fleas. We are taking him tomorrow to be defleaed. He has been very restless at night and I have not been sleeping as well as I used to, partly because of the discomfort. Too much is coming at me all at the same time these days.

Margot Peters called when I was feeling terribly ill to ask me whether I could talk to Norton about possibly offering a contract on her biography, although she is contracted to Knopf "for a second book" after her biography of the Barrymores.

Lately I am faint sometimes when I get up from a chair and find that I ask myself whether it is worth crossing the room to get a Kleenex or something I need; when one is as ill as I am one has little pugnacity I suppose is the word, very little gumption—a good New England word. So, for instance, when my car—which was almost new—burned last year it was still on the warranty but I was so panic-stricken at the idea of not having a car that I went and bought a new one from the same place the next day and never took the warranty and never said, "You owe me a new car!" I did get five thousand from the insurance company but it did not pay for the new one. That is the failure of nerve of the very ill. It is not worth the fight.

At first I had said to Susan that I thought somebody else should do the pruning of her book, but now I think I have to do it myself even if it takes a longer time than she would like. Naturally she will want to get it off now. She has worked so long and hard on it.

A little poem which I do not know the author of, but I think may be Herbert, has been haunting me lately.

> I brought thee flowers to straw thy way
> I brought thee boughs off many a tree
> But thou wast up at break of day
> And brought thy flowers along with thee.

It is a poignant poem and I thought about it quite a lot when Susan was here last weekend doing so much for me. She brought roses as she so often does. I wanted to greet her warmly and embrace her but she brought her flowers "along" herself and I had no flowers to offer because I was so ill.

I feel a failure as to friendship these days. It is a hard time, and I keep saying to myself that it will pass. Dr. Khanjani is convinced that the problem I have now is getting rid of the toxic substances in me and that when that is done I will feel much better. She comforted me yesterday by saying that quite a few of her patients are in the same phase as I, so she said, "It is very hard on me," which made me laugh a little since it is we who have the pain! But it is she, of course, who gets the complaints and has the responsibility. I do not envy her.

Thursday, October 3

THURSDAY IS the day Eleanor comes to clean, so I had to get my breakfast and make my bed and hurry. Hurrying right now is really bad for me, so I gave myself a present. I decided to blow the check Jimmie Canfield and her daughter sent me for flowers and get some right away because Susan's roses are beginning to go. I went to Foster's. There were a tremendous number of things I craved including bunches of purple anemones. I bought a yellow lily and some asters and brought them home to light up the whole house. I added one branch of something that is called, of all things, Kangaroo's Ears, an irregular branch with little yellowish tufts all along it. I have picked a few branches of peonies which turn the most wonderful bronze color. They are now both in the Japanese jar under my mother's embroidery and look very beautiful and very Japanese.

It is a struggle. I told Dr. Khanjani that one of the hardest disciplines for me now that I am so ill and in so much pain is to manage to get a real dinner for myself. Today I am going to stuff a Cornish hen, and I simply do not know how I am going to summon enough of myself to do it. But there is also the discipline of dressing, of not letting oneself go to pieces just because one feels rotten. Not, in other words, to become a rotten apple.

Friday, October 4

A BEAUTIFUL autumn day. Everything now is turning. It is one of the most beautiful autumns I remember. It is before everything has turned and there are trees that are still partly green. It is shot through with life. One forgets every year how beautiful it is.

Lots of bulbs have come. What bliss it is to have a gardener who will put them in for me because I am still ill and in pain every day. From four o'clock in the morning on I am miserable, so by the time it is nine, as it is now, I have had five hours of pain, and I am tired. Yesterday, Dr. Khanjani said, "Of course, you are exhausted. You must realize that it is all to the good and you are going to feel much better when this is over," but she does not tell me how long "this" is going to take.

I am about halfway through the Rose Macaulay biography which is a bit too long I think, but nevertheless extremely interesting. She was a curious character, so sensitive to the pain of others that she threw up and so could be of no help. When she tried to work in a settlement house she was so distressed she became too ill to work. You have to be tough in this world, and there was one part of Rose Macaulay that was not tough enough. Her kind of wit and the kind of social life she enjoyed, which was brilliant conversation, living, if you will, by good talk, are not entirely endearing. Halfway through the book I am slightly disillusioned. But this temperament also explains very much what makes her books so fascinating. They are extremely detached.

I wish I had more to say, but I feel emptied out literally by nine o'clock in the morning. Yesterday I started crying very soon in the day. It was bad when Judy Harrison, who will be replacing Nancy on the first of November, came, and I could not help it, I started to cry. She was very understanding and warm, and we are going to get on very well. But it was not a good start to the day which had actually begun with my having to get the plumber at seven in the morning, and hence to be pressured at the beginning.

Sunday, October 6

WE ARE HAVING a miserable day. Wild wind and rain. It is unfair because it was not predicted. It was supposed to be a beautiful autumn day. I had lunch with Royce Roth and Frances Whitney. This is the fourteenth year they have come to Dockside and spent ten days or so, and always it is a tremendous treat for me because there are very few people with whom I talk who are as much in tune as they are with all the things I care about, from books to politics. We had an excellent lunch. I had steamed clams, and they had clam chowder, but as I am not allowed any milk or anything made with milk or cheese, I could not have that. It did not matter because I was revived by seeing them.

Meanwhile, I have felt weak and sorry for myself, I am afraid. I decided that what I must do is try to realize that I am doing not too badly, considering that I am seventy-nine. I am proud of the fact that I keep to such discipline as it took, for instance today with bad cramps, to get up and get my breakfast, carry it up on the tray, have it in bed, and then get up and make my bed, and finally decide what to wear. That is always a problem because part of the discipline is to keep myself fed and keep the house more or less tidy on weekends when I have no other help, and part of it is to try to look well, as well as I can. As I have said before, the routine is what keeps me from going to pieces. I might be crying, but if it is a little after four, as it is now, it is time for me to get up and go up to my desk and do something positive. About an hour later, it will be time to come down here, open my bed, and lay out my pajamas as if I had a servant to do that, lay out the book I am going to read, and the slippers that I am going to need for going down to get Pierrot in and put him out which happens over and over again during the night. It is really hilarious, my slavery to this magnificent cat.

Now in the late afternoon I have gotten through two-thirds of this day not too badly. I did manage to make several long-distance calls including one to Marilyn Kallet to talk a little about the essays on my poetry which she is gathering to put into a book which the University of Tennessee will publish. What an act of friendship it is on her part! Luckily she is feeling better after a bout of walking pneumonia.

Tuesday, October 8

AND A glittering autumn day it is, though cold. Although it is going to be much colder later, now with the temperature at about fifty, I feel chilled to the bone even though I have the furnace going. I am still immersed in Rose Macaulay. Last night I read about her relationship with Virginia Woolf, which was a little prickly on both sides. Perhaps each was jealous of the other for Rose Macaulay was famous when Virginia Woolf had not yet become a classic, but already had an elite on her side. There is no doubt that writers are jealous of each other. It has been hard for me to admit this, but I know it is true. It is hard to hear another writer praised, especially a woman writer, if one is a woman.

In the course of what was said about Virginia Woolf and Rose Macaulay, there are quotes from an elegiac tribute that Rose wrote after Virginia Woolf's suicide. The biographer says Rose used an extended metaphor to describe her dazzlement at the stream of Virginia Woolf's conversation, how she mocked her visitors while assuming the pose of the recluse yet was eager to hear their fine stories of the world. I was always amazed when I went there for tea that Virginia Woolf plied me with questions as though she was truly interested in the young unknown writer I then was. It was enormously flattering. What she did is exactly described by Rose Macaulay as follows:

> To tell her anything was like launching a ship on the
> shifting waters of a river which flashed back a hundred
> reflections, enlarging, beautifying, animating,
> rippling about the keel, filling the sails, bobbing the
> cork up and down on dancing waves, enlarging the small
> trip into some fantastic Odyssean voyage
> and amusing beasts and men.

Thursday, October 10

ANOTHER BEAUTIFUL DAY. I am so happy for Frances and Royce that they are getting some real Maine, October weather, and I feel deprived because I am too sick to enjoy it. This is the third day when I am too ill to function. On Tuesday and Wednesday I simply had to stay in bed. Anyway, finally, in the middle of the day yesterday I did have a release of all that accumulated stuff in my insides, and now, unfortunately, this morning I am in tremendous pain and the stuff is still coming out. All this is good news, but it makes me extremely weak. I could not move yesterday. I slept and fought off a housefly that nearly drove me mad.

It was the typical day of an invalid old lady. Everything small has gone wrong. The housefly was maddening. A little later there was one of those wasps going up inside the screen, and I was afraid of it, but I also did not think I had the strength to get up, get it into a Kleenex, and drown it. But finally I did. That was a relief. Then I went downstairs because there was a package for me, and I needed to open it. It was then early afternoon, and I could not find the big scissors that always hang in a certain place in the kitchen. I knew that Joan, a wonderful helper who comes twice a week in the morning to make my breakfast, had used them to cut off chrysanthemums that needed cutting, but I could not find them. I looked in every drawer in the kitchen and went to every possible place where they could have been. I went to the flower window more than once. Finally I called her at the hospital and asked her, and she said she had used those scissors in the middle of unwrapping a package. I looked in the rubbish which fortunately had not gone out to the garage, and in the rubbish I found that my new scissors which I had paid a goodly sum for had been thrown out, probably fallen into the wastebasket from my bed. I guess that nightmare had a silver lining in that at least they were not thrown away. After I put them down, I decided the other scissors must be somewhere, so I looked again and there they were on the back of the sofa that faces the fireplace.

I tried to get Margot on the telephone, but I was not able to. And finally the last straw was that my electric blanket has given out, and I felt cold. I did make myself a hot water bottle. Luckily, Dr. Khanjani called me in the middle of the day and said, "You know, May, you have done so much with your life, and you must now realize that you are very, very tired. You have been through a great deal with this treatment, and I think you must let yourself rest." So I did finally go back to sleep in spite of the fly. At four I decided I had better get up, make my bed, look at the news, and get myself some supper because I had only had a piece of bread and peanut butter to eat for lunch. I did all that.

What a wonderful thing it was to go to bed in the nice bed that I had just made and begin to read some more of Rose Macaulay's biography which has certainly sustained me through these days.

Saturday, October 12

THIS SEEMS to be about the darkest passage of my life. I am not only in more pain than I have been in for over a year and more exhausted in consequence, but it is as if the foundations were crumbling; I realize more and more that the foundations have been friendship. And the friends, naturally enough, are getting fed up with my being ill and never getting well. There have been a few incidents recently that rubbed this in, so I have gone back to that bitter poem by Robert Frost, "Provide, Provide," which I remember reading when I was in my twenties, and I had thought, What a terrible man. What a wrong poem. Now that I am almost eighty and feel abandoned, I reckon that the poem is true, and I am glad he wrote it.

Yesterday Edythe brought me an electric blanket to replace mine which had given out. She knew they were on sale, she went and got it, and I had it before yesterday afternoon. I was warm and delicious all night.

But now on the last leg of my journey at a time when there is no one nearby, I have grown nostalgic for my English cousins. They are only very distant cousins, but there is something about blood being thicker than water or perhaps it is more common for blood relations to have a built-in affinity. At any rate, late in my life I have come to treasure them and to love the landscape of Suffolk, province of my Elwes grandfather and his ancestors.

Yesterday, at least in the late afternoon, I was completely absorbed in the hearings around the nominee for the Supreme Court, Judge Clarence Thomas, and chiefly a very long interrogation of Professor Hill as to exactly what happened and how she was sexually harassed. It was so painful that I felt ill during most of it; I am sure every woman who watched it did. She bore herself with such dignity and openness; she was so much not on the defensive. For instance, when an antagonistic senator asked her how to explain that she did not complain at the time, why she waited so long, she said, "I don't really know myself." We know so little about what happens to women who have been sexually harassed, and very often, it has to be buried or is buried because it takes such courage to fight and is so risky as well. She must have become, in the eyes of many, many people, a hero. There is no doubt that the attitude in the United States about sexual harassment will change because of her courageous testimony.

Sunday, October 13

MAGGIE CAME YESTERDAY to stay overnight, and it was balm. She brought sweetbreads from the farm and beets from her garden, and we had the most delicious supper of them plus brown rice and Fanny Farmer's apple brown betty. My mother used to make it. So it was altogether a feast, but more important than that, it was Maggie being here and our friendship that was restorative. We have been friends for a long time; certainly ten years. And our friendship has grown richer with every year. I can never forget it was she who rescued Pierrot when he appeared to be totally lost in a blizzard and turned up in a part of the cellar that I did not even know was there. It was Maggie, determined to find him, who is responsible for my having this comfort in my life.

I say "balm" with reason, because I am wounded, and it is not anyone's fault. I feel ashamed of myself. It seems as though I have reached a new phase in my long struggle with pain. I was moved to find in the Sunday New York Times Book Review Aristotle quoted as saying, "Pain upsets and destroys the nature of the person who bears it." Until now I have been rather proud of the fact that I have managed to accomplish something even while in almost constant pain for months, more than a year, but now in this last month I am worse. It has made me difficult and cross, difficult with friends whom I cherish. Relentless pain is making the psyche ill as well as the poor old body. I am in a bad way.

Today, like yesterday, has been dominated by the Thomas

hearings. They have made me proud to be a woman because Anita Hill was so persuasive and dignified in her hours and hours of cross-examination by the loutish, brutal, and inept senators. With almost no exception they behaved like boors. One exception, I am glad to say, was Kennedy, who was the first to praise Anita Hill after her long ordeal and to thank her for what she had done. He said that it would make sexual harassment a much harder thing to engage in than it has been. I wonder if he is right, but at least it was nice to hear it. He spoke again to the four witnesses who had this afternoon testified to Anita Hill's honesty and corroborated the time frame of her ordeal, the most notable being the woman judge from California who was superb. In fact the other woman also was marvelous because she was so honest. When they asked how it could be, if what was said against Thomas was true, that Anita Hill followed him from one job to another and did not resign, this woman said, "Well, I was harassed, sexually harassed, and even touched by my harasser, and I did not resign." The upshot of this being—it came up over and over again—that a woman does not have a chance. She has no option. If we look at Anita Hill and see what her coming forward is costing, it may well keep many women who do not have her courage, as well as a tenured position, from charging their harassers.

The worst is how these hearings have shown up the mediocrity and, I would like to say, the evil of the Senate. A set of less palatable men it would be hard to imagine.

Tuesday, October 15

STILL UNDER the shadow of the hearings. The White House brutality, their way of doing what they have chosen to do, is very much like what Bush did with the attacks on Dukakis; they go for the crazy man's estimate that Professor Hill is mad. This is an easy way out. The end result, as far as I can see, is that the American people are pretty fed up with the Senate. An article on the front page of the *New York Times* today says:

> Although many on Capitol Hill have stepped up to the thicket of microphones in the last few days to pretend themselves seekers of truth in the harrowing contest between Anita F. Hill and Clarence Thomas, very few people in Washington are seeking truth at all.

That is what is so shocking, as well as the meanness of spirit, shown especially by Spector and Hatch, whom I shall never forgive.

Sometimes in the mail something so delightful and inspiring comes that I have to include it in the journal. I got a letter from Deborah Straw today with a quotation from Henry Beston whom I have not read for a long time although I have always admired him. He says:

> We need another and a wiser and perhaps a more mystical concept of animals . . . the animal shall not be measured by man. . . . They are not brethren, they are not underlings; they are other nations, caught with ourselves

in the net of life and time, fellow prisoners of the splendour and travail of the earth.

That really is a marvelous statement because on the one hand people tend to overpersonify animals, to put into the animal's mind what is in their own, and it is simply not true; on the other hand, people are apt to call an animal soulless and brutal. Here we have a way of looking at animals that is totally sane and kind.

Sunday, October 20

GOLDEN SUNRISE today; yesterday it was crimson. That is amazing. Karen Saum was here when I was vastly depressed because I had been having too much pain, about twelve hours of it. By the time she arrived I was not in a good state, but I was so glad to see her and very excited because Martha Wheelock had sent me the video of *Portrait of a Marriage*, the book that Nigel Nicolson wrote about his mother and father, Vita Sackville-West and Harold Nicolson, including her famous love affair with Violet Trefusis, an infamous love affair actually since they ran away from their responsibilities, especially Vita's two small boys.

Portrait of a Marriage is not an appetizing story, but the photography is marvelous. It made me homesick for England, for European life in general and, of course, the magnificence of Sissinghurst, which was beautifully photographed. The woman who plays Sackville-West, whom I had never seen before, was extremely good, tall and thin and always wearing those enormous hats that Sackville-West liked. The femme fatale Trefusis was not quite as good and unfortunately both the writing for Harold Nicolson and the performance were weak and inaccurate. The writing makes him into a wimp which he certainly was not; he was a rather witty man, both brilliant and loving. One of the things I find depressing about the whole situation is that Vita Sackville-West was apparently so susceptible to flattery, and Trefusis certainly laid it on. I cannot imagine falling in love with somebody who did that.

Karen agrees completely with me about the hearings for the Supreme Court and was just as depressed as I. She was high, though, on the fact that she has just organized (at H.O.M.E) and brought into being with great success, a congress of liberation theologians from Brazil. They came up, people came down from Canada, and they enjoyed a great exchange of news.

Karen comes, and the whole house lights up. It reminds me so much of when she was here. For one marvelous year she had a job in Augusta and came back every weekend from Thursday to Monday. She wrote some wonderful things here—memories of her childhood in Panama. I was disgruntled when the *New Yorker* turned these pieces down. She has not been able to get them published, excellent though they are.

The other good news is that Jamey called me yesterday and that her life in New Hampshire begins well. She is among good people who already, I'm sure, like her. They offered to put her up for a few days and are determined to get her a job so she won't be so harassed.

Thursday, October 24

I HAVE NOT been putting anything into this journal recently because I have been doing a tremendous job cutting Susan's remarkable book *Among the Usual Days*, which Norton has contracted for and which is made up of excerpts from journals and letters of mine that go back sometimes to when I was five years old, and is, in essence, her way of defining my reasons to live. It is a remarkable collection of excerpts, but the trouble is that she has been lured into overdoing it a little. I have done in three days work what I had told her at some point would take a month, and when I said that, I was too ill to do it so we had agreed that Timothy Seldes might. He has always been a very bright, tough reader and would agree to the cutting, but I wanted to have first go at it and to see what was possible and what I think about the book. It is going to be very beautiful with lots of photographs—at Eric Swenson's request.

I would not have been able to do it, not at all, had I not suddenly become well three days ago. After a year of never, almost never, being without pain on any day, sometimes for fourteen hours, the last three days I have not had pain. It is extraordinary. It is like suddenly being let out of prison. It shows itself in small ways, such as when I left Dr. Khanjani today I still had energy to go and buy flowers and to get some things at the holistic food store. I would not have been able to do that last week.

I have finished Katharine Hepburn's *Me* and have sent it

off to Lee Blair. It is a mixed bag, though there are some kind descriptions and some heart-warming statements, and somehow you cannot help but like her. But it is not a great book, and maybe that is why it is number one on the best-seller list. She is aware herself that she is primarily a personality and not an artist though there are great actresses, great movie stars who are primarily artists, singers like Piaf who was, no doubt, a great personality but was an artist also. Yet, at her best as an actress, Katharine Hepburn was moving! I was touched when I realized that the last film she and Spencer Tracy made together was *Guess Who's Coming to Dinner* in which they were both superb.

We are having extraordinary, romantic autumn days. It is warm. The leaves have not all gone, and for once the oaks are brilliant. They usually look like dry blood, but this year they have a little orange light in them. The great oak on this place is glorious now.

Pierrot is in ecstasy and stays out all night as there will be a full moon, I think tomorrow. It has been rising later and later. At eight o'clock tonight it will be on the brink of rising. And of course the light is going quickly, so it is dark a little after six these days.

We put the clocks back and suddenly autumn is over and winter, especially today with high, cold, icy winds, has come. The jays are at the feeder. In the autumn when so many birds are gone, it is good to see them. So far no raccoons have pulled the feeder down, but I expect them any day now. The double maple in the front yard, which is half purple/half red, has dropped all its leaves so the house looks like Sleeping Beauty's house when you come in.

Susan was here for the weekend for the first time in a month, for us a great celebration of everything. As usual, she made me wonderful soup, we had long talks, and we both worked. I am still writing poems, often in the middle of the night they come, and this is wonderful for me. But I am also in a kind of palpitating suspense before Nancy leaves, which will be on Friday. Then everything, all the routines, will have to be changed.

Tuesday, October 29

YESTERDAY I had a visit from Parker Huber, that delightful man whom I have not seen for a year. Parker is an original. If you looked at his life absolutely objectively, you would say that he really has not succeeded very well, but the fact is that he is an extraordinary person who gives a great deal and is passionate about nature. He climbs Mt. Monadnock every Thanksgiving and every Christmas. He had just been up a few days ago, he told me. He takes groups on trips—for instance, once in California following Muir's Road. He is constantly educating people about the environment in a spontaneous way that is his own invention, like the White Knight in *Alice in Wonderland*.

Of course Parker does not make a living by his trips, so now he is getting an M.A. at Lesley in counseling, which he is a little sheepish about. He will be a good counselor partly because he is no longer young. Somewhere in his forties, tall and blond, he looks like a Norwegian to me and is charming in an extremely modest way. He has given various seminars on my work. We have been in touch for years. He published a good interview with me in a little magazine some years ago, and he gave me an award. It is called the Richard D. Perkins Award, in memory of a friend of Parker's. He defines it beautifully:

> This Award celebrates life and art. It does so by honoring people whose work and creativity arouses in us a deep respect for human greatness. People whose being and imagination delights, inspires, and heals. People whose compassion and nourishment moves us in the direction of our dreams.

I have great admiration for this man.

Otherwise, I am afraid I consider the best news is that Sununu may be in trouble because of that bank scandal. It appears that he was involved, and William Safire in the *New York Times* yesterday asked for a prosecutor to be appointed. It is showing up the amount of lying that goes on in the Bush administration, because Sununu was asked by Gray, the legal counsel to the president, whether he had been involved, and he denied it, and the president supported him. Theirs is an arrogant way to go about things.

It is suddenly cold. The water heater Huldah gave me years ago to keep in the birdbath must be found and used again because today there was ice on the water.

Wednesday, October 30

WE ARE HAVING tremendously high winds from the ocean. Suddenly at five the door under the porch in my bedroom blew open; it was quite startling. There must be a gale out at sea. It was blowing cold air in and tearing leaves off so what with dark coming so early now, around half past five, the autumn is racing away, and we want to keep it back.

Pierrot is excited by the wind. He came in, then wanted to

be let out again in the middle of the night. And when he came in early this morning, he flew all over the house in the excitement of the wind. On the ornamental cherry the yellow is exquisite now, and pretty soon it may be that the cedar waxwings will come. In some years, a whole flock of cedar waxwings comes to eat that food and then flies off. How do they know it is there? A downy woodpecker comes every day to eat it, and I saw a chipmunk for the first time this morning. The paperwhite narcissus are more beautiful than ever. In fact, the house at the moment is a glory of flowers, the flowers from Susan Lord who came yesterday at four bringing orange lilies and anemones—beautiful! This was our first meeting but I hope not the last.

Yesterday was special because I was able to finish the poem "All Souls" which I had to write because of four articles in the *Manchester Guardian Weekly* about the children of Iraq and the numbers of them who are dying, fifty-five thousand of them, fifty-five thousand in the bombings, then five thousand a day partly of starvation, and partly because, according to an international team of doctors who examined the children, they are the most traumatized children of war that have ever been described. These children never smile, they cannot cry, they live in a state of absolute terror all the time, trying to forget the terrible things that they have seen. And that, of course, is what we did and what President Bush said he had no responsibility for. So he kept the sanctions on, and the food is not getting there. I was in a rage after I read that, and thank God I am a poet because I was able to use it and write a poem that may be of some use.

That was the beginning of the day. I had bad cramps because of this intense emotion. And then a great event took place. Doris Grumbach drove all the way from Sargentville so we could have a talk and see each other after a long time. When I had hoped to invite her to come I never had been well enough. Seeing her, talking with her, I felt warmed to the cockles of my heart. We had a good talk about everything including her recent, fascinating book on becoming seventy, *Entering the End Zone.*

It was quite a day because at four Vicky Simon came. I had a book to give her for her birthday a couple of days ago. I have not seen Vicky for a long time. She is a therapist dealing with very difficult cases, often people who have been sexually molested or harassed and worse, tortured. And she has to be detached enough so that she can listen and support and lift these people. After all this I found last night I was too tired and did not sleep well. It was the first time that has happened in a long time.

On a branch of the ornamental cherry there is a small finch's nest.

Tuesday, November 5

ANOTHER OF THESE GRAY, cold, miserable days. One has the feeling that winter is closing in like a door closing, and it will not seem warm or dry for a long time. By four-thirty it is dark, and that is one of the hardest things, the day drains away and where has it gone? But I am in splendid shape and I am writing poems. All the leaves have not fallen yet, but almost. You begin to see through the branches, see the structure of the tree.

Yesterday David Levitt came to put on storm windows. That was one thing. He came with a friend called Steve, a very tall, very nice man. And once again I find these men, workmen, providers of kindness, of warmth. Levitt said almost at once, "You are looking so much better than you were last year." The people who see me all the time do not know what the change is, but when somebody has not seen me and notices the change I realize that I am much better. Curiously enough, a woman whose name I do not know but who is about my age and who always speaks to me said at the IGA, "You have so much verve, you are a different person." I tried to persuade her to go to Ferida Khanjani because she has back trouble she told me.

Precious things have happened. At the very end of the year in the garden there is an old-fashioned rose bearing a few late blooms. I have three by my bed now, and they are sweetly scented, a pale pink rose which is adorable, like a tiny cushion and somehow more of a treasure now than in the summer when there is a great mound of them. And the Kousa, Chinese dogwood, has been showing the most marvelous color, a deep orange. The Kousa has been a great joy because in the spring it is covered in magnificent white flowers and now the leaves are magnificent orange and red. When the leaves go I have a much larger view of the ocean. I see it from my bed and to the left of the house—there are two maples there, and when their leaves fall the ocean can be seen.

I have been writing poems. What inspired one poem was the story in a book I am reading called *The Souls of Animals* which Deborah Straw has given me, a fascinating book by Gary Kowalski. Willem de Kooning one day was shown some drawings, did not know who had done them, looked at them quite carefully, and said, "Well, they're very interesting. They remind me a little bit of Japanese calligraphy, quite sophisticated. I don't think they were done by a child." And the person who gave them to him to look at said, "No, they were done by an elephant, sir." Nothing has delighted me more for a long time. Siri was an elephant in a zoo who was seen making drawings with her trunk in the dust, and her keeper said, "Well, we must give her a chance to draw." But the head of the zoo thought he was crazy and would not do anything about it, so the keeper on his own bought charcoal and large sheets of paper and laid them at Siri's feet. Lo and behold, she went at it at once with her long sensitive trunk and would concentrate for as much as an hour in perfect bliss.

Wednesday, November 6

EVERYTHING SEEMS to be in an uproar getting things ready for the winter. The storm windows are on. Tomorrow the electrician comes at eight to be sure that the electrical outlets up in the office will carry the word processor, and at nine a man comes, at last, to fix the copier. I have missed it terribly because I wanted to get the poem out on the Iraqi children. I have sent ten of them, but I did not have any more. Tomorrow everything is going to change when Judy, who is a most cheerful and cheering person, is going to put the word processor together and be ready to get started. She may get started by Friday on teaching me how to use it. It is going to be very exciting.

Today I sent Margot Peters about ten cards with names and addresses of my friends who are in their seventies or eighties whom she might like to talk to about me. There are very few people alive who knew me as a child at the Shady Hill school, very few who knew me as a theater director, and so it is going to be interesting, and I hope she will enjoy hearing what they have to say and that they will enjoy talking about me.

It is a soggy November week. It has been one day after

another with no sun. Half the leaves are gone, but there still would be beautiful color if there were sunlight.

I ordered, after a review in the *New York Times,* a book of interviews with women of the twenties such as Lady Diana Cooper and Juliette Huxley, the latter of whom I was thrilled to see. That is why I ordered it. In the interview with her she appears as the widow of Julian rather than as herself, which is too bad. I blame this to some extent on the interviewer. Juliette did talk about the sculpture she did; she is extremely talented. But her life with Julian was devouring, especially the years in Paris when he was the first Secretary General of UNESCO, so she never did what she might have done.

In spite of all the irritating devouring of time, deep down I feel happy, rich and rewarded by friendships and what is happening now to my work. I wish I could feel a little better physically. It is as though something new were being added, and I wonder could it be cancer? I do not know. The doctors are not able to do very much, but it does always make me feel better to see Dr. Khanjani even though this seventy dollars a week is a lot of money to put out. On top of all the other expenses, it is a crusher. I mostly think about money. Money will come in time, if I can keep on working.

Tuesday, November 12

AT LAST. The sun. It has been a most dismal week and yesterday was one of the darkest days. It was dark at three o'clock because of the heavy skies and rain. They had snow elsewhere, and poor Susan who was here for the weekend had to drive back to New York through slushy snow. The plows had not yet come out in Connecticut and Massachusetts, but she did get home safely, as I was glad to hear when she called me. We had a wonderful, peaceful weekend. She cooked a delicious meal using a vegetable I can't remember the name of right now, perhaps Jerusalem artichokes, with shrimp for once, and that was great fun. We had swordfish one night with cauliflower, lots of parsley, and melted butter, and we saw the last two hours of *Portrait of a Marriage,* the film about Vita Sackville-West's love affair with Violet Trefusis and finally her coming back to Harold Nicolson. It is a powerful film, aesthetically one of the most beautiful I think I have ever seen. All the scenes, the sets themselves in the 1920s in London, Paris, Knole, and in the countryside all around, are magnificent and worth seeing several times to savor.

The costumes are a marvelous evocation of the twenties. The actress who played Vita was extremely good, except that I think the savage side, the brute side of Vita which was very clear in the writing of the book, is only bearable to the reader or the audience if it is fiery enough. Vita twice attacks Trefusis savagely—once because the announcement of Trefusis' engagement had appeared in the *Times,* and she had not told Vita; and once when Vita thinks that Trefusis had sexual relations with her own husband. Vita's understanding was it was to be a platonic marriage. But it is shocking, partly because the actress is not able to master that side of Vita Sackville-West that makes her much more understandable. And, of course, she wanted so much to be a man because of Knole. She would have inherited Knole had she been a man, and her bitterness was there all the time. Also she was perhaps the most truly androgynous woman I have ever heard of. She looked like a man dressed in man's clothes; and then looked like a queen dressed in evening dresses.

Judy Harrison and I were to have worked on the computer, the word processor, but something went wrong with it.

Today she is coming to get it and take a part of it into Portsmouth and have them go over it with her. I guess it is more complicated than I thought, and so I begin to get rather frightened about it. But also, it is not as easy as it looks to transcribe the vocal dictation that I make on a cassette. My voice is not loud and clear, and doing this requires a special talent and a wide frame of reference of my life, which Judy lacks. I think she had trouble at first because she was trying to type it off directly, whereas Nancy first wrote it out, and that allows the writer to correct names and things like that. So maybe it will go better now.

It is unbelievable to see the sun. It is going to make a huge difference.

One of the things Susan and I did was not only to see *Portrait of a Marriage*, but also the film with Robert DeNiro called *The Mission* about Jesuits in South America. It is an absolutely remarkable film. I was too tired to see it all, but what I saw was very moving. What happened coincidentally was that a new issue of *Sojourners* had just come with a whole essay on the founder of the Jesuits. He was a Basque, and the family of the last head of the Jesuits was also Basque. My parents and I spent a summer in the Pyrenees after a long, lonely winter when Mother and I were in Belgium and my father had to work on a book and stayed in Cambridge. We had a marvelous summer together, a green summer in the Pyrenees. We went to the birthplace of Ignatius Loyola who now has a tremendous monument which contains thousands of little windows behind which are relics of saints. It is impressive and a bit shocking to a non-Catholic. When I read the issue of *Sojourners* and came to a small section called "The Features of Ignatian Spirituality," I felt warm inside because I recognized every one of them. One: grounding of everything in profound gratitude and reverence. That is beautiful, and I believe it. Two: continuous cultivation of critical awareness. I could not agree more. Three: confident expectation of empowerment to accept and exercise responsibility. Four: unequivocal commitment to action. Five: recognition that the Gospel of Jesus Christ is essentially countercultural and revolutionary in a nonviolent way. Of course that is being played out in South America now with the radical Catholic liberation theology. It was moving to find this beginning of the Jesuits.

I am discouraged because I do not feel better. The weather was too terrible for me to see Dr. Khanjani. It was like a hurricane. The first time in six months that I have missed being there twice a week, and it was a relief in some ways. I have been seeing her two days a week, and I am in suspense between visits. I don't know why. It takes about half an hour, and I feel better after, but somehow going to her creates suspense and tension, and there is so much tension now about other things. Maybe that is why I don't get better. It is discouraging.

But the big news yesterday was that I talked to Juliette Huxley again on the telephone. She sounded perfectly herself. She was out shopping when I first called, and she's ninety-five, or will be December sixth. I talked to Alan Best, the nephew of the Alan Best whom I knew back in the '30s when he was an intimate friend of the Huxleys and worked at the Zoo. Alan told me that Juliette is remarkably well, and I am glad I found out that she drinks only red wine, not white, so I am planning a case of burgundy and a case of claret for her December birthday. It is wonderful to have pounds in England; I am rich in pocket money there, though not here.

I called Juliette partly because I so much enjoyed reading the interview with her in a book called *Looking Back*, and she is called in the book "the grande dame of European letters." That made me smile, and I am sure it made Juliette smile, too, when she read it. It is not quite true, but this is a good book in spite of the extraordinarily strange name of its editor and writer: Shusha Guppy. What delighted me in the interview with Juliette was something she says at the very end. "But what is life after the flame of life is burnt out, except perhaps memories—*une petite fumée de souvenirs."* Isn't that lovely? And so like Juliette. There I heard her voice.

Thursday, November 14

IT SEEMS to be harder and harder to find the moment when I can talk to a cassette, and it is a day or so since I have done so. Today was a tiring, busy day, but I am a little better. Thursdays are always hard because that is the day Eleanor Perkins comes to clean, and therefore nobody comes to give me my breakfast. While I am lying there in bed trying to pull myself together, I plan the day. The hot water bottle is a great comfort. I realized suddenly that what gets me up, makes my life worth living these days, are two things. One is that I am writing poems again at last and these I do late at night after I have let Pierrot in at one A.M. There is a wonderful silence. There is no pressure. Otherwise these days my life is pressure. Anyway, the poems first. Then it is imagining things to do for friends. This morning I was thinking and thinking about Eleanor, whose husband is dying of cancer. She looks so tired. What could I do for her? I suddenly thought, Well, I can give her books. She does not have all my books, and she is a great reader. So that got me up this morning to climb up to the third floor and find four or five of my books. I think she has not read *Anger* or *Crucial Conversations,* and she has not read *Harriet Hatfield.* So that is what I did. I signed the books, and that started the day.

The sun was out. It makes an enormous difference. I did manage to write a long letter to Georgia Peters in Philadelphia whom I hear from only about two or three times a year. She works so hard. She is the one who knows all about word processors who works tremendously long hours as a legal secretary. Her daughter is graduating from high school, and her son is now, I think, a junior at Cornell and doing extremely well. His shoulder was badly hurt in a soccer game, and he had to come home and be operated on. Sports should not be so dangerous. There is something wrong about that.

And, of course, the catalogs pile in, and Christmas is on my mind. It is a lovely thing to have on one's mind.

It was a great day yesterday because I had the first lesson on the word processor. Judy is an excellent teacher, and what we did was to sit and watch Norton Textra projected onto the screen. It tells you exactly what you will have to do. It was interesting. Also terrifying. But I am determined not to let myself panic, and I think that when I am alone here and can fiddle with it every day for half an hour, little by little I shall come to be able to take it more or less for granted. It should be easy compared to what I have to remember to set my tray in the morning. There are something like twenty different objects that go on it, including medicines. All these things I do manage to remember, as well as all the checks for the people who work for me here. I have a payroll every week of over two hundred dollars which means the writing of six or eight checks, and all this I manage to do even though my poor old head is still not what it was before the stroke five years ago. I manage, and I am quite proud of myself. Today I had to rush to have my lunch and then run to the doctor's, do errands on the way, pick up fish for my supper and flowers on the way back. When I got home at half past two, I still had to arrange the flowers. By the time I got to rest at three, I was tired. But I had been up since six, so that is not too bad.

Friday, November 15

THE SUN ROSE today again, and, oh, what a difference it makes
to the whole mood of the day! Yesterday was also a very good
day from that point of view. Susan's roses are on the way out
now, but they are still lovely.

I must be one of the few literate Americans who has never
read Scott or Helen Nearing, but I was sent the proof for the
book she had written after Scott's death. It is rather a mish-
mash, but there are wonderful things in it. One of the things
that moved me was the extraordinary generosity they showed
in welcoming people to come and see their houses, especially
the one in Maine after they had become famous. On one Saturday she gave lunch to twenty-seven people who had turned
up. They also apparently answered most of their mail, for
which I have the greatest admiration. They were extraordinary people, quite extraordinary. She, of course, is still alive. I
read her with something like shame. I would not have the guts
to eat twelve apples a day, as they did after coming back from
one of his lecture trips having gained ten pounds. They lost it
in two weeks. But the mood of the book and what stays with
me after finishing it is what one or two people can make happen.

Here was Scott Nearing, because of being a pacifist during
the war, ostracized, losing his job as a professor, not wanted
on lecture platforms because he was dangerous or radical during that terrible McCarthy time, and thus finished. That is
what it looked like, finished when he was about fifty. What

were they to do? They decided to go and live on the land.
They built houses and greenhouses and grew all their own
food. I cannot imagine a better book to read to give courage.
They really were unsurpassably brave and able to cope, never
complaining. The fact is they loved their life, and that is the
big lesson of the book. If you love your life, you can stand
living on apples for a week.

There is an interesting contrast between Helen Nearing's
book and the one on Gertrude Stein and Alice B. Toklas which
was sent me recently. It is not a wonderful book, but it has
told me a whole lot about Gertrude Stein's childhood that I
never knew, and I find it interesting. Gertrude and Alice's
was a good marriage, a marriage as good as Scott and Helen
Nearing, and for the same reason. It was a marriage of two
very different people, two very different temperaments which
fed each other and which created a unity where dissension
would have been the other possibility. Alice B. Toklas was
content to walk in Gertrude Stein's shadow, although she was
a person in her own right, the power behind the throne.

Monday, November 18

THIS IS the second day with a beautiful clear sky. The moon is
about three-quarters full. So far we have not experienced the
beauty of November. It has been so gray and somber, so miserable, but when the sun comes out and we get the structure
of the leafless trees, it is beautiful. The trees are like seaweed
in the air, floating on the air. It was like that when I got up at
four or five to let the cat in. Such a peaceful, soundless morning waiting for the sunrise!

Deborah Straw was here overnight on Saturday. We had a good time. It is a great pleasure for me to see someone who reads as much as she does and thinks about it as intelligently, so we have good conversations when she is here. She comes ostensibly to help me on the weekends because I used to be afraid to be alone, even three months ago, over those two days. I thought somebody should be here in case I had another stroke. But now I feel a good deal better. I have about decided that the time has come for me to take the weekend as a time of solitude. So many people come to do work for me all week long that it is moving to have days when I am not pressured to get a meal like yesterday evening. I feel a wild excitement at being alone again. I feel like an armadillo all curled up in a shiny ball. The fact is that nothing interests me as much, perhaps, as myself at this stage of my life. I have so much to think about.

Now the requests or recommendations for the Guggenheim are coming in. I look forward to recommending Nancy Mairs. Nancy Mairs is a prisoner of a wheelchair because of the MS, but the amazing thing is that nothing of the extremity she faces every day is in the poems. It is a sign of her genius, this energy within the crippled body, and I hope she will get a fellowship.

Yesterday there was an avalanche of phone calls, and I got rather tired, but on the other hand it is wonderful to think of friends scattered all over the place. Eleanor Blair called, it was wonderful to hear her voice, always so full of life. And much to my joy and amazement, Liz Evans called. She has been having a terrible time, a cyst on her spine causing frightful pain had been operated on, but she is on top of it now and well into her book on Tyler, which is her next biography. Liz wrote the critical biography of me, *May Sarton Revisited*. I want to send her the Iraqi poem, she will be thrilled to see it. I am getting a wonderful response to the poem. Deborah Pease is going to try to get the new poems read by the poetry critic of the *Paris Review*. It is great to think they might be acceptable. Connie Hunting is most enthusiastic about them. She also called yesterday. Joy Sweet called. I have not heard from her for such a long time. Ann Warner called from York because I asked her to find out if the library could use a few of my books that I have extras of and which I want to give them.

At any moment the proof of my journal will arrive. I am really dying to see how it will sound to me now after nearly a year of not having looked at it. So it is going to be a full week.

Tuesday, November 19

WHAT AN extraordinary sunrise! Very black clouds and then just at the horizon a strip of crimson, a long slash of crimson. I was able to see it when I took the rubbish out.

Yesterday was a depressed day, mostly through my own fault and clumsiness. The battle with machines and forgetfulness—I lost my glasses and I need them. What I have not found, which is almost as important, is my private telephone book. Fortunately I have another one down here, and most of the numbers I use all the time are in the one downstairs. It is heavy gray-green metal, one of those you push up according to the letter. It might have been thrown away by mistake; Joan is quite absentminded sometimes. I have looked and looked.

I decided to do my duty which was to work alone at the word processor for half an hour, and I got totally tangled in it. All I could think of was that marvelous cover of a *Life* magazine years ago, a large photo of a pig which had been made neurotic. It was all wound up in pieces of string from which it could not extricate itself and had a look of horror. I was that pig all day because I could not get the word processor to do what I wanted. Then I thought, Well, I'll do something easier for me. So I tried to put a new toner cartridge in the copier. I did not do it right, and it has now stopped dead. I am waiting for a call from L&L to see when they'll come. I need the copier badly now because of the poems. So all together the day really was a nightmare.

Then I cooked some haddock and it was not good. I baked it with a little bit of onion and used some of the soy milk—maybe that was the trouble, the soy milk does not taste right—and some crumbs and some olive oil. I cooked a little turnip and mixed it with the rice. That was quite good.

I had cramps all day yesterday.

Sunday, November 24

A DISMAL DAY steady, grim rain. For once Pierrot did not go in and out most of the night but came in at half past one and did not go out again until very early this morning. So I did have an especially good night's sleep.

I have finished *Gertrude and Alice*, by Diana Souhami, that fabulously interesting book. Gertrude Stein believed in her genius absolutely and in its service justified allowing Alice Toklas to run things and to take care of her; Alice did supremely well and became more and more of a power. Finally it was she who decided whom Gertrude should see, typed all the books, and was the arbiter of their publication. All of this she obviously enjoyed. The fact is that Stein was a genius. That is what is remarkable because so many people think they are and are not. But here was a genius who invented a powerful form of expression in the English language. The more you read the book with her intonation and her repetitions, the more grooved you become. I began to talk like Gertrude Stein after I had read a few pages. And then the other thing is that there is a lot of wisdom in her handsome Roman head. I was startled by, but agree with, her three stories about roots. She made me think about my own roots. Stein says:

> Roots are so small and dry when you have them and they are opposed to you. You have seen them on a plant and sometimes they seem to deny the plant if it is vigorous— Well we're not like that really. Our roots can be anywhere and we can survive because if you think about it we take our roots with us. I always knew that a little and now I know it wholly. I know because you can go back to where they are and they can be less real to you than they were three thousand, six thousand miles away. Don't worry about your roots so long as you worry about them. The essential feeling is to have the feeling that they exist, that they are somewhere. They will take care of themselves and they will take care of you, too, though you may never know how it has happened. To think of only going back for them is to confess that the plant is dying.

I think it is true, and we do have the experience of going back to remembered places with great excitement and then finding that they are not there, or they are not there as we imagined them.

The only thing hard to take about Stein was her voracious appetite. She really did eat a great deal and she was enormously fat. The strange thing is that that heaviness became her and in a strange way was quite attractive partly because

she got the young Balmain, then unknown, to design her
clothes, and she wore those sweeping Buddha-esque gar-
ments that gave her the air of a monk rather than a woman.
That, of course, delighted Alice B. Toklas.

Wednesday, November 27

I AM UNABLE to answer all the mail. Everything seems to be
racing fast and Christmas will be here before we know it. The
sun is out, as it was yesterday also, and the chickadees have
finally discovered the suet, Maine Manna, and are loving it. It
is very cold, about twenty above today, which is cold for the
season, and I imagine there will be snow tonight. Just a little
after Susan arrives would be perfect.

I have decided, after much thought, to see Dr. Khanjani
only once a week instead of twice a week. I have been seeing
her on Mondays and Thursdays at one-thirty, and on each of
those mornings, I was anxious and unwilling to spend my last
ounces of energy. There are only about six ounces of energy in
my mornings. I am tired when I come back and am late for my
rest. I get back about two-thirty. So the whole afternoon gets
swept away. I think I need the time more than the benefits of
a chiropractic session. We shall see. She believes I am not
ready yet to cut it down; I must feel my way.

I have had depressing days, but I have an idea that I am
getting better. My energy is a little greater although I have
not managed to write the poem about guilt which I think
about a great deal. I wonder whether when we are very old
we can reassign that burden of guilt we all have from the time
we are infants. If you look into a baby's eyes the first day of its

life you see only deep innocence, no guilt. Later, the guilt begins. Why did I do that? Why didn't I do this? By the time you are my age, you have done not only good things but a lot of things you regret, and those are the things which come to haunt. There is such a thing as neurotic guilt. There is also the propensity of humans to think that whatever children do is the responsibility of their mothers. That may be sometimes true, but it often is not. No one can control everything, and that may be one of the things which we can lay aside as we get closer and closer to death.

It is a huge pleasure to have the Christmas poem to send out. I think it is beautiful this year, and I am happy that my friends who will receive this message will see that I am writing poems again because they will know what that means. They will know that it means that I must be better; I could not have worked in the middle of the night on a poem six months ago. And this I owe to Dr. Khanjani. I must not forget.

Thanksgiving Day

When I think of all the things to be thankful for, there are so many I cannot count them. I am first of all thankful for my friends and for their support through these hard times. I think of each one and their faces rise up before me in a great host of love and smiles. Beautiful! Angela Elliott sent flowers; I was so touched. And, of course, Susan arrived at half past eight with great glorious bunches of roses, two of which are now here in my bedroom scenting the air. She has already set the table, phoned Edythe, and Edythe has made a lemon pie.

I am deeply involved now in *Pride of Family*, a remarkable book by a woman of color who records three generations of middle-class colored people in Charleston before the Civil War. They had originally come from Santo Domingo. It is a fascinating record of a middle-class family which was always liberal and distinguished. Her great-aunt was a doctor and is one of the people who dominates the book. Her grandmother ran a famous restaurant in Saratoga. The book has made me realize again, though I think I have always subconsciously known it, how very difficult it is to be black in white America, partly because being black itself is very complex. Are you born with straight hair? That is to be an aristocrat, of course. Are you very light? Much of the author's family was mulatto so they all were fairly light. The reader can see the infinite gradations and subtleties of what still remains an undercurrent. It is a very recent book, well worth publishing. Once I got into it and into her search for her great-grandmother, it became very dramatic and one pulled for her. But how difficult to always feel conspicuous. I remember a black woman saying to me once that she was always conspicuous. If you walk down the street with a black person everyone who passes will note the black person and probably never note you.

And of course our present government is not helping matters at all. Sununu is a real menace, and I cannot believe he will be there long unless he really has something on Bush. It is a dirty business. All this has made me feel that I have to give more than usual to the American Civil Liberties Union because we are in a real struggle now, and one must back whatever organizations can help.

Wednesday, December 4

YESTERDAY WE HAD one of the worst storms that I have been through here. I do not feel ready for winter. It is not lovely fluffy snow, but a mixture of sleet, snow, and rain which was at first about six inches of slush; Mary-Leigh very kindly had it plowed for me and shoveled off the path. But the trouble is it was most dangerous to go out in it and I decided I could not go out even to the garage, so, for the first time, I left the rubbish out all night. I was pretty sure no dog or any animal would come last night. Pierrot, in spite of his infected eye, was determined to go out and went out at about eleven, then would not come in. I kept going down and calling, but he was safe in the shelter of the front door and would not come in. It was irritating. Finally he did and seemed happy to be in. He came up on my bed and purred. It is three in the afternoon and I have called Edythe. We talk every afternoon at three and catch up on what has happened in the last twenty-four hours.

One of the nicest things about York is Tony at the post office. This man knows everyone's name, but, far more than that, though he is businesslike and gets everything done in record time, he really cares. During this whole long time of my illness, he has more than once lifted my spirits in an amazing way by telling me that my whole attitude and the vigor with which I attack everything helps other people. I have no idea what it does to him when I walk into the post office. That kind of imaginative kindness is overwhelming.

Monday, December 9

THE SUN is out. It has been a dismal six weeks. We have hardly seen the sun at all. On the weekend I was low in my mind. It was not being able to get into the garage and get my car because the electric button which opens it did not work. Not a good idea because it is going to be much colder and it is the cold that freezes it up. When it gets below zero, I shall be helpless. It is a time of annoying happenings. Suddenly all the light bulbs began to give out. Why does that always happen at the same time?

At the moment there are very few flowers in the house and I miss them. But in a way my flowering these days is in writing the Christmas cards and thinking of all my friends. That makes every day exciting. Pierrot's eye is better so I think I will not have to take him to the vet as I thought I would.

Remarkably I am pretty well set for Christmas! Yesterday Edythe came. She always cheers me up. We went to Stage Neck Inn and sat in the bar there. It is so nice looking out over York beach. We had a delicious lunch. I even splurged on vanilla ice cream with hot fudge sauce. I seem to be getting on quite well, and I think there is no doubt that I am on the mend and may be well out of the woods by the time I go to England. That journey looms. I am trying now to track down Durrant's Hotel where Edythe and I stayed four or five years ago.

I am in the middle of—well not the middle, it is an enormous tome—about a fourth of the way through Margot Peters' *The Barrymores*. It is full of anecdotes and incidents. Obviously an immense amount of research went into it. But somehow or other, the book does not interest me very much. Perhaps because the Barrymore legend seems based on a series of accidents. None of them had a real vocation. When Ethel had a try at *A Doll's House* and did badly, she gave Ibsen up completely and proclaimed that Ibsen was boring and morbid. This kind of self-enclosed arrogance gets to me. Certainly when Margot deals with me she will have more materials about an inward life. There is next to none in *The Barrymores*. Her biography to come of me scares me, and I think a lot about it—what I must say and not say to her. I want to tell the whole story, but it is complex although there is nothing to conceal.

I am still stuck on the poem about guilt. I guess the chief reason is that my mind is on the Christmas poem. It was wonderful when Larry LeShan called the night before last in a great state of excitement over the poems. I sent him just two: "Rinsing the Eye" and the Christmas poem which is called "Renascence." I have no idea about their quality. I only know how marvelous it is to be able to write poems again. It is a true rebirth of my self which has been buried for so long. There is cause for rejoicing this Christmas.

Sunday, December 15

WE ARE HAVING unsettled weather so one never gets settled in to anything. On Friday and Saturday we had deluges of warm rain, straight, heavy, an utterly depressing gray, gray day. Then, at one o'clock this morning, the lights went out, there was no heat, and meanwhile a bitterly cold wind had begun and was screaming round the house. I have rarely felt so cold. I was miserable until finally the lights went on at seven. Fortunately, because Maggie was here, I did not have to drive out or get an alcohol stove going to get our breakfast. We had our usual breakfast, unusual in having fresh eggs from her farm and French bread which she had made. It was heartening and helpful to have Maggie here this weekend. It always is. But this weekend was particularly difficult because I am not feeling well.

Meanwhile Christmas looms over everything, and Maggie helped me get the tree up. It really is an adorable tree this year. I think the smallest I have ever had, not more than five feet, maybe a little less, but very round and thick and a beautiful shape. As usual I could never have done it alone. It was wonderful to have Maggie's help.

Meanwhile upstairs in my study, whenever I go for an hour or two a day, I am absorbed in writing the Christmas cards and remembering all the people to whom I am sending them. What struck me this morning was that I shall probably never see most of these people again. Many of them I met on lecture trips or on a boat to Europe . . . and it suddenly made me feel shaken. It also made them more precious than ever. I had a call this afternoon from one, Carol Olch, who had just received the poem. She used to garden for me the first year that Raymond Philbrook could not come any more. Carol is a tall thin girl, woman I should say, in her thirties. She loved to garden, and I knew that all the time she was working for me she was intensely happy because she loved doing it. Now she lives in Tucson and works in a bookstore where she meets many friends of mine. That is fun to hear about.

In spite of attending the wedding of her youngest daughter, Maggie brought extraordinary food, as she always does. We had two sweetbreads for dinner, and peas which had been pushed through a sieve and with a lemon-and-orange concoction to follow. There are many marvelous things to say about Maggie, but what jumps into my mind after she has been here is how she always notices what I need and then later provides it. She noticed that the timer was pretty banged up and so, lo and behold, she arrived with a new one yesterday when she came, soaking wet. The wedding had taken place in woods on a bridge over a foaming brook and it was pouring rain. Very hard luck on the married couple.

Thursday, December 19

CHRISTMAS HAS ABSORBED all my energy these last days, and I have not been good at recording anything. It is a matter of time; I am in a whirlwind. Just as I am, for instance, getting my supper, the phone rings and somebody, maybe in Oregon, wants to speak to me; at the same time a delivery comes to the door with more flowers. More come almost every day. It is exciting. But packages pile up, and when I go down from my rest around four these days, I am tired, and there are three or four packages to deal with. This is one of the hazards of being as frail as I am. My hands have no strength at all and undoing a package covered with reams of sticky tape that I have to pull off becomes exhausting. I feel a little like a small child reduced to tears when given something frustrating. Sometimes I leave it and ask dear Nadine or dear Joan to help if they are here. Sometimes I leave the big packages for one of them, and that is a great help.

And Judy Harrison, my new secretary, has been wonderful about taking packages and mailing them for me. Generally

I am beginning to see that what I need is a governess. Judy is beginning to help me tidy up the study, and that is important.

The Christmas tree is, I think, the most beautiful I have ever had. It turned out to be such a wonderful shape, round, although not broad. It is exquisite. I am ashamed at how many presents there are under it, all dressed up in beautiful wrapping waiting for me to open. I am a spoiled old lady. That is a fact.

But the spoiled old lady would be better able to cope and respond and give as she wants to so much if she did not feel so ill. I am having a bad time. It may be that the sulfa drug I have had to take for a bladder infection is affecting my whole intestinal tract. I have been in a lot of pain and am afraid of falling.

Susan arrives tomorrow at last, Susan with roses in the snow. We have had a beautiful Christmas snow, just the right amount of fluffy white. All last winter when she was here taking care of me, I do not believe we ever saw a real snow; the fact that they now announce that there may be sleet tomorrow is devastating. Let us hope they are wrong.

Saturday, December 21

SUSAN IS HERE, so everything seems pleasing and beautiful. Everything is love in this house. As usual she brought several dozen roses. By my bed I have brilliant diminutive yellow ones. Another friend from Albuquerque sent a dozen pale pink tulips. Glorious! Yesterday also Judy Harrison sent some magnificent flowers. Roses of two colors, red and white together, and very dark blue iris and one large red-and-white lily with buds. It is a stunning bouquet and came with a dear message. We have made a good start. And yesterday Judy suggested that she might tidy up the piles and piles of catalogs that were in my study in total disorder and chaos. This is something that Nancy did for me, and I am grateful that Judy realizes that what I need is a governess as well as a secretary!

The most Christmasy thing this year is the tree. The next most Christmasy thing is that I got a card today about coming to see me here from Connie, Judy Matlack's sister who is now ninety-one; Judy's nephew and his wife, Tim Warren and Phyllis, will come with her. They are the closest thing I have to family in the United States, and when they come it is so full of sweetness, it is so full of the past of our wonderful Christmases at Fourteen Wright Street, Judy's and mine. At that time we lit real Christmas tree candles in the Danish candle holders that Eva LeGallienne had given me, and it was beautiful but of course dangerous. I certainly would not do it now after the fire here, which was not from candles, but terrifying. I shall never forget it, the way the tree went up in one second, nor ever forget that I managed to get it under control so fast once I got the fire extinguisher working. It was like a miracle. Finally I had to run upstairs and get a second fire extinguisher. Mary-Leigh supplies one on every floor which is certainly kind of her, and I managed to put it out.

Judy Burrowes, who was here at the time of the fire, does not know the area well. I had told her, "Call the fire department. I've got to put this out." It was thick, black smoke. I could hardly breathe. And she kept trying to drag me out because she was afraid I would be overcome. But I knew I had to stay there. Within five minutes it would have gone up into my bedroom. The ceiling would have gone. It was touch and go. Luckily it did not affect the books. They all had to be dusted off of course. Insurance covered nearly everything—eight thousand dollars' worth of damage.

Connie, Judy's sister, has just lost her beloved cat and her son has given her a new one. But perhaps she was not quite ready. The new one does look lovely and is a treasure, I am sure. But it is very hard. I mourned Bramble for nine months. And I was not ready for a new cat for quite a while after that.

Not enough perhaps has been written about the death of animals, and it is very touching to see that the clinics which have to put animals to sleep often send a letter of condolence a few days or a week later. They appreciate what the loss is. I suppose it is partly that the animals are totally dependent, even one as independent as Pierrot. But he does depend on me for his food, for his warm place to sleep. Now, because he was so plucked, all the knots in his fur having been taken out by the vet, he is shivering in the cold, whereas he used to go out with splendor in his thick glossy coat when it was nearly zero, and not mind. I am hoping it will grow back.

Christmas Day, Wednesday

THE SUN rose above a bank of clouds at the horizon and it is now a brilliant morning. There is still a cover of snow, unlike last Christmas, which was brown. This is a white Christmas and a much happier one as I am so much better than I was then.

It has been a festival of flowers. When it seemed there could not be another bunch or another plant, the truck would drive up and another bunch or another plant would be given me through the door. What a treasure of friends it all represents and how touched I am! Among the marvelous flowers are some of the ones that I love best, anemones. One of the last bunches that arrived, from Betty Andrews, was an extraordinary gathering of spring flowers, deep crimson tulips, anemones of every color from purple to pale pink, and brilliant dark blue iris. It is a stunning sight. Last night I felt I must have it up in my bedroom where I could see it. Now we will take it down to be by the tree.

There are almost too many presents under it for one old lady. Little by little I open them, and rejoice, and thank in my heart all the dears who have imagined something I might like.

Pierrot is very friendly these days and spends a great deal of time under the tree. He loves it. And of course the whole house is alive in a way that it is not when I am alone because Susan is here. Every room has its reason, so to speak.

Yesterday, among all the marvelous things that happened, a very large red hibiscus was delivered from a friend of mine, Betty Everhard, who is in a wheelchair from polio and who is one of the most life-giving people imaginable. A great giver and a great thinker about politics.

Everything will soon be in order and the chicken in the oven for dinner, for Christmas dinner in the middle of today. We did have one moment of stillness and of feeling what Christmas was all about late yesterday afternoon when Susan listened to the Christmas poem, and we sat in the library.

Renascence

> For two years
> The great cat,
> Imagination,
> Slept on.
>
> Then suddenly
> The other day
> What had lain dormant
> Woke
> To a shower,
> A proliferation
> Of images.

> My Himalayan cat
> Sits on the terrace wall
> Back to the sea
> His blue eyes wide open
> Alive to every stir of a leaf
> Every wing in the air
> And I recognize him
> As a mage.
>
> After long silence
> An old poet
> Singing again,
> I am a mage myself
> Joy leaps in my throat.
> Glory be to God!

But what haunts this Christmas for all of us is the homeless. I felt it very much when I looked out into the darkness past the crèche which Lee Blair had made for me some years ago, and it was as if all those faces, the thousands of homeless, were out there looking in at all this peace and security, and I felt for them and for all the people who had just lost their jobs—seventy-five thousand at General Motors. I cannot find it in my heart to forgive Bush, who would not even admit there was a recession until now when he has been forced to. Why? Because the polls say that his popularity is dropping.

Every day now there is an extraordinary early morning sky. Before seven today a band—it looked half a mile high—of bright orange sky and then a little streak of cloud and the color turned to a strange pale green. It was a marvelous sunrise. But it is terribly cold, and the cold gets to me so that I feel I shall never be warm. It is colder than I ever remember at Christmastime. The worst cold here usually comes in February.

It has been a peaceful holiday. I do not know when I have had so untroubled a Christmas. There have not been any tragic events among my friends. We have been given a rest from horrible problems, except the homeless are still homeless, and those thousands of new unemployed who have been released by General Motors. These things are never far from our minds.

But yesterday Susan and I were invited to have lunch with Margaret and Barbara. Barbara is just back from Europe. In Salzburg her group sang with the choir, accompanied by the organ that had been used by Mozart. They sang the Coronation Symphony which I do not think I have. She said it was the most moving experience of her life. The sound in the great cathedral echoed after the final words of the mass, which are *"Pace, pace, pace."* Those words, "peace," went on and on through the cathedral while tears streamed down the cheeks of every singer, she said.

It has been a wonderful Christmas, a most loving Christmas. I must mention two of the presents, from Deborah Pease, because they are so special: a small silver squirrel and a small silver quail, and there they are now hanging very near the top of the tree, two wonders. And another wonder, a wonder of another dimension, came from Susan Atherton in Belfast, Maine, who sent me George MacDonald's *At the Back of the North Wind.* This is a classic children's book which my mother read to me. I can hear her voice in every line of it. It was like being in the past in the most beneficent and moving way. I remembered also the vivid illustrations. Susan found one, of the mother in the book sitting with her little boy, that she thought looked like my mother. And it does remind me of her.

I spent two hours yesterday with the help of Judy trying to revise an interview. I had a sense that the interviewer for the Weber Studies had not read the poems attentively. She said she found them not concrete, which is nonsense. It is hard when an interviewer says something that would take a chapter of a book to answer and you have to say "Yes, yes" or "No, no."

I worked hard all morning yesterday and was tired when we came back from lunch at Barbara and Margaret's. Their house is full of paintings; most of Margaret's family including herself are painters, her mother a very prolific one. It is a house full of life, looking out on an incredible view of ocean and beach. There are many gulls and bufflehead ducks at this season. I love to watch the ducks dive under. Margaret and Barbara are among the very few people who ever invite me for a meal. But it is more than that kindness. They are true friends of the spirit in a way that I have few of here in Maine. I am grateful for them.

I must mention one other Christmas present in this Christmas of silver. Maggie Vaughan gave me a beautiful little silver container for salt with dark blue glass inside so the salt does not hurt the silver. Very pretty. And a pepper shaker, too. I had my boiled egg this morning with the elegant salt and pepper on the tray.

Tuesday, the last day of 1991

IT IS unbelievable that a whole year has past. A whole year in which I have lived in a prison, although it is a beautiful prison. I have been nowhere, in no city except York, for a year, except for that week in the summer when I go to Rene's on the Cape. But I have not been out for dinner or to a movie or out at night at all. So it was especially precious yesterday when I had to pick up some medicine, to do it after dark so we could see the lights, the people's lights. The sunset featured a perfectly clear, deep orange sky. And the river was burnished with something between vermilion and gold. Magnificent, and peaceful.

That was the end of a remarkable day and a remarkable night before. Two days of nostalgia because of two things: *At the Back of the North Wind,* as I have related, and we have been looking for two days at what I believe is the most beautiful film ever made, *Les Enfants du Paradis,* which Lugné-Poë directed in Paris during the war while the Germans were occupying France. Deborah Pease told me she thought they had been able to use Jews in certain scenes, Jews who would otherwise have been deported. But that is not the point of the film. The film is the most poignant, romantic film that has ever been made. Jean-Louis Barrault is unforgettable as the Pierrot in long white silk pajamas and black stocking cap, his absolutely white face, his crimson mouth, and those burning eyes. And Arletty is marvelous. In a curious way she took me back a long time to what I felt for several women who became muses and who were responsible for my books of poetry. I have been in a state of dazzlement because of this film.

The weather continues to be cold but brilliant. Pierrot is not eager to go out. This morning he would not go out when I went down at four as I always do. Then he did want to go out at half past four.

Judy and I have been struggling with one of the very few interviews I have ever had which was uncomfortable to the point of my wishing that I could withdraw from it. But Judy comes today and we will make a final copy of the changes I made. Reading it over I caught myself in a lapse of memory, a bad one, having confused Circe with Medusa. Medusa turned the people she looked at to stone; Circe turned people into pigs and animals. There is quite a difference! My poem "Medusa" is quoted in the interview.

Friday, January 3

YESTERDAY, January 2, is a red-letter day that I have to remember the rest of my life. It began as so many of these days
lately have with a perfectly clear sky and the sun rising on a
brilliant winter day. But the main event was, first of all and
most important, a letter from Eric Swenson, my editor, who
has finally finished cutting Susan's book *Among the Usual
Days*. At first he thought it was much too long. Not at all. Now
he says that he barely cut anything, he found it so fascinating.
Great news because I believe this book will be much more
moving and beautiful than my last journal, which comes out
for my birthday. I imagine that this one will come out in the
spring of '93. That is the first great news.

And the second was a letter from the *Paris Review* saying
that they have taken four of the new poems. This made me
happy because I am not sure about these poems. How could I
be? As ill as I am and eighty, and all the rest of it!

The third thing is the most remarkable. I went to my rest
quite tired because I had gone to see Dr. Khanjani and then
stopped to do a brief shopping for food. I was finally lying
down desperate for rest because I had also shopped in the
morning for flowers, and the phone rang. It was a man's voice.
He was calling to tell me that I was in the final game for five
big prizes. It was quite funny. And then it turned into so many
requests for buying things and sending small sums to cover
their expenses, and I was not about to do that.

Saturday January 4

It is a wild northeaster, but fortunately rain, not snow. And Morgan Mead came bringing soup for lunch. I have not seen Morgan for about two years. The last time I was very ill in the hospital, and he brought me a primrose. As always we had a good talk. He has known many of the people whom I have loved. He stayed with Juliette Huxley, and his family has a place very near Center Sandwich. He is now teaching again. This is a man who is a born teacher and loves it. His eyes light up when he talks about it and how interesting and exciting his students are to him. Last year he was teaching the ninth grade and this year I think the tenth or eleventh—a little bit older anyway. They are reading *Huckleberry Finn* amongst other things. But he is still in the real estate business so he makes quite a lot of money.

While talking to all these people I am hearing that Margot Peters has written to them. She had written to Morgan. But it makes me constantly think back, I'm afraid, as if I were writing the biography. What came to me this afternoon after Morgan left is that I suddenly remembered an Italian painter called Cagli whom I knew through Giorgio de Santillana and who read my fortune with Tarot cards. I was perhaps thirty years old. Certainly not much more than that. I was having, as I remember, rather a hard time in every way. The fortune told was quite amazing because he said, "You will have hard times but everything will come out at the end—money, fame, love." It is the best possible fortune to hear because it is way off there in the future and you can keep thinking that however bad things are now, they are going to get better. The truth is that they have gotten better and that the end of my life is such a happy one due to Susan and the dear readers who have made my work known to each other and who have told me what it has meant to them. Because of that, after sixty-five I began to make a great deal of money so I am able to give, and that is my idea of heaven. It seems almost unbelievable this can be true. I have been thinking it all over. This beautiful house, flowers everywhere, wonderful Pierrot asleep on my bed now as I am dictating this, and outside the rain beating against the windows. Soon I shall go up to my desk and pen thanks to some of the friends who gave me such marvelous presents this year. I hope to look at the draft of the poem about guilt which I have been trying to write for a long time.

Tomorrow Edythe comes to take down the tree with me as she has for many years now; it is one of our traditions and one of the things that makes this house a home. It will be a kind of celebration.

Morgan talked about hearing Nigel Nicolson the other night give a wonderful talk about living as a child in Sissinghurst. Apparently Nigel said that often, in making the garden, important parts of it had to be planted late at night because Harold Nicolson had to come back from his London office and after dinner they would start planting, among other things a great yew hedge which grew very tall. It appears that it is a little bit crooked. There is a sort of notch halfway through, and this is because it was dark; great gardeners have seen it and said how clever it was to make it not absolutely straight. He described how antisocial his mother was, how they were always trying to get her to invite people from the neighborhood and she never wanted to. I wish I could have heard him. He was, according to Morgan, extremely charming and modest and a joy to behold.

Diane Johnson, in the *New York Review of Books,* has a fascinating long essay on the books about gender; there have been a lot of them recently. The one most widely read is probably Robert Bly's *Iron John,* and on the feminine side, *Backlash,* by Susan Faludi—the subtitle is *The Undeclared War Against American Women.* Diane Johnson is so brilliant and draws together and makes clear so many things that I have been puzzled about that I found the article absolutely fascinating. She speaks about somebody I did not know anything about before. "Richard Tarnas," she says, "in his interesting history of Western thought [*The Passion of the Western Mind,* Harmony Books, 1991], in a part reprinted for distribution to Harvard undergraduates, refers to Jung's prophecy of 'an epochal shift . . . between the two great polarities, a union of opposites: a *hieros gamos* (sacred marriage) between the long dominant but now alienated masculine and the long-suppressed but now ascending feminine.' " And, Tarnas says, " 'this dramatic development is not just a compensation, not just a return of the repressed, as I believe this has all along been the underlying goal of Western intellectual and spiritual evolution. . . . The feminine then becomes not that which must be controlled, denied, and exploited, but rather fully acknowledged, respected, and responded to for itself. . . . This stupendous Western project should be seen as a necessary and noble part of a great dialectic, and not simply rejected as an imperialist-chauvinist plot . . . [a] tradition [that has] painstakingly prepared the way for its own self-transcendence.' " Isn't that fascinating? I am going to have to get hold of Bly's book I think and perhaps one or two of the others. I have been thinking about gender myself, and I hear this on all sides.

Tuesday, January 7

THIS IS the day when I have to drag the bin with all the bottles out of the garage in the dark and I went out at six-thirty to play with Pierrot, but then it was so beautiful. A streak of crimson just at the horizon and above that ominous clouds which have now gone. But it was really exciting out in the darkness with Pierrot dashing along beside me because he loves to get into the garage and snoop about. He is delightfully affectionate these days. But he does not like his food, even the most expensive cat food called "Sheba," and I am ashamed of buying it. But then over and over again he will not eat. What he wants is fish and what I want is fish, but there isn't any right now.

I feel terribly pressured. There is never time. And I wonder whether there is not some psychological way to handle it better. Yesterday is a good example of what my life is like because I had gone to get a new ribbon (which I had bought in Portsmouth when Karen drove me in) to put into the typewriter so I could work on the poem about guilt that I have been making notes for over the past month. I went up and opened the ribbon. It was not the right one! What was there to do? I decided that I had to have it so I stopped at a shop that is having a sale here in York, but they were closed at half past ten. I shot into Portsmouth, managed to find a parking place not too far from the stationer, and they exchanged the ribbon but did not have an all-black, just a black-and-red, but that is not important. What was important was that the whole morning went by. And when I got back I still had to read the mail! I was upset and driven. That is the trouble, driven, because if I do not have my rest then I feel ill. And these are difficult days from the point of view of digestion. I do not know why. Maybe because I have not been able to get fish. One night I had a boiled egg. That was all right. Yesterday I had a prepared TV dinner. It was stuffed chicken breast, and it was not bad but of course not half as good as a dinner cooked from scratch.

I then tried to make various phone calls, none of which got through. I tried to call Margot Peters, who is able to come here in March and work with the files when I am in England, and that is good news. I tried three times to get her but there was no answer. It was one of those days. There must be ways of gliding over the frustrations, but that is easier said than done. Because I have so much I ought to do, if I miss an hour, if I miss a morning as I did yesterday, I feel I am so far behind I shall never catch up. Today I want to write to Jabber, who sent me one of those spring gardens that blossom little by little, and now I see purple crocuses, two tulips, and three magnificent blue hyacinths out.

The only triumph in all this is that I managed to get hold of Alysan Hooper's number. Alysan is not a dear or old friend, but I like her and we have met a couple of times. One day when I was feeling ill, she woke me in the middle of my nap with a phone call, and I said she should not call me at this time and should know that, and hung up. She wrote me a note of apology; this was all a month ago, at least, and I realized I did not have her address or her telephone number, and I could not remember whether she lived at Biddeford Pool or at Kennebunk. Of course this is all ludicrous: this crazy old memory that lets me down. Yesterday I decided to try Biddeford Pool. I got her phone number and she answered. We had a good talk and I apologized and got her address so I can send her the Christmas poem.

One wonderful thing happened. I had no more copies of the Christmas poem and was desperate because there are so many people who send me cards. I sent out two hundred and twenty-five of them and thought they were all gone, but then I suddenly discovered a cache of about eight. This was riches.

Meanwhile, Nadine has called and said she has driven off the road and her car has to be towed so I have to go down, get my breakfast, and lug it upstairs. Then I shall leave it up here and let her make the bed when she gets here because Judy comes today and we will have another lesson on the word processor, which I had intended to practice, but I simply have not got out from under the pressure.

Monday, January 13

IT IS Carol Heilbrun's birthday and thanks to Susan (she has a way of getting roses flown in from Ecuador) I am able to send Carol three dozen roses, mixed colors. It is going to be lovely, I hope. I have not been able to dictate before today because I have been awfully sick. Saturday afternoon, because I had been suffering most of the week from acute pain, I decided that it must be diverticulitis, which I have suffered from before and been in the hospital with more than once. Dr. Gilroy was willing to prescribe an antibiotic which I am now taking. In some ways I am better. I do not have quite as much pain, but I think the antibiotic is constipating so I am back in my ordinary torment.

Four long, important letters came from four people I care about very much, and needed immediate response. The trouble is there is too much coming at me right now and I am stupid to feel so pressured since what does it matter if I wait two days to answer? I have got to learn not to believe I have to do everything immediately. It is a psychological hazard and has to do perhaps with a fear of death—one could have a heart attack—and also with the fear of life in the sense that the next day there will be even more mail and maybe things that I need to answer even more.

Over the weekend Maggie Vaughan was here, such a help, and made scalloped oysters for us. Over the weekend I managed to do the fourth of the four letters, to Christopher de Vinck, who had talked to me openly in a beautiful letter about his beginning to understand what friendship is all about partly due to his great friendship with Fred Rogers. The most exciting answer for me was to write to Betty Voelker, who had sent me a box of thirty or more transparencies of the work she has been doing this year. She is an extraordinary painter. She has not had a break, although she has been bought by important institutions such as the Phillips Gallery in Washington. But somehow she has not found a dealer who can help her. She has to earn a living and so only gets three or four months a year to paint. These transparencies she has sent are more powerful and compassionate than anything I have seen of hers. There are a whole series that look like homeless people or people in a concentration camp—isolated, helpless people, people in misery. Very moving. For another series, she has invented a way of using plastic trays to support the canvas. She is extraordinarily imaginative. My impression of the Bunting Fellowship Board is that they are particularly interested in women with academic backgrounds, so someone like Betty Voelker who is a free-lance painter, however distinguished, does not get a break. It is tragic that she has not gotten a Guggenheim; I seem to be the kiss of death for that as no one I have ever recommended for a Guggenheim has gotten one. I warn people that they had better not ask me.

I went into a real tailspin when a lot of letters came in one day, also a request from an old friend that I sign, pack, and mail a book which she wanted to give someone. She sent me a blank check. She would never have done this if she had realized in what extremity I am. I have the energy for at most two hours in which I can work at my desk in the morning and possibly an hour in the afternoon. Signing a book, packing it, and getting it to the post office is more than I should be asked to do. This request took about fifteen minutes out of my two hours, and that is why I cried. I burst into tears because I thought I could never answer the many needs. I am caught in much too rich a life for somebody who is ill and as old as I am. I never get a moment's peace. I rest for two hours in the afternoon. That is a physical necessity, so the actual time I have in which to run errands and keep the house going, and at the same time tend to what is turning into a huge career I am in no way capable of handling, is terribly little. Judy comes only twice a week. Nancy came every day. I cannot afford more, and Judy is at the university and so probably could not come as often as that in any case.

What I have to do is look on the bright side of this and try to persuade myself that I simply must not worry if I cannot answer four important letters in one day. My real friends know that I am ill. It is the people who call out of the blue who distress and badger me. Yesterday two people called whom I did not expect to hear from at all. One wanted to talk about Eva LeGallienne in order to give the official biographer of LeGallienne a lot of material. She wrote a play which LeGallienne had hoped would go to Broadway, but never did. That call took a lot out of me. At the time I was in the middle of sorting out the checks at the beginning of doing the income tax.

This afternoon is going to be cut off because Raymond Philbrook is coming. He called me on Saturday, and I was very touched because I have not seen him for a long time.

I am at a loss for something commanding to read, but I am into a delightful gardener's book which Tom Barnes sent me for Christmas.

Tuesday, January 14

THE CLIMAX of all the holiday festivities was certainly yesterday afternoon when Raymond Philbrook, who for nearly twenty years was my gardener, came with the delightful young Irish woman, Madelyn Gavin, who for the last twelve years has been taking care of him. It seems like a miracle, and never was one better deserved as Raymond tended and took painstaking care of the gardens all around this piece of coast. He is the most meticulous gardener I have known—I have not known that many, but he certainly puts to shame anyone whom I have had since except my present one, Pat Robinson. It was such a joy to watch Raymond plant. In the days when very well off people lived in this house and flagstones on the terrace had been laid down recently so the grass that grew up between them was not that high, Raymond clipped it on his hands and knees with scissors. He was also a master at cutting the big field that looks down to the sea. Raymond, on a small machine, cut it so that it looked like a lawn. When he cut the rectangular bushes that are in front of the house, he did it by eye and they were as flat as a tabletop. No one has been able to do that since.

He looked awfully well though he has a form of Parkinson's disease which means that he falls, and that is, of course, serious. He described one terrible afternoon when he fell forward and scraped his knee and then could not get up. He was near the barn at the back of his house and had to drag himself on his stomach into the house. He somehow did that but still could not get up. Fortunately Madelyn, who is highly attuned to him, was at home and had the strong feeling, even though she was about to have her dinner, that she must call Raymond. It was so strong that she did call and whether he got to a phone somehow, I do not know. She came and rescued him and got him standing up again, but his knee was still swollen.

We sat down. I know Raymond does not drink, but Maggie had made brownies and Raymond is a chocaholic like me, so we had brownies and cider and a very good talk remembering things and laughing about them. One of the things Raymond did for me every Christmas was to write me a poem, and I think one of the reasons he wanted to come to see me was to show me an interview that came out in a local newspaper. It was an excellent interview and with a very good photograph of him. The interviewer, when he showed her *The House by the Sea,* my journal, in which quite a lot is said about Raymond and one of his Christmas poems is cited, insisted on putting it into her interview, which delighted Raymond. It is the life of a highly intelligent man who could have done anything, but growing up during the depression it was hard to find work, and he found that gardening work was easy to get, so he became a first-rate gardener. He also worked for some years at the Navy Yard because of the depression, for a dollar twenty-seven an hour. Much of his talk in the interview was, of course, how times have changed and how everybody thinks only of money these days. Raymond would never send a bill, that was his only fault, so he was, I am sure, underpaid. I would ask, "What do I owe you? I want to know where I stand." And then I would give him a hundred dollars. I probably owed him five hundred. He would never give me an account. I am glad that Pat Robinson does charge me a definite

agreed-upon amount, four hundred a month for five hours a
week. She is well worth it.

Raymond loved Tamas. I could hear him talking to Tamas
in the garden. At one time he had a great many pets, but he
does not anymore. His sister Viola, who is a little older than he
(Raymond is one year younger than I am), is in a nursing
home and has to be fed entirely intravenously. It is costing a
fortune, and very soon when the money runs out, she will
have to go on Medicaid. And Raymond has to keep something
for himself now that he is retired and not well. It is wonderful
to think about Madelyn, that dear young woman who has
come into his life when he needed her most. Sometimes life
does pretty well by us.

I entirely forgot to say that yesterday was a red-letter day
not only because Raymond and Madelyn came, but because
Marilyn Kallet sent me the most exquisite flowers to thank me
for finding the worksheets of some poems she had asked for.
This bunch had three blue delphinium in it, three tall white
iris, one yellow lily which had four buds, and three or four
rich, full yellow freesias. It was all yellow and white and blue.
It smelled delicious, and made the whole day a festival in
spite of heavy rain.

Wednesday, January 15

I HAVE had my nap, and went out to the garage hoping that it
might be a little warmer and the door would open. It is frozen
again. I pushed the button. Nothing happened, which means
that I do not have the car. This happens when the temperature drops very fast. What is chilling today is the wind, with a

twenty below zero wind-chill factor, as they say. It feels like
it. So maybe it will warm up when Eleanor comes to clean and
if she is able to get a car—hers is being fixed after that accident—she will pick up the mail. I have left a message with
Sylvia Frieze, hoping she can take me to the doctor at ten-
thirty. I have to play it by ear, and not get too agitated. But
the cold does take it out of me. I have on long johns and the
house, at least, is quite warm. The flowers that Marilyn sent
are as fresh as spring.

I am trying to work out why it is that I am so agitated and
driven. It is because every single day something happens that
demands a response having to do with my work. Yesterday or
the day before, it was a request for the two three-act plays
that I wrote years and years ago. Judy and I managed to find
one of them, but the one that was published had been filed in
a different place with published things. I had lunch with
Nancy, and that was wonderful, and she offered to try to find
it, and she found it right away. So now we can send that off to
the people who wanted it. This morning I had to find a photograph for Marilyn Mumford's book that the University of
Michigan is publishing and to answer some of her questions—
whether I approve of the title, for one. I love the title of
Marilyn Kallet's book, *A House of Gathering*. But I am not
crazy about any of the ones Marilyn Mumford suggests. Apparently the University of Michigan is bossy about titling a
book and wants to choose its own. By the time I had gotten
things together for Marilyn, the morning had gone and it was
time to go out for lunch.

What encourages me a little is to think of all that I have
managed to do besides thanking people for kindnesses. But if
about forty percent of one's life is spent in thanking people, it
does not seem a viable life. The whole problem is energy. I
discovered yesterday—I am now doing the income tax—that I
have given away sixteen thousand to friends, not deductible. I

have no regrets; I am glad that I could. But it is appalling to see what everything costs, and I am depressed because I do not have my car. Luckily Joan was here; she got the mail and she also got two prescriptions from Wellby's for me. Nadine will be here on Friday which will help. She can get the mail and so on. It is certainly very necessary in the winter to have these helpers. I am lucky.

Sunday, January 19

On these cold days all I can think of is the homeless, the numbers of people who are going to die out there when the wind chill is twenty or thirty below zero. The sun is out so that from inside the house it all looks glittering and there is mist over the ocean showing that the air is colder than the sea. However, I do *not* wish to go into the sea to get warm today!

Susan is here so the house is filled with the scent of roses and the flowers that Marilyn Kallet sent me are still marvelous, so everything is beautiful inside. Susan is making wonderful meals as she always does and also brought food from New York, from Zabar's, some delicious vegetable soup that we had yesterday.

When this cold spell began, and the garage door stuck, I was hopeful that the weather would change as it usually does in New England. You know, "wait a minute, it will change" is certainly true about New England weather, but it has not changed. We have now had almost a week of this extreme cold from Canada with icy winds, which make it much worse. I decided to wait it out. I asked Eleanor Perkins to bring the mail on Thursday; she comes to clean on that day. Nadine comes on Friday, so she is able to get the mail for me. The problem was I had an appointment with Dr. Khanjani on Thursday. So I called Sylvia Frieze, a near neighbor who has asked me a dozen times to call on her if I ever needed help. I called her with some trepidation and she said, "I'd love to do it. I've plenty of time." She came and got me, and took me to the doctor, but there I got a blow because Dr. Khanjani made it clear that she thinks I am wrong to cut down my visits to her to one a week. She said that twice I have had to be on antibiotics, once for a bladder infection and now for painful diverticulitis; it is not as much the diverticulitis, which the antibiotic has helped, but that the antibiotic itself is making me nauseated. Worst of all, I think for the first time in maybe a year, I was not able to do one thing at my desk. I tried to find an address and the search made me feel quite ill; I have been through every address book including the one just for fans and did not find it. These are friends of mine in Vancouver—the Tillmans. So yesterday, except for good talks with Susan, it was a rather miserable day. It is miserable to feel nauseated and yet not throw up.

But Sylvia and I had such fun; it was a pleasant time we spent and she was even able to do a few errands with me so that I did not have to do quite so much on Friday because Susan will be here. I shall certainly dare to ask her again. Meanwhile I decided that I had to have help on the door, so on Friday at seven I called Henry's Garage Doors and at about nine an old man—he looked old to me—found that the door was frozen, the button frozen, and there is no door except the mechanical door into the garage. Very cheerfully he took his own ladder with him, forced a window open, and got in through it. I was amazed, but he kept saying, "Don't worry, it's all right, I can do it." And he did. Now he has fixed the button so it is even lit up at night, and it works though I was skeptical and did not let Susan close it on Friday night when she arrived because the birdseed is there and if by any chance we could not get in the birds would starve.

Friday gave me the proof that I am getting better because in spite of the nausea and feeling quite ill, I wrote my first solo letter on the word processor. Today I am going to try to write one to Maggie. It is such fun once you get the gist of it! I did that and then went over some things with Judy, so many things, so many demands.

This reminds me that I must try to find some more drafts of poems for Constance Hunting, who agrees with me that for her speech at the Westbrook Conference next June, which is to be on May Sarton the editor, she can use one set of drafts on a poem and show that revising a poem is a kind of editing. When that was done, it was ten and Karen was there, as well as the man for the door, so it was complicated. I had to do a huge shopping at the Golden Harvest and try to get sole for Susan and me. The Weathervane is the only fish market open and it is at some distance in Kittery, but I got it. When I got back there was everything to unpack, and Edythe was ready to go out for lunch. She had noticed that our old haunt, now called "One Fish, Two Fish," was open on Fridays. This is good news. We made a beeline for it and had one of their elegant soups, a scallop soup with tomato, which I should not have had but I do not think it did me any harm, and an absolutely remarkable dessert: lemon cake with white chocolate striped into it. Very, very good. I got back, had my nap, and then emptied the icebox. It is always filled with things that should have been thrown away. In Susan's honor I cleaned out the vegetable bin and arranged all the new vegetables and made a list for her. Then I cleared her desk, which is where I did the income tax, and packed all those checks away until Tuesday—she leaves tomorrow. After all that, I still had to get my dinner and I must say by then I was very tired.

But I am greatly enjoying Moseley's book. It is a remark-

able novel which takes one through the history of the last
ninety years. It is called *Hope for Monsters*. It takes place, at
least in the beginning, in Cambridge, England. It is wonderful
to have a book which one is eager to read. It makes me see
that I do have a head because it is an intellectual novel, the
most primarily intellectual one I have read since Aldous Huxley's *Point Counterpoint* years ago.

Friday, January 24

IT IS now, I am ashamed to say, Friday, January 24, and it
must be days since I have put anything on record here. That is
because the antibiotic I have to take for diverticulitis has
made me terribly ill with nausea and other side effects hard to
handle. Now I am through with that dose, forty of them, and I
am hoping to emerge well. Dr. Khanjani says that she never
thought I could do as well as I am doing now, apart from this
infection. She is proud of me, she says. "We have done it
together."

There are so many events these days! One is that Bill
Ewert sent me the twelve poems which will make a little book
for my eightieth birthday, to be called *Coming into Eighty*. I
am happy about it. Twelve new poems is not nothing. Marianne Moore offered only twelve poems in one of her last
books. Mine will not be a bound book, but it is going to be
lovely, and it will be wonderful to have it to give to friends.

A great event has happened. Almost a year ago, I received
a catalog of a show by a painter called Joan Gold at the Lisa
Harris Gallery in Seattle. A reproduction was sent of something called *The Camus Quartet*—four abstract paintings that
belong together and which are notable chiefly for their bril-

liant color. I felt that it was distinguished and somehow airy and life-giving, so much so that I have had the *Camus Quartet* pinned up by my bed ever since. I have now heard that in her new show there is to be a series called *The Sarton Quartet*, and I asked a friend in Seattle to go and look at it and see what she thought because I might be interested in buying it. Kay Bullitt wrote me a good letter describing the four paintings, but then I never heard anything else. I thought it strange that the gallery did not get in touch with me, but then I forgot about it.

Lo and behold, yesterday came a long letter about Joan Gold, who is a fascinating person. She spent twenty years in Venezuela, now lives in California, and color is everything to her. She talks about a blue as not being just blue but *blue* itself. And I think this is a real affinity because it is, of course, the color which got to me in the four paintings that I have lived with all this time. So I went through a crisis of saying that I had no business to buy paintings for myself. But then I talked with Margaret Whalen on the telephone, and she said, "You must do something for yourself, May." I decided after all, it is also for the painter. I want to support Joan Gold.

Yesterday afternoon I called Lisa Harris and we had a talk and I made an agreement by which I would pay half this year, half next year, and then whatever is left as a result of the framing and the postage, which is enormous, but I am to have them right away as soon as I send the check for fifteen hundred on February first. I am terribly excited. I think I know exactly where they will hang, but there are various possibilities and we shall have to try them in several places. This feels like a tremendous event. I am exhilarated. Whenever I have bought a new car, as I have done maybe five times in my life, I never felt any joy. It seemed so materialistic and had no soul in it. Whereas having made this tremendous decision to buy something I obviously should not afford, I feel nothing but joy.

Monday, January 27

THE BITTER COLD goes on. It is a harsh winter indeed. A little snow would soften it, but this relentless cold . . . This morning when I came down to write out a list of what Joan might do when she comes to get me my breakfast I looked at the temperature where my chaise longue is and it was fifty. So I put on an electric heater with the thermostat at eighty. It was only seventy in the rest of the house. It is really cold, there is no getting around it. And when I think of all the people who are suffering from it, it shakes me to the core.

I had a hard weekend. I felt extremely ill. I think it still must be the side effects of the antibiotic. As it works itself through my system, I seem to get worse rather than better and have a great deal of pain. I finally called Dr. Khanjani because my bladder seems to be affected, and she had me drink a lot of Cranapple and also a glass of water with one tablespoon of vinegar in it twice during the afternoon.

It was a hard weekend, too, because Susan was unable to call when she was in Florida to see her mother, and I waited and waited for that call. Nancy did not call on Saturday or yesterday morning either, so I got quite anxious. I felt sick and rather abandoned, but Susan finally did call and was disappointed that I do not feel like having anybody over this coming weekend. I have to think only about getting well, and that means resting a lot, eating only what I want. It is a low ebb. January compounded by sickness and bitter cold.

Soon Judy will be here with the mail.

Friday, January 31

IT IS a relief to get this awful month over. In two days we will see what the groundhog has to say. I have been bad about dictating lately because I am sick. It seems so boring to keep saying the same thing over and over. It is clear that I have an intestinal infection, and that is what is making life harder than usual. But I keep reminding myself that a year ago I was much worse off. Yesterday the mail brought ten letters that should be answered immediately—a little overwhelming. Karen was coming at ten-thirty to take me to do a big shopping in Portsmouth at the place which has wonderful herbs and vegetables, and I had my usual appointment with Dr. Khanjani at one-thirty. Also on Thursday Eleanor comes to clean. Nobody makes the bed or brings my breakfast on Thursday so I had to do all that. Then I managed to write two long letters, went out and did that big shopping, rushed back, had a quick bowl of the vegetable broth I made under Dr. Khanjani's direction (it tasted awfully good), and rushed off to see her. I must admit I did collapse then when I came back.

One of the things that happened was a tremendous event. That was the arrival of Deborah Pease's first book of poems, *The Feathered Wind*, which Connie Hunting has published at the Puckerbrush Press. I saw these poems as they were being written, and they were being written in an extraordinary way. Almost every day one would make its appearance. It is a little bit like a journal, but it is not a journal, not at all. I have now reread the whole book in bed with my breakfast, and I find it

one of the most powerful books of poems I have ever seen.
This is an extraordinary thing to say, even an extraordinary
thing to feel. Deborah, I think, must be about fifty now. She
was a student of mine at Wellesley College many years ago,
and we have become good friends. What is wonderful about
this book is that it is a direct speech in poetry that I have not
heard before. The voice is haunting. It envelops you. It is your
self talking to your self in some ways. I think I must ask her
permission to copy out at least one of the poems. There are
two which are particularly haunting because they speak to
everybody. The genius of these poems is that they are at the
same time original and universal. I feel the poems are for me.
The first one, I think, shows what I am trying to say:

> Sometimes I try to console myself
> For my human failures
> By comparing my behavior
> To certain traits of animals in the wild.
> The main features are: shyness
> And a solitary life
> So I assume the tawny form of a cougar
> And vanish at dusk
> Into mountainous terrain
> Seeking safe places in trees
> Or the interstices of rock.
>
> I spend twenty hours a day sleeping.
> The rest of the time I look for food.
> Once a year I conjugate with a male
> In a spar of love
> After which he leaves, to my relief.
>
> When I give birth to cubs
> I tend them carefully;
> They are my poems.

Here is another:

Once, my face protected me: a mask
Of youth and health and even prettiness.
The mask preceded me.
It led me down pathways
And across valleys
And into the arms
Of harm and villains, magically
Eradicating dangers
(One would have thought otherwise).
Now the mask is dented and cracked.
It bears a patina of fatigue
And a moral quality
(In the sterner contours)
It lacked before. It's a mask
No longer: it's me.
Human and open to attack.

I think I am feeling a little better, but it is still such a struggle and I am exhausted by the long list of personal problems that do not go away. Dr. Khanjani says it is not surprising that I feel tired but that I am getting better. She is supportive and gives me faith that I am. All I have to do is remind myself of how terribly ill I was a year ago and realize that I have made great strides.

Yesterday was a marvelous day because I heard from Jamey. Good news from people in real trouble is so rare that when I opened this letter I began to cry I was so relieved because she has been struggling for two years to get a job. She works with crippled children and also adults who need special care, and is a genius at it, but she is ill a great deal of the time and has been unable to get help. It has been a worsening situation now for this past year and is improving, at last, due to the intervention of a wonderful therapist, a woman doctor who have become interested in her case, and finally a neurologist who has become interested for purely medical reasons;

one of her problems is rare. She is going on disability with Medicaid, which is to say that she gets a considerable sum of money, enough so that she can keep afloat every month. This is the end of such an incredible struggle for so long, I cannot get over the relief that she will be taken care of and at the same time I keep thinking how terribly important it is that we have better health care for everybody in America. We have got to do something about it.

Deborah Pease, who is the publisher of the *Paris Review*, sent me a few earlier copies and in one of them was a good interview with Donald Hall in which he remembers the several times that he saw Marianne Moore and Robert Frost. Something he said about Marianne Moore really struck me. He says,

> She was tiny and frail and modest, but oh so powerful. I think she must have been a weight lifter in another life— or maybe a middle linebacker. Whenever you're in the presence of extreme modesty or diffidence, *always* look for great degrees of reticent power, or a hugely strong ego. Marianne Moore as editor of the *Dial* was made of steel. To wrestle with her over a check was to be pinned to the mat.

The last sentence was because she insisted on paying the check when she took him out to lunch. And I recognized this at once and tried to think of the people I know who are extremely reticent and powerful. But I am not going to name them.

He also talked about Robert Frost. I was quite fascinated by several things he said about Frost:

> Frost was a political animal in the literary world. So are many of the best poets I run into, and it doesn't seem to hurt their poetry.

On the contrary, they have become more and more aware that without being a political animal you do not get anywhere, and I am an example of this.

Saturday, February 8

I AM AFRAID I have neglected the journal because I am so driven by the material on my desk that I never seem to be able to make the time. It is now nine o'clock on Saturday. Saturday is the day when nobody comes to help so I have gotten my breakfast, taken it up and eaten it, and read a piece in the *Maine Times* about an extraordinary Maine town in which about thirty-five percent of the people are retired or are over sixty, but they are all active retirees and very good and eager to help, so it is a civilized town indeed as well as beautiful. It is good to read about this and realize how important a town like that can be. One of the people interviewed had gone to Florida first and didn't like it and said that one of the things that was precious in Maine was the quiet. Of course I feel that very strongly myself.

I associate the observing of flowers and the enjoyment of having flowers in the house very much with silence. I don't look at them in the same way when I have a guest. Right now by my bed, thanks to a Christmas present from Joan Jansen, I have the most exquisite bunch of spring flowers: six anemones of six different colors—oh, they are so beautiful!—with three deep rose tulips and two very blue iris. I watched them open, the anemones, and now I can see their black hearts, all except the white one which has a greenish-white heart. In some ways

CREDIT: DON CADORET

Looking at flowers

they are my favorite flower, but I have said that about others.

I almost let out a scream yesterday when the Jackson &
Perkins catalog had on its back cover a photograph of the blue
poppy, Meconopsis, which I saw at Sissinghurst against a low
brick wall, a sight I have never forgotten. I have even tried to
raise it from seed, but that seems impossible. Now Jackson &
Perkins advertises root plants. They are expensive, but I think
I have simply got to have it. I am not a greedy person except

about flowers and plants, and then I am afraid I become fanatically greedy.

One of the few good things about February is Valentine's Day, and I have been having a lovely time because for once I found some time for writing Valentines yesterday afternoon. It is not much better than any other festival when cards are sent, but there is no other day for such an effort. It made me remember one of the teachers whom I most admired at the Shady Hill school, Miss Putnam, who taught science. One Valentine's Day I made for her a map of the world in the shape of a heart; I copied it carefully out of a book. I thought you never should tell that you sent a special Valentine. She was very anxious to know who had sent it and asked several times. I never dared to say it was I, but I minded terribly. I used to make all my Valentines; that I have not done lately, and I must say that many of the Valentines you can buy seem rather cheap and not very beautiful.

It is a stressful time, and I am beginning to realize why. It is at least in part because I am being forced to look back on my life, and the way to live well when you are eighty is to live in the present and the future. I do not want to look back, but because Margot Peters is writing my biography, she naturally asks questions, and I am forced to look back. She has left me very much alone, but the fact that she is thinking about my life makes me come to terms with it. She brought up the name of the first woman I ever shared an apartment with, and now I have to think about that and what I should say. It brings everything back, you see, and what I really want is to look out at the gray sea through the falling snow.

One nice surprise yesterday was that the taxi driver in London whose cab I hired four years ago, and to whom I wrote to ask whether he would drive Maggie and me in London and what he would charge, called me on the telephone yesterday. He will certainly meet the plane, which is good news.

I am still deeply involved in Moseley's *Hope for Monsters*. It is a long, dense book, dense in the sense that there is an enormous amount of information in it. It brings alive many of the chief moments and preoccupations of the century— from the Holocaust to the Spanish Civil War, from Hemingway to the Bloomsbury circle. So one is constantly living over the past in that book. Brilliantly done. It is never didactic, partly because we see it all through the eyes of two young people, a man and a woman, and they are living through it all; they are not recounting it as history. I can highly recommend the book, but it does take an effort; it is not an easy read.

Gloria Steinem is not getting very good reviews on her autobiographical book about self-esteem. It seems clear from the reviews that the trouble is that far from letting us into her own experience as she realized that she had very low self-esteem in spite of all her fame, what she does is give a step-by-step way of conquering low self-esteem just as a dozen "how-to" books that have come out in the last year do. And one cannot read them, or at least, it seems to me, the people who do are crazy. I suddenly realized what it is about my journals that may be valuable. I never tell people what to do. I cannot imagine making a step-by-step analysis of how to live in solitude. I describe a way of life. Sometimes it affects someone and has actually changed the way of life of quite a few people.

The other day I got a charming letter, one that feeds me as much as any I have ever had because it is such a simple kind of influence that I am told I wielded in this case. It is from a woman who decided after reading *The House by the Sea* that she would go and buy a bird feeder and set it up, perfectly confident that birds would come. Of course they might not

have, but lo and behold, the next day there were every sort of
bird you can imagine, birds I had described—chickadees,
bluejays, nuthatches, and God knows what. And isn't it delightful that if I am asked, "Do you influence people?" I can
answer, "I influenced someone to buy a bird feeder."

Wednesday, February 12

WE HAD a respite from the bitter cold yesterday, and it was
amazing how much energy I had as a result. But in the night
icy winds came in from Canada, and it is now five above zero
so I think the wind chill must be well below zero. I have on my
long johns, and even so I am cold.

There is a lot of talk about self-esteem these days. Gloria
Steinem's book is following a trend, or perhaps making one. In
either case, I doubt that it is a good idea. I do not think Americans need more self-esteem, I think they need less. However,
to use a fashionable word, I was filled with self-esteem yesterday because for the first time in months, I was active all day
doing an enormous amount of walking and getting in and out
of the car. All these things take it out of me, but in the warm-
ish springlike air, it was possible.

The day began in the dark when I went to take the rubbish out before seven, and by great good luck the truck came
at seven. Very often I have left it for Nadine thinking they
would never come on time, but the fact that I had dragged it
out and they came was a wonderful start to the day. I had
already made my breakfast at about half past six and had
eaten it. Then I went back to bed to stay there. I was having

bad cramps, so bad that I was not sure I could get out to the garage in time. But I did manage, and ultimately got dressed and made the bed and washed the dishes and then set out at eight o'clock for Portsmouth to see Dr. Dinnerman, my dentist. Because I have lost so much weight the partial dentures have slipped and one of them had to be cushioned, so he needed to have it for one day. When I was doing so many public appearances and had all my teeth out about ten years ago, I thought I had better have a spare. So I simply used the spare and was comfortable all day.

When I left Dr. Dinnerman about nine yesterday I went to the A&P and got two six-packs of pineapple juice, heavy for me to carry, and then, in great pain, cashed a check, got the mail, went to Sesame Tree to get some medicinal things that I need (they have health foods), and got home about half past ten—triumphant! I then even had the energy—and this is marvelous—to think about people who might blurb the new journal, and I asked Susan to suggest some names. It will be published not long after my birthday.

Then I had my lunch, but I was still in pain. I think it is interesting that gaining a sense of self-esteem showed that I could do all this, even when I had bad cramps. At two-thirty Sylvia Frieze, so kind, came to drive me back to Portsmouth to pick up the teeth. And I must say by then I was tired and grateful for a driver. We had time even to stop at Eberle's for me to get some things, a typewriter ribbon and manila envelopes. When I got back at five, I really was tired, and it was hard to stand and get my dinner, and there was no time to relax until I had eaten it, cleared things up, and gotten into bed.

Michele, who substitutes for Nadine, was here this morning and is a charming presence in the house. Unfortunately, she cannot come on Friday, but Susan comes Friday night and all will be well.

Saturday, February 15

SOMETIMES THE TELEPHONE can be a hazard because one does not properly explain something. A new friend of mine named Norma Allen, a doctor who lives in St. Petersburg, Florida, called when I was terribly depressed—that is the trouble, you cannot not answer—and she was quite upset and wrote me a delightful letter which made me laugh so much that it got me right out of the depression. She said, "You may feel like a drowning mouse now, but maybe you are a strong, able, good mouse able to swim and last the terrible storms and nibble on some cheese." That made me laugh partly because cheese is not on my diet, but mostly because at the end I thought, What is an able mouse? What is an unable mouse, especially? And what is a bad mouse? But I guess I am a pretty good able mouse on the whole, and I certainly am better than I was even a month ago.

Susan came last night for the first time since New Year's with, as always, an armful of roses. Most wonderful on Valentine's Day! Red, white, pink. Just beautiful. And before that she had sent a whole bunch of different-colored tulips. A delight for the eyes!

I felt very spoiled yesterday, and today it is heaven to have Susan here. She is off getting the mail now. And today we have a video of *Doctor Doolittle* which I am dying to see. When I was a child it was one of my favorite books.

Now everything begins to come together as I have to be thinking about London, about getting this house in some kind of order, and about clothes. I did manage to get three jackets from a shop in Portsmouth. Up to now I have been wearing "elephant clothes" since I have lost so much weight.

It is a little warmer today. This morning Susan read a little of the journal, the new one coming out. She thinks it is just as good as the others, not worse, as I had feared. That is a great comfort.

Monday, February 17

IT IS President's Day. Susan has left. I think it has been the most perfect weekend we have ever had together. Susan always arrives with an armful of roses. Here she is, in the middle of the night—it seems the middle of the night to me after about nine o'clock—between nine and ten, this slight figure with a great armful of red, white, pale yellow, pale pink, every rose you can imagine in her arms, and her little white fluffy poodle, Cybèle. We had a radiant time, a weekend full of Valentines.

The afternoon before she came there were two deliveries of flowers, overwhelming. One from somebody called Ben Franklin; I haven't the foggiest idea who he is, but I am enjoying the flowers just the same. And Susan, as usual, has brought from Zabar's marvelous soups, a leek-and-potato soup that was quite fine, all kinds of chocolates, and goodness knows what.

We are so happy to be able to talk, and a lot has occurred. But the two great things of the weekend, very different but equally marvelous, were, first, that I received the bound proof of the new journal, and whenever Susan was not doing things for the household (which she always does) she read it. I have been extremely nervous about it; it was dictated because I was much too ill to type. When I started to read it I was overcome by the memories of how ill I had been, so I could not read it. And I was worried about it; I wondered if there was too great an emphasis on illness, and whether it flowed. Susan said that it is in some ways the best of the journals partly because it is dictated, which created a special kind of flow. And also because it is Proustian, as she says. More than ever before I have brought in childhood memories, memories as they have come to an old woman. Apparently this is successful. What a relief to have some hope about the new journal! Eric Swenson, my editor at Norton, has always been enthusiastic, and so has Tim Seldes, my agent. But you never know. And of course we see all the faults, and I know how ill I was and how difficult it had been.

The other great event was seeing the video of *Doctor Doolittle* which Susan brought with her. It is one of the best movies I have seen. It is a perfect part for Rex Harrison who, as Doctor Doolittle, was passionate about animals and learning their languages. Of course every animal is in it and they all are charming. I do not know where they ever got them all. It must have been an immensely expensive production. It ends on a floating island somewhere on the ocean, one does not really know where. It was such a delight I could hardly bear to have it end, and I miss it already. I feel as if there is a wonderful kingdom that I have lost but will never forget.

It has been a remarkable weekend in every way, including the weather. It was so warm the cat stayed out almost all night.

Friday, February 21

SUDDENLY IT has started snowing, and I had forgotten how mesmerizing it is. I have been sitting here watching it fall. It is sticky and wet, not fluffy and dry, so wet it might even change to rain. I hope it doesn't.

For some reason this seems to be a time of crisis for a lot of people I know. Yesterday was a calm day all around because it is the day Eleanor comes. It is the day I have to make my bed and make my breakfast, and so on. I was thinking about hiring more help, so it was rather a shock to read the mail and find that one good old friend of mine, an artist, is having to declare bankruptcy. She is a wonderful woman who has been subject, if that is the word, to a mean divorce in which she gets nothing after the daughters graduate from high school. After twenty-seven years of marriage, her husband fell in love with a young woman and later they were married. In the meantime, my friend Catherine, who married young and therefore had no chance to acquire tangible business skills, has found herself at fifty in the terrible struggle of trying to make a living.

The second letter I opened was from Pat Keen, a dear friend, and she is in trouble with the British tax people because she had an accountant who did not tell her about the mistakes he made, and while she was paying U.S. income tax, federal, state, and city when they were doing *Nicholas Nickleby* in New York, the British IRS was not notified. I called her this morning to commiserate and also to talk about our trip. She is going to get tickets for us to *Uncle Vanya*—I am simply thrilled—and for a wonderful Irish play. She said she would drive me to Suffolk to see my cousins; this is a tremendous gift because I was going to have to get the train, she told me, at the new Liverpool Street Station and to walk miles.

Yesterday I was in a state of anxiety about friends. Dr. Khanjani was very upset with me. The trouble is that I need to be soothed and to have a chiropractor treat me and I was upset by her tone; it did not do me any good, not at all. Things will work out in time, no doubt. But it has been one of those days when the heart is heavy because there are so many people you love whom you wish you could help and cannot.

Tuesday, February 25

NADINE IS BACK! She has had two weeks off, and it is awfully good to see her. She is so helpful and efficient. She knows the household routine. She is also an upbeat presence, and because she has had the same problem that I have, she is understanding when I have bad days. Fortunately Maggie Vaughan was here this weekend. The pain was so bad that I did not know what to do with myself. Yesterday morning I finally did break the spell and had a movement, but during the day I was in great pain. So last night and today I have felt as if my colon had been stripped and was bleeding, which it is not, but that is how it feels.

Maggie is such a marvelous presence that when she is here everything looks better. She keeps the bird feeder in good condition for me. She actually has bought new insides for it, so it has been rebuilt over and over again after the squirrels gnaw it to pieces. She did that and, heaven knows, lots of other things as well. Fantastic meals. She brought sweet-breads from her farm and marvelous spinach—I do not know how she does it—cut up very fine. Maggie does things with a little garlic and a small thin-skinned potato cut up very small so she can cook it fast. And it is delicious. And then grapefruit.

Friday, February 28

TOMORROW IS that extra day that comes only every four years, and something great should be done with it. Susan will be here, and that in itself is a celebration.

What a mistake it is not to trust one's judgment! For a long time deconstruction has been fashionable; the new models for criticism in France were Foucault, Barthes, Derrida, and Lacan, who followed Sartre. I felt completely distanced from them, and could not understand what was happening. Friends in academia considered me very backward. Now, at last, there is an article by Marc Fumaroli in the *Times Literary Supplement* called "A Walk in the Desert," with the subtitle "The Ghosts in the Ruins of the French Literary Tradition." I had not realized that in French education now the emphasis on the past, the history of French literature, on which French civilization itself is based, is no longer common in the schools. The average French child does not know about Montaigne. So there is a terrible barrenness. The article states:

> In the twentieth century, the destructive role once played by the French Revolution devolved on the defeat of 1940, the German Occupation and the epuration fol-

lowing the Liberation of 1945. Whole areas of the symbolic legacy of French culture, and the literary schools that had given it vitality, disappeared because of their complicity with the Vichy regime. By contrast, the tired remnants of Surrealism, allying themselves to the Communist Party, together with the coterie around Jean-Paul Sartre, coloured by nihilistic anarchism and Marxism, suddenly acquired disproportionate significance. They became rivals and accomplices, as Jean Paulhan said, in a literary Reign of Terror. An abstract symbolic system, atrophied and artificial, was the progeny of this literature of arrogant camp-followers: the New Novel and Structuralism, cleverly inflated products of a sect.

It almost seems as though something of the same sort happened at the same time in China with the Red Guard and the destruction of the whole of Chinese culture, and I wonder what this is based on.

Today in the mail I had beautiful photographs of one of my adopted Greek daughters, Mando and Dinoula. I had adopted them through one of the associations where you send money once a month, but little by little I got to know them. It is not allowed, but I went to Greece and I met Angeliki, their mother, and we have become true friends though I have not been in touch for a long time. I hoped Angeliki would marry again because she was having a hard time when I adopted them, and she did marry again, in part because of the small dowry I was able to provide. Angeliki's husband, Alekos, is a kind, dear man who wants to call me "Mother." She wants me to come and live with them, which of course I cannot do, but it is comforting to think they want me. A blessed day . . . but I have been having pain and intestinal trouble, and I wonder if I will ever get to London. Never mind! I intend to go, willy-nilly.

Monday, March 2

PEOPLE SOMETIMES ask me why I live here in what seems like a remote place, and the answer could be because of the York Hospital, which is only a ten-minute drive from me. When Susan came late Friday night, she was bothered by a pain in her chest and of course we both wondered if it could be her heart, and so on Saturday, after lunch, she went to the emergency room at the hospital. I was terribly anxious. Fortunately, perhaps because I have an unusual problem myself, I lay down and figured out that she might be gone a few hours. She came back in two hours to tell me what a wonderful hospital it is. She marveled at the amount they did in two hours. Dr. O'Neil, a woman doctor who helped me once in an emergency, was there, and they did an EKG and then a much longer test of the heart and found nothing troubling and ruled out the heart as the problem causing the pain. X-rays were made of course and how great it was that her own York doctor was there in the hospital to give her a prescription, so Susan went off to get a pain killer which worked well. She went back to New York Sunday morning. It is incredible! I mean, here is this hospital ten minutes away, with an atmosphere of so much kindness and goodwill in this sorry world we are in. Overwhelming!

We had a good weekend, in spite of everything. I am anxious about going to England because I am having such bad pain. So I have started, out of sheer desperation, to go back to my medical doctor to see if something can be done about a pain killer which would help me through the ten days.

Wednesday, March 4

YESTERDAY I finally wrote a letter to Bill Heyen, a great poet and friend of mine, who had sent me his book, *Pterodactyl Rose: Poems of Ecology*. He is at the top of a list of people I want to write to for one reason or another but each day they all get pushed aside because there is something of immediate necessity. I sat at my desk and read the book through for a second time. He has a power that is very rare, to write real political poems without ever attacking the reader. I enjoyed one which I read again yesterday, called "Harpoon."

> Now that blue whales are as few as two hundred,
>   I want the last one dead.
> I need to forget them right away,
>   before the last reports:
>   ships stripping lost codes of flesh,
>
>   the last calf wandering away, &, later,
>   are there any left?
> Before the last eye is cut out, dumped overboard,
>   & floats away,
>   & what it sees. Kill them now, please,
>
>   before politics can't save them—
>   the fountaining overtures
> the biblical jaws the blue tinge fathoms deep
>   the evolutionary curves our
>   predecessors' pitiful & beautiful last songs.

Saturday, March 28

IT IS March 28, and I am home again after an extraordinary adventure—flying to London on the fifteenth to see Juliette Huxley, who is now ninety-five and, I suppose, my dearest friend on earth. It was risky, and the first thing that happened was that our plane had trouble and we were first told that there would be a delay of four or five hours and then we were finally put on the plane and sat in it for four hours and then were told, "We're very sorry, but we have not been able to solve the problem tonight and have to bring in another plane in the morning, so you will be put up at the Hilton Hotel here in Boston and your flight will leave at nine-thirty tomorrow morning." Of course this was simply terrible. We had to get off the plane, find our luggage, get a taxi to the Hilton. I was afraid that I would be too ill then to manage the whole trip. But we managed, Maggie and I, and of course she was a tremendous help. In the morning we had breakfast sent up and then were told that the flight had been put off as they had not been able to get the plane from Dallas—the carrier was American, incidentally, which had only just begun to fly to London—so we were told to wait and that our flight would be at twelve-fifteen. Luckily we had reserved on business class because of me, because I was not well enough to travel in the crowded sardine box of coach as I always have before. Because we were in business class, which I am afraid I shall always do, however much it costs, we were able to use the lounge. It was a comfortable lounge, so I could even have a

snooze and could read in a comfortable chair. But the whole
thing was an ordeal. There is no getting around that.

The worst moment came in the middle of the afternoon
when we thought we might still be getting off, but the wait
seemed interminable. Suddenly Maggie and I both had the
same idea. Let's have an Alexander. I have not had an Alexander since I was in Florence when I was nineteen, so you can
figure about sixty years ago. But we managed to persuade the
bartender to make one, Maggie described how to do it, and
this was a great moment. That is the fun of having a friend
with you, as I have rarely done. This time it was necessary,
and it was wonderful.

So finally after all this we did land at Heathrow in London
at one A.M. on Tuesday morning; we had left here on Sunday
afternoon at four! I could not believe it that my darling friend,
Pat Keen, was there to welcome us in the empty halls. She
first tried to meet us at six-thirty A.M. on the morning before
and then was told that it would be one before we got in. She
was there, as was Hyman Kern, the taxi driver whom I had
written to after remembering that I had his card in my purse
from another visit. There he was in an absolutely deserted
airport. There was not a taxi in sight. We went fast through
Customs. We just walked out and there were these two adorable people, Pat with flowers for me. She followed in her own
car and we got to Durrant's Hotel where they also were most
welcoming. In my room I found flowers and chocolates from
my cousin, Alan Eastaugh, and a beautiful shawl from a friend
and fan, Carol Ebbs, and daffodils from her garden. So it was
a wonderful arrival, after the stress.

Here I was in London. I had not believed this could happen. It did not seem possible. But here I was in London. I was
called at seven at my request and had a Continental breakfast
at seven-thirty. It was delicious, one of the best breakfasts I
ever had because I had decided that on this holiday I was

going to forget about my diet. I have not had a cup of coffee for nearly two years, and so I ordered coffee and hot milk and had a croissant and pineapple juice. After a little while, at about ten, I called Juliette Huxley, who was a bit bewildered since I had been expected to call the day before. But I said, "May I invite myself for lunch today?" She said, "Yes, you may, but I thought you were coming for tea, but that's all right." So, I called Hyman, and he came and got me and drove me to Hampstead through Regent's Park where I passed so many of the beautiful Nash houses, at least two of which I have visited. One was H. G. Wells' and one of course was Elizabeth Bowen's at Two Clarence Terrace where I first met Virginia Woolf and watched her walk across the room to long French windows and look out on the park. I thought, How much more beautiful she is than any photograph shows!

London was not yet in full spring, but the grass was emerald green and there was something I had not seen before, that is, lakes of crocuses, planted so densely they were a carpet of purple and white. Very beautiful, but it would only do in a park, not in a garden. Daffodils were out everywhere. The cherries and plums and pears were blossoming under a gray sky.

Suddenly there I was at Thirty-one Pond Street and there was Juliette, looking not a day older—a pink angel. Her cheeks have become quite full, cherubic. The greeting was so warm and loving that I felt totally at ease at once. The first day it was just warm enough so that we could go out into the garden, and Alan Best (the young Alan Best) said to me, "My uncle is out there in the garden having a rest. He just arrived." And his uncle (old Alan Best), now eighty-one, I knew very well in the days when I first knew the Huxleys fifty-five years ago. It was amazing that he should be there that day. And there was Juliette's garden with the camellias out and pink vibernum, which I had never seen before, and forsythia

and all along the border of the garden were daffodils, anemones, and crocuses and all kinds of small flowers like the rich
border of a tapestry. It felt chilly. Juliette kept saying, "Aren't
you too cold, Alan?" to young Alan. Her present housekeeper-
companion who comes from East Asia would say, "Yes, and
you can just move in to the dining room." But the extraordinary thing was the sense of spring in the air. There was a little
bee and the most marvelous butterfly. For some reason the
butterfly landed on the tablecloth, something I marveled at
after leaving wintry Maine two days before.

It was a superb time altogether. It is extraordinary to be
with somebody ninety-five who forgets almost everything but
then suddenly remembers everything and is still so full of
charm and humor and love that to be with her is a sheer
blessing and joy. So it was well worth it to make the journey.

I saw her once more before I had to go to Suffolk to see my
relatives. My mother's cousins are in Farmington, and near
Ipswich at Dakon's Cottage. The first time I was driven all the
way to Ipswich from London by Pat Keen; nothing could have
been kinder because, as I mentioned, I would have had to
walk a long distance had I taken the train. But to be picked up
at the hotel in London and driven in a little less than two
hours was a miracle.

We managed to stop at an elegant terrace hotel where we
had a delicious lunch and then onward to where I stay, as I
always have, at the White Horse Hotel, where Dickens stayed
and wrote *The Pickwick Papers,* I think, and where my
mother always stayed when she went to see her mother.
There I was picked up by my cousin Isobel Strickland, who
drove me to her parents, May and Richard Pipe, who have
made over an old cottage, Dakon's Cottage, an absolutely
charming, ancient, stone cottage surrounded by a lovely garden.

Richard Pipe is a radical politically, so we get on very well, and May is a charming woman who loved my mother and talks about her. We had a very good talk and tea with all kinds of goodies that May had made.

Then I got back to the hotel and realized that I was suddenly tired, so I called Pat and suggested that we have dinner sent up to my room and that she come over and have it with me. It was a very bad dinner. A Spanish omelet that bore no resemblance to any I've ever eaten, and I thought, What am I going to do; my digestive system is going to be totally upset. But the extraordinary thing was that during all those days in London, I was well. I had hardly any trouble—in spite of drinking coffee for breakfast.

Sunday, March 29

IT IS rather hard, I find, when you come back from a journey, to write in a journal, because the journal is about today. It is not about the day before yesterday or a week ago. Yesterday I did dictate a piece about the trip to London, but today I think I am going to skip that and go back to it tomorrow because I am anxious to talk about reentry into my life here. It is always something of a shock because there is so much mail, so much that has to be attended to.

But this time it was a fabulous reentry because Susan was here. I did not walk into an empty house. Pierrot was fantastically affectionate, would not leave me alone, wound himself around me, purred very loudly most of the night, and altogether was extraordinarily welcoming. The house was filled with bunches of spring flowers and plants—crocuses, a blue hyacinth, and a whole bunch of freesias of all colors in my bedroom. Such extravagant beauty. Lilies, yellow and orange, in the front hall. Purple anemones and yellow tulips by my chaise longue. It was all superb.

And then it was wonderful to be able to tell Susan all about what had happened, to share, to come home in fact to someone. Coming home also of course to things that have to be done. Some of them were wonderful. One I must do today is thank Bob Hale for the marvelous blurb for *Endgame,* my new journal, which will be out very soon. I am so touched that he did it, partly because I so admired his novel that came out last year. He really is a superb writer, and praise from him means a great deal.

I brought back with me things that I have done, like reading—*Keeping up Appearances,* by Rose Macaulay, is the book I took with me to London. I rarely read a book that makes me laugh aloud, but this one did, so I have been finishing it since I came home. It takes time to bridge the transitions, I found, and this did it well. I want to send it to Huldah. One of the events since I came back was a call from Huldah, who has been too deaf until now to telephone, so it was wonderful to hear her voice, a voice that has always moved me, a deep voice for a woman.

Yesterday there was a check for an option on a movie of *Kinds of Love.* It would be splendid if that novel could be made into a movie. What a meaningful part Christina would be for Jessica Tandy, with her husband, Hume Cronyn, as Cornelius. It is a dream come true to have that novel chosen as a possible movie. *As We Are Now* still is on the brink of being filmed, but is not yet under firm contract.

I have called a lot of people, a great circle of friends all over the country; I talked with many of them yesterday, and everyone is so happy that I am better and that I had a good time. It brings tears to my eyes. It is wonderful *not* to complain about health, *not* to have to say, "I am having a strug-

gle." I am somewhat on top of things at last. The fact that I
was able to drink hot milk and coffee for breakfast in London
and not have severe digestive problems as a result is tremendously good news for me.

Just before I left I heard that Ruth Pitter had died. She
was over ninety certainly. One of the things I found in my
hotel room was Carol Ebbs' beautiful shawl, which she had
made for my eightieth birthday. She also had put the obituaries in my room . . . Ruth was ninety-four I see, a magnificent
poet. It said in one of the obits something I liked very much:

> Pitter, capable of discerning beauty in a bat, could not
> but be conscious that she possessed the irrefrangible soul
> of an artist:
>
>> Hate me or love, I care not, as I pass
>> To those hid citadels,
>> Where in the depth of my enchanted glass
>> The changeless image dwells;
>> To where forever blooms the nameless tree;
>> For ever, alone and fair,
>> The lovely Unicorn beside the sea
>> Is laid, and slumbers there.
>
> Pitter's beautifully contrived utterance calls her readers
> to attention; her seamless simplicity holds them trans-
> fixed. In her ordered scheme neither obscurity nor ba-
> nality had place.
>
> Her poetry combines grit and tenderness, hardness
> and fragility, sensual experience and intellectual vision.
> Yet somewhere behind these multiple antitheses, she
> would hint, there lies the single unattainable truth.

She wrote some marvelous poems which I go back to over
and over again. Who are the poets to whom one goes back
over and over again? Certainly Ruth Pitter is one, and then
Yeats has always been one, Robert Frost is one—more than

any other perhaps, strangely enough. Though he was such a terrible man, he was a great poet.

I am getting ready to go out for lunch with Edythe, who is my best friend around here, to whom I must tell all my news. She herself twice accompanied me to London.

There was also in the mail a transcript of an interview which I did not altogether like and had to read over and correct.

I had a letter from a woman who, as I understand it, wants to take photographs to put with excerpts from different books of mine. Her name is Linda Carter. She sent me one absolutely exquisite photograph, a self-portrait sitting by a canal in Holland—so nostalgic!—and quoted what I want to quote to myself now from *Plant Dreaming Deep:*

> Solitude itself is a way of waiting for the inaudible and the invisible to make itself felt. And that is why solitude is never static and never hopeless. On the other hand, every friend who comes to stay enriches the solitude forever; presence, if it has been real presence, does not ever leave.

Of course that now tells me something about Susan because when she is here she does so much around the house—I suddenly discover that a whole cupboard has been cleaned out, everything is in order, all the vases for flowers have been washed—extraordinary. I can almost hear her footfall on the stairs and the echo of Cybèle's bark when she thinks that Pierrot wants to come in.

Now I stop to write to Linda Carter.

Monday, March 30

I HAVE just finished listening to a recording of a Mozart piano concerto, Number 24, which I used to play over and over again, and also Number 18. This is an event. It has taken place since I came back from London—I am able to listen to records again, and I have been playing Mozart since I got back. It is like returning home after a long time in a foreign country where there was no music. Now when I put a record on I do not cry as I used to because I could not write poetry any more. I did not think it would ever come back, but now of course it has. It is like a miracle. The feel of the music in this room is marvelous. In fact my life seems to be such a continuous miracle of good things happening these days that I sometimes wonder when it will stop, or if I am due for a sudden bad spell because the good spell has been so long.

I wrote a letter to Kathy Gale at the Women's Press because I have come up with a good idea of what poems they might choose to publish, namely putting together the last three books. It would show a poet who has kept her intensity into old age, and that is rather rare. The poet who comes to mind of course is W. B. Yeats, who kept his intensity, his rage, and his passion into old age. Now at eighty I do not have quite the rage or the passion, but I am still very much alive. So if Kathy Gale wants to publish these three, the book would begin with a book of love poems, *Halfway to Silence*, written when I was sixty-five, and end with the last book, *The Silence*

Now. I think it would be interesting, and I hope very much that she will do it.

It has been hard to focus back on London, but I must say a word about the wonderful time we had together, Maggie and I. Pat Keen had her little car and drove us around so I did not have to walk more than a hundred yards. We had a splendid dinner at a restaurant called the Pelican before seeing the hilarious comedy *Dancing at Lughnasa*. The play has won three Tonys in New York. It is humorous and also moving—a conservative Catholic family, all spinsters, and what happens when they are given a gramophone and suddenly there is music to dance to and they get up—wild with the freedom of it—and start screaming and dancing, an extraordinary sight. Into this scene comes an uncle of theirs, a priest, who had been a missionary in a leper colony in Africa, and who comes back convinced that the native rituals are just as meaningful as Christian rituals. This naturally causes a good deal of trouble. It is a delightful play.

But the biggest excitement was a great performance of Shaw's *Heartbreak House.* I have always thought it one of his best plays, a very moving play. He wrote it during World War I when he was a pacifist, and unpopular of course. It is a play about the disintegration of Western Civilization brought on by greed and sexual freedom. Written in 1913, it is almost descriptive of what we have experienced in the last ten years. It was magnificently played by Paul Scofield, and Vanessa Redgrave had one of the leading parts. It is a long play—three hours—and for three hours my attention never wavered for an instant.

The third thrill of those days was going to a concert in Festival Hall that Alan Eastaugh got tickets for. At first we thought it would not be a very interesting concert, a concert for chamber orchestra, because the selections seemed trite—a

Mozart clarinet concerto which I know almost by heart and a Haydn trumpet concerto which I don't think I have ever heard. It turned out to be pure delight. Anyway, I love Papa Haydn. But I really had not expected such pleasure nor that the trumpet would be so small. It was played, or I should say, blown, by a very young man. The sound was so clear and spoke so purely, so loudly that he would have wakened the dead. A real thriller.

In the Mozart Concerto for Clarinet and Orchestra, the clarinet was played by a woman. I have never seen a woman play a clarinet with an orchestra who was not sitting. She came on in evening dress with her long instrument in front of her standing up on wheels so that it looked extremely odd. Then she began to play standing, her face of course expressionless because she was blowing with her mouth and her hands were busy way below; it became extremely comic. I was afraid that I would burst into laughter. But she was brilliant and the concerto of course is lovely.

When we came out of the National Theatre it was pouring rain so it was a luxury to have Hyman there in his taxi to take us back to the hotel.

I do not know whether I have talked about my cousins, but it was a joy to see them; I felt so related. For the first time I felt *en famille* with my real family, and I had a very good talk with Evelyn Mann, who is ninety now and blind. She talked about my mother and about me when I was small and stayed with them when we were refugees from Belgium and I spoke only French. I have come back from London a new person, able to hear music and feeling much better. From now on it will be what the journey is really all about. my days very rich and peaceful in the old routine.

Tuesday, March 31

THERE IS a slight lifting of the air so I can smell the earth for the first time, and yesterday I again took possession of my life here. The thing that did it was picking a few snowdrops, the only thing in flower now, and putting them in little bowls on the table and then rearranging the wonderful flowers with which Susan welcomed me home, and stopping at Foster's to get a few replacements after seeing Dr. Khanjani. She is pleased with me and is allowing me to have General Foods' Café Français, a mild powdered coffee. Milk has been completely off my diet, so to start the day with a *café au lait,* as I did in London, is a treat. Otherwise I am to stay with the diet, brown rice, fish, and steamed fresh vegetables, and see her twice a week until the end of April.

I am beginning to sort through an immense amount of second-class mail. The thing that is different and better than it has been for a long time of pain is playing music and writing postcards because it is one way by which I can answer some of the good letters from people who read me. What I am finding is that I can write a postcard quite easily, and listen at the same time.

Pierrot still gets me up about three times a night and when it is raining outside I listen for him to meow. He can give very loud meows when he wants to be let in.

But I rather love the night and being able to be awake in it. Yesterday morning there was the beginning of a wonderful sunrise, then it clouded over and began to rain. We are not having spring yet, but it will come.

I am reading a manuscript for a book about the history of Elderhostel. I was on the Board of Elderhostel near the beginning and was thrilled by the whole plan, but I could have no idea of what a huge success it would be. There are now Elderhostels all over the world, and many people in their eighties are attending a few weeks in a college here or there, overseas or in the United States. Many go to one every year. It is helping to change the whole way we look at the old. The old who go to Elderhostel are independent, go for long walks or take courses at universities, and make friends—do all the things that you are not supposed to be able to do after you are eighty. So this is a valuable contribution, and I am pleased to be asked to recommend the book, which I shall certainly do.

Otherwise there has been on my desk a book of poems about the women of Buenos Aires whose daughters disappeared in a terrible way and who have marched for years in protest, trying to get the torturers punished. Little by little perhaps this is going to happen. These are powerful poems. It is important that poetry keep alive something which our tendency is to wish to forget. So I must write a note to the author of these poems today.

I must also write to my English cousins. I have many letters on my mind this morning, so I am going to go upstairs, begin to write, and play some music.

Thursday, April 2

THIS MORNING I got back into my feeling of quiet desperation that my life is a chaos and nothing can be sustained, especially anything creative. So I decided this afternoon to find out what really does happen to the morning. Thursday morning is always somewhat driven because it is the day Eleanor comes to clean, and therefore no one brings me my breakfast. So the day begins, as today did, with getting the magazines out for Eleanor, to whom I give magazines every week, and I noticed that one of the two fluorescent lights on the ceiling of the kitchen had failed. So I went into the cupboard where the long fluorescent lights always have been kept to see if one was there; I found one, though I was not sure it would fit. Of course I cannot climb a ladder here alone, so I hoped that Eleanor could do it, and she did.

It all seemed to take a lot of time, and when finally she came with the mail at nine, I was already tired. I had gotten my breakfast, had it in bed, made the bed, had a bath because I see Dr. Khanjani on Thursdays, and washed up the dishes. I wanted to go back to bed and go back to sleep. Instead, I took the mail upstairs to my study and looked at what had come.

There was a letter from Ellie Friedman, a student at Harvard who is going to do her thesis on some aspect of my work. She wrote to say that I had offered to see her, and she wanted to know if she could bring her boyfriend with whom she talks about everything, she says, and would I make a date. First my heart sank. It is more difficult and more tiring to talk to two people than one, but I decided that this was a generous thing to do, so I called her up and made a date. They will come and talk with me sometime next week.

There was also a note from a young woman who asked whether she could send me *The Fur Person* to sign. She explained that it was the first of my novels she had read. In a fit of impatience about people asking things when they do not really know what they are asking, I wrote her a postcard. This is not my good day. Later in the morning I knocked a glass of water all over the desk, wetting the beautiful cards I had bought at the National Gallery, and that was the last straw.

I was in the middle of saying what it means to sign a book for somebody. I have already remarked elsewhere that it means driving it from the post office, climbing three flights upstairs to my study, unwrapping the package, signing the book, wrapping the package again, taking it to the post office, and mailing it. The minimum time to do these things would be fifteen minutes, and the energy involved is a great deal more than that because one has to remember that I have energy for only about two hours of work at my desk. If I give fifteen minutes to sign the book, that leaves me only an hour and three-quarters, and it is simply maddening. People do not realize.

So now I am upstairs and I am about to call Jamey. She is in the hospital for all kinds of tests. I called last night and will call every day while she is in the hospital. I want to do it. I love Jamey. But it also means one more thing that drives me, and I cannot play a record because I am thinking about that.

I did play a little Mozart this morning and typed off a little bit of the poem on the trumpet concerto of Haydn that we heard in London. I hope that I can have that poem "come out," but it is not going very well simply because I do not have clear time. I also am imagining a novella about the luncheon with Juliette and Alan Best that first day in London. This would be really a fascinating short novel if I can do it. So I think up names for the three characters. That is what I am doing now.

Monday, April 6

THIS WEEKEND has been dominated hanging Joan Gold's *Sarton Quartet*. The four paintings have been standing in the hall now for two weeks; in fact, they arrived and were unpacked before I went to England. I kept looking at them and wondering how I would ever get them upstairs. I had intended to put them in my bedroom, but they would have dwarfed everything there and I would have had to take down Anne Woodson's painting of the cemetery at Nelson where my ashes will be buried under Barbara Barton's phoenix, which is now here in the garden.

I knew the paintings had to go on the wall of the stairs by my study on the third floor. Mary-Leigh and Beverly came to help me. Beverly has had an operation on her knee and had real difficulty with the stairs. Susan was here too, which made it all much better and more fun. We sat there on the landing for an hour, with the good workman Barry Jandebeur, expertly getting everything together. It would have been much easier to hang them vertically, but they were meant to be seen horizontally. So Barry had to work out a way, and he did it marvelously.

I lived for a whole year with a reproduction of Joan Gold's *The Camus Quartet*. Now *The Sarton Quartet* is hanging on

Hanging the Sarton Quartet

the wall of the stairs as I go up from the second floor to my study on the third floor—a large expanse of white wall which is lit by windows high up above. The light is beautiful, especially in the afternoon, and it is also wonderful at night to see them in the shadows. What an event it has been!

Otherwise, I did not feel well. I do not know what is wrong with me. I was having hot coffee; when I got up this morning I decided I really needed to have it. Yesterday afternoon after Susan left, and we had a lovely weekend in spite of my being ill, I did manage to do a lot of work, including send-

CREDIT: SUSAN SHERMAN

May and Mary-Leigh Smart

ing a letter and the last check for the paintings to the Lisa
Harris Gallery in Seattle. I decided to pay it all this year.

On *60 Minutes* last night there was an astonishing segment on women who live in cars in Bel Air, that rich part of
Hollywood where so many stars live. These women are in
every case divorced without alimony. In California, alimony
only goes on for six years, I think, so after six years each one
was without it. They are too young for Social Security, so what
we saw was four remarkably interesting and charming

women who had been reduced to living in their cars, and we were also introduced to a woman volunteer who tries to help them by showing them where they can park. They have to find a place to park overnight, if possible under trees or near bushes so they can relieve themselves. They also learned to go into laundromats and use the bathrooms there. They go into bars and eat a few peanuts; if you go to four or five you might get a small meal that way. They are deathly thin, but none of these women will go to a soup kitchen because it is too embarrassing. They are horribly embarrassed by being homeless. One, the most endearing, lives in her car with a large dog and a gray cat. The last shot was of her covering the back window of the car so that she could not be seen at night because that is the bed, and she was getting into the car and saying, "I'm home, kids," to the cat and dog.

One of them finally had had it and took an enterprising step as a housekeeper for an elderly couple. The interviewer, who was very good, asked her how she managed to handle that at first. She said, "For the first four days I kept saying to myself, 'It's an experiment, and it may not work,' but I find that it is working." And of course she has managed to have shelter at last and, I imagine, a bathroom.

I was so glad I had seen this segment about the women living in cars; it made me understand even better what my dear friend Catherine has been through. She has had a terrible time trying to find a job. I am so proud of her. She now has two jobs. One just breaks into tears.

Wednesday, April 8

IT IS quite warm. The birds start singing early in the morning, and the sun rises at about six so I feel I must be up and doing. But I do not feel at all well; it is discouraging. I have so little strength that after I get dressed in the morning, I wish I could go back to bed.

This goes back to something that happened on Friday. When I came back from a brief shopping trip in town, I walked into the house and I had been thinking for the last half hour, I can soon have some hot soup. It was hard for me even to carry in a small, light bag of groceries. When I got in, there was a note on the table saying that the lights had gone out at eleven. It was then twelve. This meant that I could not heat anything because the electric stove of course would not work. It had been windy and cold outside, and I was chilled to the bone, but more than that I felt knocked over the head. I felt strange and found it impossible to put the food away, but I did do it. Then the lights came on, in an hour I think it was, and I made myself a cup of hot coffee and hot milk because I thought I must have a stimulant. I now believe that it may be that I had a small—I do not know what you call it, not a stroke—but that something happened with my heart.

At Massachusetts General Hospital at the time when I hoped I could have a pacemaker—it turned out that my heart was not strong enough to take it—a doctor told me that my heart had suffered several "insults." I thought that was a wonderful way of saying "small heart attacks" because I guess that is what he meant. I wonder whether I did not suffer an "insult" on Friday which might explain why I feel ill. It is different from trying to keep going, which is an effort anyway. If I feel ill, then it changes the whole ethos, if you will. It forces me to slow down—not by choice.

It was a great blessing to have Joan here today. She brought me a delicious breakfast with some whole-wheat English muffins.

I am beginning to read the journal of last year when I can. This journal you are reading will end after the conference at Westbrook in early June, so I have to begin now to correct it and to think of photographs. And today I must at last try to do the blurb for the book about Elderhostel.

I must go up and send Angeliki, the mother of my adopted Greek daughters, the address of a florist because she wants to send me flowers for my birthday. So dear of her. The whole family called me on the telephone and asked for the address last week, and it was quite a strain, but I enjoyed hearing their voices.

I had a letter from Deborah Straw this morning enclosing a small essay by a friend of hers, a charming essay about cineraria. She had found a small passage in one of my journals about them; it is one of my favorite hothouse plants. In California it makes a great show of blues, purples, pinks, and whites out of doors. This year I am sorry to say I only managed to find one at a florist. They seem to have gone very fast. In this essay, the friend buys a cineraria for herself and one for Deborah, who is her teacher, and describes it all very charmingly. I enjoyed reading it, and I enjoy thinking that something in a book of mine has persuaded a woman with four children who never spent money on herself to go and buy a cineraria. That is the kind of influence I like to have.

Friday, April 10

CLOUDY AND COLD. I have been reading last year's journal and I realized that spring then was in full swing; it was an early spring and very warm, and here we are with the grass still brown and nothing out except the green spikes of the daffodils, which I suppose in another two weeks may come out. Don Cadoret was here to photograph, and unfortunately I had had a sleepless night, which is quite rare for me. It happened because I had to have on a machine to measure whether I need oxygen. I am quite sure that I do not, but it has to be proved to Medicare before the tank is removed. This machine puts out a little tape which makes an ugly, rather loud sound every thirty seconds for about three seconds. Each time as I was falling asleep I was wrenched back. It was torture. I do not suppose that I slept more than about an hour or two at most through the whole night.

I feel rather ill, and I think it is not only because of not sleeping last night. I think something did happen exactly a week ago today when Karen and I walked into the cold house with the electricity off and I suffered a shock, more of a shock than would seem reasonable under the circumstances. I am beginning to wonder whether I had a slight stroke. I have certainly felt strange and ill ever since, on the verge of tears all the time.

But Margaret and Barbara sent a great bowl of planted daffodils, a garden of daffodils that came while Don Cadoret was here. He is a longtime fan who has never been to the place before but offered to photograph me as a birthday present. He says we have met at least once when I read poems at Colby College, which was many years ago, so I warned him that he would see a very old lady now. He is an extremely endearing young man who, he told me, has a three-year-old son, a man who has had the courage not to go to the top in a company of which he could have been president. He decided he did not want the rat race, so he is the chief photographer for a newspaper in Connecticut. He takes every Friday off, and goes off to do something for himself. He loved the house and went around photographing things, and I am glad to say that the flowers he had sent so generously two days ago, pale pink tulips and very brilliant deep blue delphinium, were still looking glorious. I am very spoiled at the moment. But I also feel terribly old, and ill, and a little scared.

Monday, April 13

BITTERLY COLD. When I went down at three A.M. to try to get the cat in because I thought he must be freezing, I put the heat up, way up, and now the house is too warm, but it seems no fair that all of this week they predict that the wind chill is going to be about twenty. The daffodils are trying to come up; they are green spears, but I do not see any buds.

Maggie was here for the weekend. What a blessing! I managed to walk with her halfway down to the sea, then we turned right at Beverly's garden and came up. The difficulty was climbing the gentle slope up the driveway. I had to lean against a tree at one point. This is the farthest I have walked in a long time. It shows that it can be done, and now I must try to do it, especially when Susan is here, every day, so that I can walk down to the sea again and back. It was a specially wonderful time with Maggie. I even did some work, and began to get out of the cycle of panic and illness I have been in now for more than a week. Though I am not very well today, I think I am going to make it.

On Saturday the great event was a letter from Vincent Hepp. He and Christiane have now moved. He retired to the Mas, that old stone farm in southern France near Toulouse. I wish I could see it now. I visited it twice when Vincent's mother, the famous writer Camille Mayran, lived there. I met her at the Huxleys in the thirties when she had just won the Fémina-Vie-Heureuse prize for her novel *Dame en Noir*. I think she is the person who has best understood my poems and written marvelous letters about them, all of which are now in the Berg Collection in New York. The reason for Vincent's letter was the joy of the birth of his first grandchild, a little girl, Sophia Marie, whom he says is absolutely beautiful. Then he says:

> A baby. To be seen as God sees each one of us who has not as yet learned to look back with pride, skepticism, self-assertion, who so entirely depends on us, who love her most particularly for that, and are thankful that she appears to us in such perfection and abandon.

I love the combination of those two words: *perfection and abandon*. It brought tears to my eyes as I read that paragraph, which is why I wanted to put it in this journal. The reason for the tears was personal. I felt that the old are much like what Vincent suggests he sees in the baby, for we are so bereft of pride and of the ability to stand up, shall we say, and we become more and more dependent. One of the things I am learning, and I am beginning to learn it better, is to accept being dependent.

When Maggie is here she takes over in the most adorable way, cooked us a gourmet meal with mushrooms on a bed of very finely cut onion with a half cup of red wine which is unusual but turned out to be very good.

Wednesday, April 15

IT BEGAN as a sunny day but terribly cold. It is hard to see the crocuses ready to open but unable to because it was twenty last night, but at least today there is less wind. There is no doubt that April in Maine is the cruelest month. It does not breed memory and desire, but tremendous frustration and constant pain because you feel things are trying to come out and are not given a chance. One day of warm sun would make all the difference.

Pat, my gardener, is coming today and I think we are going to plant the Meconopsis, the blue poppies, which, if they flower, will be a heart's desire come true, but the earth is still very cold. However, they arrive as what looks almost like bulbs but actually are roots, and it is possible that she will be able to plant them, as well as do some pruning and raking. Little by little the grass is getting less brown, and the green shoots of the daffodils are about a foot high.

Yesterday was a muddled, chaotic day. I was no good to myself or anyone else because I was so agitated and torn in pieces by all the things I had to do. The worst of course was reading in the *New York Times* that Mandela announced today that he is separating from his wife, Winnie, after forty-three years of marriage, affectionately referring to Mrs. Mandela by her African name of Nomzamo. Mr. Mandela said, "My love for her remains undiminished," but it was clear from what followed that they disagreed fundamentally on too many things, and it is rumored that she has a young lover, but more than that she was impossibly arrogant and has not been able to change what she was. Nothing can diminish her bravery and courage in the twenty-three years when Nelson Mandela was in jail, when she was tortured, imprisoned, always under surveillance by the police, banished to a remote town where she was to be in touch with no one, and where perhaps she started to drink. That seems to be one of her problems.

I felt darkness creeping over me, and it stayed with me all day. The Mandelas' is such a tragic story, and in many ways such a noble story, but the darkness which invaded me came from my feeling for Nelson Mandela himself and the awful pain this must be for him. At the end of his speech to the leaders of the African National Party he said, and for the first time nearly broke down, "You do understand I'm sure that for me this has been frightful pain." It is now questionable whether Winnie Mandela will keep her position in the African National Party. Reportedly it would be better if she does not. One must remember that she brought up two daughters who are doing very well, who have not inherited her temperament which was always volatile, and nobody could possibly inherit her charisma which was quite overwhelming. A long piece about her in the *Times* yesterday said, "The conflict in her personality caused conflict among those who know her. Many of her supporters, especially in the United States, experienced only the warm, loving, very charismatic Winnie Mandela. The sense of love she gives is so powerful that many have found it impossible to resist her or her demands. Those who knew her other side also rushed to obey her with a compulsion that came from fear. It was the fear that prevented people from telling on her and perhaps prevented Nelson Mandela from knowing what was really happening."

I believe as deeply I think as I ever have that her political act was a choice that colored yesterday black and today gray.

Saturday, April 18

WE ARE in the middle of the gloomiest Easter weekend I have ever imagined or known; it actually snowed on Thursday night but we only got an inch. They had six inches in Kennebunkport so Judy could not come to work but will make it up next week.

Very unusually Susan is here, and because we were both so gloomy she decided she was going to give me my birthday present that night, which was Thursday night. She terrified me by saying, "It is really quite a present, and it will take you some time to get over it." I could not imagine what it could be. I think we were both terrified when I did take off one wrapping after another, finding at first silver paper and then gold paper and then finally a magnificently bound book with the title *Forward into the Past*, which is a quotation from my poem after Virginia Woolf committed suicide, "I send you love forward into the past." I opened the book and saw that it was a *festschrift* of words, a paragraph up to a page about me and what I have meant to a whole group of people all distinguished in the arts or literature or theater who go back into my life so far that even John Summerson, with whom I fell in love when I was twenty-two, is there. He is now eighty-seven. Sir John Summerson. He wrote a simply delightful poem. We lodged in the same house in Bloomsbury on Tavistock Street, and he played the harpsichord. Next door to me while I wrote poems a concert went on for most of the day. I thought of it as a kind of wooing, but it turned out that he was engaged to somebody else so that never came to anything, and I saw him only once after the war.

What pure delight the book is! There are so many wonderful passages that I hesitate to enumerate them. Joanne Woodward is the last. She said, "From one of your greatest admirers," and that certainly sent me on a leap of joy. Much to my amazement and delight, Vartan Gregorian wrote among the best of all the entries, a very imaginative and beautifully expressed tribute. So I complained about not being recognized! I went through the book with tears streaming down my cheeks, tears of joy, and now I have to say that I *am* recognized, and it makes my heart sing.

The tremendous problem for Susan, who devised and orchestrated the whole project, was hunting down the addresses of all these people, some of whom I had not communicated with for thirty or forty years. Irene Sharaff, for instance, who designed the original production at the Civic Repertory of *Alice in Wonderland* and with whom I spent a month in Florence in the early 1930s. I have not been in touch with Irene for fifty years or more. A letter was sent out around December tenth by Susan to the list of people and then she began waiting for the answers, and what amazing answers came flooding in!

A friend of the work who does not want to be named is paying for all of this, a tremendous sum I am sure, for every contributor will be given a copy of the book, and I will be given twenty-five. What a birthday! Nothing can come up to this in the days to come. I cherish it. I keep picking the book up and reading it again and again and wondering who the lucky twenty-five friends of mine will be who get copies.

At least today the birds are singing. They were not singing yesterday. It was too grim, pouring rain, and still a little snow on the ground.

Easter Day, April 19

BY A MIRACLE the sun did come out about noon. Until now, we have had the most dreary weather imaginable. It is now about half past four. After my nap I decided to cheer myself up by going out and seeing what was happening in the garden. It was not a very good idea because the first thing I went to look at was twelve species tulips which Pat planted for me in a high rocky nook where I thought the deer would not get them. They were flourishing on Wednesday when Pat came and began the year's gardening by doing some pruning. This afternoon every one was eaten to the ground. I nearly cried. I then went to the magnificent yellow de Rothschild azalea across the lawn, and I think the deer have eaten all the buds. It is hard. The daffodils which should be out are barely beginning, and they are not very tall. Some of them have been blighted by the cold and the snow in the last days. I managed to pick four which I will put by my bed, three of them in bud and one in flower, so it is going to happen little by little.

But I cannot help feeling rather low in my mind. Also of course I miss Susan, who left today, but soon I will be in a rhythm. An awful lot of things are happening, people coming, letters, an extraordinary one yesterday, a letter from a Japanese outfit in New York asking me whether I would be willing to give an interview on May fifteenth. They want to fly from

Tokyo an interviewer, a well-known Japanese writer, a critic, the translator of my book, and two women photographers because, and this is the amazing thing, *Journal of a Solitude* is having such a success in Japan! I was not even aware it had come out. It was bought some time ago through my English agent. This is very exciting! Tomorrow I shall learn whether they can manage to do it on the fourteenth because on the fifteenth my adopted brother Charles Feldstein is coming from Chicago to take me out to dinner. I do not want to get too tired, so I begged the Japanese to try to make it the fourteenth. They will let me know tomorrow whether that is possible.

Patriot's Day, April 20

BY ACCIDENT I tuned to the wrong TV station and someone was reading the Declaration of Independence. "We hold these truths to be self-evident, that all men are created equal." It shot right to my heart. How could we for two centuries pretend that that wasn't true? It is staggering.

Again a dismal day and I feel depressed.

Friday, April 24

IT ALWAYS HAPPENS. Suddenly! After waiting and waiting and thinking the spring would never come, suddenly it is here. And yesterday the temperature went up to seventy for the first time this year. There was a blue sea at last. A beautiful blue sky and all the daffodils burst open in a great hosanna. I picked some. Is there anything more exciting than picking the first daffodils? I picked four or five different kinds to put in my room. In fact I did that the day before, but the great outburst was yesterday. Now this horrible climate has given us three days of rain and cold winds. It is not fair! It is so hard when we have waited and waited and waited, to have it taken from us.

Yesterday was so beautiful, but a difficult day for me because I had to do a big shopping. Also the first copy of *Endgame*, the journal of my seventy-ninth year, came. It looks stunning except, and it is a serious exception, Susan's marvelous photographs have not reproduced well in this journal. I do not know why; in the other journals the photographs have done very well. It must have something to do with the paper.

Monday, April 27

WONDERFUL TO HAVE Joan here to bring me my breakfast. The week had been very hard. Yesterday I had to give up living, so to speak, and it was terrible because then I cannot do anything at my desk. The only thing I managed to do late in the afternoon was write the checks for the people who work for me all week. I did not get even one letter written because I was in very great pain. I think I am going to die, and I am not sure why but I think that something hurts too much. Stress all the time. At almost every mail there is some kind of problem that I have to try to solve. The other day I was sent a botched biography of me which was so full of mistakes it made me quite ill because I did not see how I could possibly correct it. It would have taken weeks, so much had been left out. Fortunately I thought of wonderful Nancy, called her, and she told me where I could find a completed, accurate biography. So I sent that off but it took me over an hour by the time I had resolved the problem.

I had a letter from a friend whose son is dying. This is truly something that must be answered, but I did not manage to do it yesterday. Today looms because Margot is going to see Anne and Barbara. Judy, my secretary, will come this morning. I see Dr. Khanjani at one-thirty as usual, and then back at half past two. Bill Ewert and William Heyen and his wife are coming to bring me copies of the little book of new poems which Bill Ewert has produced for my birthday. It is so exciting! I hope I can live until four.

I feel very, very ill and I need to go to the hospital, but that is not possible. The fact that the weather continues to be so bad does not help. It was below thirty last night. It is gloomy again today, but we might see some sun. We have had in the last two weeks one warm, sunny day when the sky was really blue.

I am going to read a poem into the journal. It is by the son of the poet Roy Fuller, his name is John Fuller, a fellow of Magdalen College in Oxford, an extremely elegant poem which is a little like a nineteenth-century pastiche, but I love it.

> Shall you revisit as ghost or shadow
> This world of waters that you wept?
> Shall you revisit, though it be narrow,
> The bed of tears your weeping kept?
> We smooth the creases in your pillow
> Where you have slept.
>
> Silver glitters in the furrow
> Where the lost coin records your name.
> Winter fastens clod and harrow
> And a cloistered queen the same.
> Though ice describes the grassy meadow
> Your tears remain.
>
> Shall you revisit as winter's fellow,
> Shut in his coldness with your fame?
> Shall you come startled to the window,
> Finding frost-flowers upon the pane?
> They will remind you of your sorrow
> And turn to rain.
>
> Though the world sink again we follow
> The pain and patience of your love.
> Though waters spread they will be shallow,
> Familiar hills will peep above.
> You will return like the shot arrow,
> Like the first dove.

Having read it once, I think one has to read it again. It is beautiful. One wonders for whom it was written.

I hope I can pull myself together enough to do a few things. I am trying to get things organized before the avalanche of my birthday, which is already beginning.

Tuesday, April 28

AND AGAIN we have sun which is marvelous, but it is still cold, so much so that when Joan came yesterday there was ice on the birdbath. You can feel everything waiting to come forward, but stopped by the cold. The green buds of the lilac leaves are not even fat now; they are little points. But the daffodils are wonderful although they have only begun, and at least the cold will make them stay longer.

Margot Peters, who is talking with friends of mine (I have already mentioned the biography she is writing of me), yesterday went to see Anne Woodson and Barbara Barton at Deer Run Farm in North Parsonsfield and had a long and I think rich visit with them from what I have heard briefly from both sides. Talking with her brought back my memories of Anne and Barbara and how long we have known each other and how much I feel they are my family.

I remembered how much Anne helped me in the hard times; when I first went to Nelson, even the very difficult time I had when Marynia Farnham became senile and turned against me. That ended in my having to leave Nelson and come here. I think I must have called Anne hundreds of times, and she was always so patient and so wise. Somehow or other, I had forgotten all that, as one forgets important things some-

times. Now it has all come back to me. I saw a lot of them in
Lynnfield, Massachusetts, when Anne and Barbara first
began to live together. I would leave my Audi with them and
then they would drive me to the airport and meet me on my
return. The airport was only twenty minutes from their home.
That was a way of catching up, of having somebody to tell
about my adventures on the trips. I miss that, but of course I
am not doing that kind of poetry-reading trip anymore.

The great joy outdoors right now is not flowers, not even
grass because that is still not green, but the birds. The gold-
finches have now all got their yellow suits on, and the purple
finches are here. I am awakened every morning by the robins
talking—talking while they are singing. So a lot is going on.

Pat, the gardener, is here a lot and put in the little blue
violas I bought yesterday. I thought I would do it myself, but I
have been feeling weak and ill.

Friday, May 1

IT SEEMS that my birthday is galloping toward me. Already
flowers are arriving, and a magnificent tree of white orchids
from Angeliki and my adopted Greek family. It is so touching,
and I am grateful for those that come early and that I have
time to arrange in a vase. But I must admit that this knot of
tension for the last month around both my birthday and all the
other demands about books that are being written about me,
as well as keeping at this journal, has taken its toll, and I feel
extremely frail. Yesterday I was determined to pick flowers
for Susan, who comes today, and I was afraid I would fall on
the way back, but I did manage. In spite of the extremely cold

White orchids from my Greek adopted family

weather the daffodils along the woods, the ones that come first, are in flower. Everywhere else is a terrible slowness. Even the leaves of the lilacs are not out. This May it is still a bare, wintry scene.

Meanwhile the racial situation in Los Angeles is getting worse and there are riots in every city; one cannot blame the blacks for rising up. It all goes back to Reagan. We have had years of neglect, of deliberate creation of an underclass, of depriving over and over again those who are the neediest so that the rich could get richer. Of course it is frightening. There was a man on the *Today* show who said that one of the reasons for racism in this country is the white fear of black violence and the fact that black crime is rising. But why is it rising? Because we have neglected to give them a chance to do anything but be violent. Where does a young high school graduate who is not on drugs find a job? Nowhere. Who cares? No one.

In 1943, after one of the first riots in Detroit, I wrote a poem which is still true. It ends: "Those who died here were murdered in my mind." We have each of us to look into ourselves for remnants of institutionalized racism or classism and to see alongside it those who died here yesterday and the day before in Los Angeles. Those who died here were murdered in my mind. We are all responsible.

Saturday, May 2

YESTERDAY, as so often happens on a Friday, while I was out Federal Express came and delivered two monstrously heavy boxes of my new book, *Endgame*, and put them in the garage. Luckily Nadine is here and was able to take them up to the third floor, because now my lovely task is to pack fifty of these to send to friends. How I will get the energy, I do not know, but I think Judy, my secretary, will be able to help me with some of it anyway. Today I hope to get *Endgame* and the little book of poems to Juliette Huxley, and that is a joyful package-making.

The sweetest bunch of flowers in the house now is one that I made a few days ago of scillas—a new scilla that is very pretty because it is a little bigger and wider than the other scillas. I had ordered it from a new place I have discovered, Van Engelen Inc., that sells wholesale—and three crocuses, one purple, one lavender and purple, and one white, and several other of the early spring flowers. This is in a little blue glass that belonged to Pat Chasse's grandmother, and the flowers looked adorable in it. By my bed I have bright blue delphiniums. So beautiful.

One of the things that has come recently is a book of reflections on old age called *The Ageless Spirit* in which I have a short section from *After the Stroke*. The authors are an interesting group of people; there are a great many big names, which does not necessarily make for a good philosophy, but there are some extremely moving ones, among them Jessica Tandy and her husband, Hume Cronyn. Here is something that Burl Ives said:

> John Steinbeck once wrote about somebody who saw the great eye of a Chinese man, and as he entered the eye he found the whole suffering world on the other side of it. So if you look into yourself deeply for any period of time, you begin to see yourself and your follies and the follies of the world. You also begin to see yourself passing on, see yourself dying. At this point I say to myself, I am not the body, I am not the mind, I am not even my emotions. I am spirit itself. When you can put your finger on that you can laugh again, because there is something remarkably freeing and joyful about the fact that every single one of us is spirit. I always end up with a little ancient prayer that goes like this: "Oh hidden life, vibrant in every atom. Oh hidden light shining through every creature. Oh hidden love embracing all oneness. May each who feels himself at one with thee know he is therefore one with every other."

I assent to that . . . today . . . just before my eightieth birthday.

Sunday, May 3

MY EIGHTIETH BIRTHDAY. It seems quite unbelievable that I
have lived eighty years on this earth. It makes no sense, and I
do not believe it. Today, here at Wild Knoll, a very English
morning with mist, the daffodils come up through the mist—
romantic, and intimate.

As I lie here on my bed all dressed, I am looking at delphiniums, the first flowers that came, which are from someone I do not know, a fan in Oregon, and they have been so
beautiful. The delicate yet brilliant blue against white walls.
What a joy they have been!

But this whole birthday is such an ascent of celebration
that I can hardly believe I have arrived, as though I were at
the top of a mountain. These last days, full of cards, many
from readers, and all so moving. I was going to say "too many
presents" simply because it is tiring opening things for me
now—I feel like a little child at Christmas who cries—but I
am so touched by all the people who wanted to remember this
particular birthday.

There are too many lists to cross off one by one because
nowadays I am sending *Endgame*, my journal, to friends. I
also have copies of the little book of my new poems that Bill
Ewert has given me for my eightieth birthday to send out.
Without Susan, who is here for the weekend, it would all be
quite impossible. She creates order out of chaos.

We shall celebrate my birthday today, doing everything
with ceremony. How rare the sense of ceremony is! Susan in a

beautiful dress last night helped my heart.

And of course I think of Wondelgem, where I was born, with the poignant sadness I always feel about it and especially about my mother. I think of the beautiful garden she created and then had to leave when the German armies invaded in 1914. I wish I remembered more about Wondelgem. I do not. I am told things, so I can see myself crawling to the strawberry bed when I was a year old and being found there covered with strawberry liquid all over my face, happy as a bee. But I do not remember that, and of course I do not remember that it was Céline Limbosch who held me in her arms before my mother did. That deep bond started very early in my life, before she herself had a child.

And I think of all the birthdays. Margaret and Barbara sent two bunches of balloons. It all brought back a birthday party my mother gave me when I was perhaps seven or eight years old in our tiny apartment on Ten Avon Street in Cambridge, balloons all over the ceiling. How thrilling that seemed to me! And I remember my twenty-fifth birthday at Jeakes House, Rye. I and a group of friends rented the house from Conrad Aiken for three months, just down the street from the Mermaid Tavern and Henry James' Lamb House. The room where I worked looked over the marshes and it was a beautiful, peaceful scene. That whole time was a magic time in my life, full of happy memories. Twenty-five is a wonderful age to be, but in some ways eighty is an even better age because you do not have to be worried about the future anymore; you can rest on the past.

When Margot started interviewing me for her biography I got very upset and in fact even thought I might have a nervous breakdown. Digging up the past is painful; there is no getting around it. One does remember lovely things, but there is always a lot of pain in the background. I got quite upset and said that I could not talk to her for a while. But this time, this

May at eleven months in Wondelgem

week, when we had two long talks, exactly the opposite happened. The past became a kind of addiction, and I looked forward enormously to talking with her. I think she is going to do a good job. She combines sensitivity and a certain toughness which I admire and which is in me also, a quality to be recognized by any biographer.

Now Susan has gone out to get the clams to steam for our lunch. Nancy is coming, and Edythe, bringing as she always does for my birthday miniature roses which I plant on the terrace, along the border inside the wall. Last year they were in flower until November. Thrilling.

But of course this spring continues to be a kind of monster. I mean, there are not even leaves on the trees yet! On the lilac bushes they are just little points; they are not blooming. And there are no violets yet.

It is very exciting to have *Endgame* to send out to my friends. Altogether it is a great time.

Pat Carroll called me yesterday—that was quite a thrill— and spoke so warmly of Pat Keen and her great talent that I felt moved to call Pat this morning. She has given me a most heavenly blue-and-lavender scarf with Art Nouveau roses on it. I have it on now. I am also wearing a silver-toned necklace which I find very charming, as sometimes such things can be when they are so obviously not real that they have a charm all their own; this a fan from Oregon sent me.

Thank goodness Pat Chasse was here when I was trying to dispose of forty pounds of asparagus sent by a fan in California who really perhaps should have thought twice because I am old and this was far more than I could lift. Pat has taken it to her church to be distributed, and I am glad.

I wish I could think of a poem that I really wanted to read for my birthday. Perhaps I can.

It is now eight-fifteen on my birthday night and Maggie and Nancy and Janice Oberacker are washing the dishes and tidying up downstairs. I suddenly felt I must get up here to bed, but before I go to sleep I also want to tell the big event—there were many, but one of the biggest events of today, in some ways the most moving, was when I went down after my nap at half past four and looked out at the bird feeder. There was a scarlet tanager! I have not seen a scarlet tanager here for twenty years. On the day that I moved in, there was a scarlet tanager in the andromeda. I never saw him again. This magic bird was there again this evening as we had supper. Maggie and Janice were excited, and then, just to top it all, Janice said she saw an evening grosbeak as she walked from her car into the house. Perhaps I shall see the evening grosbeak tomorrow.

The whole day has been a festival of love and friendship. And as I say goodnight I think of my mother and of how glad she must have been when I finally came out of her, alive and all right, and she took me in her arms.

Wednesday, May 6

MY BIRTHDAY goes on and on. What splendor! And by a miracle, today, although they had foreseen rain or at least mist, there was a deep blue ocean, and the daffodils are dancing! They are out and beautiful although very cold. The cold is hard. Everything is waiting for just a little warmth so it can flower. I have not seen the magic bird again, and Anne Woodson, who was here for lunch with Barbara, when I described the great apotheosis of my birthday, said she thought scarlet tanagers migrated north and that he probably was passing by and I happened to see him. Wasn't it wonderful that I did?

This birthday was extraordinary because Anne and Barbara brought Persephone home. Ten years ago I commissioned from Barbara a sculpture of Persephone rising from the sea; it was my idea of changing the myth so that she went down into the sea for the winter and came back for the spring, and Barbara did a most extraordinary sculpture which was placed at the end of the terrace wall so that when you came to the house you saw it in the distance at the end of the terrace. Four or five years ago in a wild storm it fell and cracked into pieces. We thought it might have been knocked over by a deer, and I still think it may have been a deer that did it. It seemed a totally hopeless mess. I told them with horror I had never had such an experience, the death of a work of art. At that time I wrote a poem about it and thought it was gone forever. But Anne and Barbara, and I am sure dear Anne's wonderful energy and imagination were responsible, came and collected all the pieces and took them home, and for the last few months Barbara has been working on gluing it together and on making it even more beautiful. In the original version Persephone had one arm raised and there was something not quite right about it. Now that arm has gone. But the curling of the ocean around her is there and so beautiful. It is a miracle to see it here again. So this is also the birthday of Persephone coming home.

I feel frightened of feeling as exhausted as I do. I suppose it is a reaction to my birthday, but I feel in some ways as though I were dying. Setting the table for Anne and Barbara became almost an insuperable task. Joan was here in the morning so my breakfast was brought up and my bed was made. As usual there was news in the mail that required an immediate answer—a friend has cancer of the prostate, and I felt I must get that written, so I did it. Then I went down and made a salad and got things a bit more ready and read the rest of the mail, which was not quite as overwhelming as it has been, but there were still I suppose ten or fifteen cards and letters and presents. A birthday to end all birthdays.

In the back of my mind there is fear because Dr. Petrovich seemed to be a bit alarmed about my going up and down the stairs so much; I had always thought and believed that this was good for me, good for my heart. When he realized how much I do it, have to do it, partly because of Pierrot, he said, "You mustn't go up and down so much, and sooner or later you will have to move your study down." Well, I have faced this, but I thought of it as something that I might do if I lived to be ninety. At that moment the phone rang and it was Connie, Judy's sister, to tell me all about her marvelous ninetieth birthday celebration. Pure delight! And I did manage to write a poem, not worthy because I was not inspired, although I love Connie so much.

I simply have too much on my plate right now. As I sit here I am waiting for Raymond, who used to be my gardener, a dear man, who is coming with his friend, a young woman who loves him and has changed his life by taking care of him and caring. She has never seen the daffodils, so they are coming in a few minutes; it is now half past five and I expect them any minute. I told him that I could not sit down and talk.

I knew I would be tired after Anne and Barbara. But I want to go back to them because always their visit is so rich in love and imagination. Every year they have given me a hanging fuchsia, which I see they took into the garage as I was afraid of the frost tonight. It is usually placed so that I can see it from the window next to my chaise longue. All summer long it flowers. Anne also brought me an enormous white pot of herbs, every kind of herb from basil to thyme. I can go out the side door and take a pinch or Susan can.

Deborah Pease telephoned before Connie. She had received a copy of *Endgame* and was very excited by it, and that is wonderful to know, but I believe that it is not going to be on general sale until the end of the month. However, it means that I shall not have too many letters to answer until June, and that is all to the good.

If I can find some way of not going up and down the stairs so much, if I can ever accept that the people who send me such wonderful flowers are never going to be thanked properly and many of the presents will never even be acknowledged, if I can accept that—but I cannot accept it. The fact is that at the moment I am living a life much too arduous for the state I am in, and this is hard to handle.

There is a wonderful moment when I go to bed and know that the whole night is ahead of me. I enjoy going down as I always do at ten to take some medicine and again at four to let the cat in and also to give the digestive juices a chance to work. It is a quiet time; I love the night. The phone does not ring and there is no mail.

I forgot to say that Anne brought two poems she had written, one a marvel about a hawk. And the bluebirds have come back to their place, and that is thrilling.

Friday, May 8

I AM at a strange moment in my life because I have a feeling that I may die within the next few days or hours. This is because I am so frightfully tired. It is the tiredness of my heart. My mind is clear, in fact brilliant. I could write poems if it were not for what has to be answered and dealt with every day. And that is driving me close to something like madness. I am so weak that setting the table for Anne and Barbara seemed impossible. The heart is very tired, but it is not be-

cause it is fibrillating. It is not the cancer in the lining of my
lung; that seems to be under control. It is not the bowel,
although I have been in a great deal of pain, but that I am
used to. What I am not used to is the feeling that I am about to
die. And against this are the pressures which make me often
behave like a crazy person. I do try to make myself time so
that I do not get so crampy. For instance, before lunch I have
arranged it so that I go down and have fifteen minutes of quiet
rest.

I have come back from shopping with Karen and have
time to sit and read the paper and not hurry. Because I was
seeing Dr. Khanjani I had to have my lunch by half past
eleven. I got back from shopping at a quarter of twelve, and as
usual the phone rang and it involved about ten minutes of talk
with a very charming man who wants an interview for the
Portland *Sunday Telegram*. I am obligated to do that for the
sake of the Westbrook Conference and the general publicity. I
liked him and was touched by what he said about my work,
which he apparently really knows, and that is too rare. By
then my "rest" time had been taken from me. That is what
happens. I forget what I am doing because I have been interrupted in a sequence which I had planned. It is like having a
piece of music brutally interrupted, over and over again.

Saturday, May 9

IN THE NIGHT I lay awake planning a dictated journal entry
about frustration only to find that I had come to the end of the
last cassette! Frustration!

Yesterday, after seeing Dr. Khanjani, I got up from a short

rest at four, determined to give myself an hour to work on the Persephone poem and play some Mozart. I came up here and remembered I had promised Greg (from the Portland paper) to send him directions as to how to get here. It should not take more than a minute, but I had not counted on my collapse under the pressure these days. Luckily I had remembered to bring his address upstairs, but it took me minutes to find the file of directions to Wild Knoll (the file in my desk is too crowded and things slip down out of sight). I found the directions, but then could not find the envelope I had addressed. That finally turned up, but the roll of stamps had disappeared! What should have taken a few minutes took a quarter of an hour and left me feeling crazy. It is not that I am crazy. I do know that. It is that the kind of pressure that requires constant minute actions about things of no real importance eats into my consciousness and ends by destroying my competence. Frustration is my hair shirt. This morning I brought my breakfast up to my bedroom having forgotten the English muffin.

I did rough out the poem in a half hour, but it needed two or three hours of work. Yesterday I was saved by playing some Mozart and this morning by remembering De la Mare's poem "The Witch Hare," one that Agnes Hocking taught us and that we acted out at Shady Hill school.

Witch Hare

In the black furrow of a field
I saw an old witch hare this night
And she cocked a lissome ear,
And she eyed the moon so bright,
And she nibbled o'er the green—
And I whispered—whisht! Witch hare!
Away like a ghostie o'er the field she fled—
And left the moonlight there.

When I was teaching poetry I used the poem to suggest how moving silence within a poem can be, that silence between her fleeing and "the moonlight there." Genius!

Music and poetry suit me well. I can handle art. It nourishes me and in my way I sometimes nourish it. What is hard to handle these days are the infinite small decisions and actions demanded of me.

Now I am playing something I have thought of listening to for days. Chausson's Symphony in B-Flat. He was a Belgian nineteenth-century composer. It is full of dark Belgian romanticism and melancholy; I recognize Chausson in my blood. As I listen I am at last back in myself after days of frustration and fear of dying. So tired is my heart that I did not know what to do with myself.

Today is the book signing, so I must hunt out some pens. Quite typically I have managed to lose the wonderful Mark Cross pen Sue and Lois gave me for my birthday. It will no doubt turn up.

That makes me remember the day in Brittany when Judy and I left our tiny rented Renault to walk on the beach. Somehow I dropped the car keys in the sand! We went back and we looked and looked, threading sand through our fingers. We said a prayer to St. Anthony, went and had a drink, and then tried again. Suddenly I felt the keys under my hand. A miracle! Alas, we never did find a St. Anthony later on so we could light a candle.

Monday, May 11

On Saturday there was a book signing at the local bookstore, Books Plus, and I knew there would be quite a few people. But it was quite amazing that I must have signed nearly four hundred books, at least a hundred of *Endgame*. It was touching to see how many books people bought, many of them paperbacks. Liz, the proprietor, had made a wonderful tea with sandwiches and the whole atmosphere was very loving and tender. Susan came all the way from New York with Cybèle, which delighted the children as she sat in a chair near me; I told them that there were pictures of Cybèle in the book. I think it shows that, sick as I feel—and I had burst into tears in the morning and could not stop crying because I feel so terribly ill just from the exhaustion of my heart—I manage and can do a lot, and that is good.

Wednesday, May 13

I am in bed after an extremely exhausting day, and I would like to record just what I have done today to see why it is that I feel so cracked up into little pieces without any wholeness or chance to be something.

I woke up with bad pain; I expect that these days. But I

Book signing

am relentlessly driven. Dear Joan was coming, so at four A.M.
I set the tray up, tidied up a little, and made a list of things for
her to do, including getting the mail, because I knew that I
would have to go out at eleven and shop for food, get something for my lunch—I am off soup at the moment—and maybe
look at flowers since I now have quite a lot of credit at Foster's. I am having my hair done at twelve. The Japanese come
tomorrow.

When Joan came back with the mail I read most of it.
There was a moving letter from Catherine Sanders, the young
Wellesley girl graduating this June who attached herself so
deeply to Eleanor Blair and was a joy and delight and great
help to Eleanor during these last two difficult years. Catherine
is absolutely desolate, desolate that she was not there as much
as she would have liked to be in that last difficult week for

Eleanor, and I gather that Eleanor, always so brave but legally blind, panicked. No wonder, because there was nobody to read the mail; she had not been able to find the help she needed so desperately. Thank God she died in her sleep because Catherine in her letter said that Eleanor had asked that nursing homes be looked into because she might have to go to one. I know how she would have hated it, and it is good that it never came to that. Catherine, just as she is graduating, suffers this mixture of grief and also I feel sure some relief, as I wrote her, because she would have worried so much about Eleanor when she got home.

Anyway, what that meant, that letter, was that I must write to Catherine today, this morning, before eleven; it was then about half past nine. There were bills to pay, three hundred dollars for medicine, my medical self takes a great deal of energy these days. No wonder I am tired. I am seeing Dr. Gilroy next week, I saw Dr. Petrovich this week, and of course Dr. Khanjani on Monday. I did pay those bills and wrote the letter to Catherine and also one to a fan from Florida who has been writing to me for years. She has now moved to North Carolina and has sent me money, which is always so difficult to handle; I always feel it has to be acknowledged at once. It will turn into a plant for the garden.

In the mail also came poems set to music; there are now two that I have to listen to. I had already put one in the downstairs record player, the only machine I have that plays cassettes, so that it would be easier to make myself listen to it later. The problem is that it takes over half an hour to listen to one, and I do not have a half hour.

I had promised David Levitt that I would give Mary-Leigh his card and tell her that his father had worked for her. He is the dear man who took off the storm windows the other day—and incidentally the house is very cold as a result. That always happens at first—it feels cold. Well, I had not done it,

and he took the storm windows off on Saturday, and now it is
Wednesday. I was afraid I would lose his card so I took care of
that, as well as writing to Catherine, paying the bills, and
writing to my fans. I also made out a check for four hundred
dollars for Pat Robinson, the gardener, who has done such
marvelous work all this month and whom I like to pay in
advance always, so she gets four hundred on the fifteenth of
every month.

Then it was almost eleven. You see, all this is a buzz in my
head. There is no continuity. After that difficult letter to Catherine about Eleanor, I did find two poems that might be used
at a memorial service: one is my poem "The Great Transparencies" and the other is a poem which comes next in *A Grain
of Mustard Seed*, "Friendship: The Storms," which is about
Eleanor after we had a fight, although her name does not
appear. Occasionally we had battles. We were both quite sure
we were right, and that caused some conflict here and there!
This is quite a moving poem, so I thought it would interest
Catherine, who for all I know may have had some arguments
with Eleanor, for Eleanor, great woman that she was, was
also a very power-driven woman and had to be right. Sometimes that causes trouble.

I leapt from that to bills to rushing out to try to get something to eat because I am against food right now. I feel ill all
the time, at the same time I am terribly hungry because I am
tired. So I went and got a piece of quiche and, very stupidly, I
had coconut pie from what used to be the IGA. Anyway, I got
some mushrooms so tomorrow night perhaps I can have a
mushroom omelet. We shall see.

Susan comes Friday night, and oh what a blessing that will
be—not to have to do everything myself! When I came back
from having my hair done in honor of the Japanese tomorrow,
it was half past twelve and I quickly heated up the quiche, ate
it greedily, read the paper, and then went upstairs to rest with

the idea that I would get up at three. Mrs. Dwight was coming to interview me about gardens at three-thirty and I thought I would have that half hour to put on one of the cassettes and listen, which I did do after Mrs. Dwight left. Meanwhile I was awakened twice from my nap by phone calls, one from one of the Japanese people who are coming tomorrow. I forgot to say that earlier this morning, the very beginning of the day, I called Pat Robinson to tell her that the last rose had come from Wayside Gardens, the rose they had left out of the delivery, and she said she would come and put it in, maybe tomorrow. This is as scrambled a recitation as the day was scrambled, and as all my days are scrambled. I quite forgot to say that I finally got off a long questionnaire and all the answers that I could manage to the Women's Press with two photographs. The questionnaire came Saturday, and I think it is the reason why I have been in such a frenzy ever since. I should not have had to do that right now, but at least it is mailed and off my mind.

Friday, May 15

YESTERDAY WAS at last a perfect May day, a gentle quiet sea murmuring in the distance, the daffodils glorious still because it has been so cold, and at the back of the house suddenly the plum tree in flower that I had feared was dead as it had not blossomed. It seemed like a good image because the Japanese people came at three and, when I was in Japan in March thirty years ago, the plum trees with their poignant scent were almost the only spring flower.

Such excitement when a white van drew up only fifteen

minutes late and there they were, coming toward me smiling and clearly moved by the landscape. It is quite a sight when one first arrives here. I always remember how taken by surprise I was when I first saw the great view down the field to open sea and thought I was in heaven, as I have been for the last twenty years.

They were Naoko Takeda, who translated *Journal of a Solitude* into Japanese; Noriko Midorikawa, the editor of *Impressions*, a magazine published by American Express for its card members; Masuko Kuriyama, representing the publishers, Misuzu; and last but not least a delightful critic, Saburo Kawemoto, the only man. We all were in a state of undisguised delight at meeting each other.

In the night I had suddenly realized how deeply I have been influenced by Japanese art so I decided that I must first show them the truth of this fact with a brief tour. We started with the Hokusai and Hiroshige prints that hang in the library, and I explained that the Japanese prints reached Europe in the 1890s. Mary Cassatt of course was immediately influenced by them, and my dear poet friend Jean Dominique (Doro) was introduced to them and taught a course on them until her death. She gave me these two superb originals and several others, one a snow scene that hangs in my study. Naoko Takeda recognized a tall vase in front of them as Japanese also. Then there were the netsuke to see and finally Kobo Daïshi in the porch where the chaise is and where I have my meals. His portrait and thin gold halo are works of art I remember as a child. It was always a presence in our apartment wherever we moved and now radiates peace where it hangs against the silvery wall in the enclosed porch.

I told them about going to Japan for a month as part of the celebration of my fiftieth birthday and how I had planned it to begin with a month in Japan, then move westward through a month in India, and finally to climb the Acropolis on my fiftieth birthday, May third. Greek civilization could seem the youngest as I had come from the Far East.

Saburo Kawemoto asked me whether I had seen the moss garden in Kyoto and of course I had, a magical place where you walk on carpets of brilliant moss.

Then we sat down in the library and I was given a present by the editor of *Impressions:* two beautiful lacquer plates, so light they are amazing to handle. There was joy in the air, partly because of opening my beautiful present and then signing copies of the Japanese edition of *Journal of a Solitude;* the interview itself was not wholly satisfactory. I did hear the great news that *Journal of a Solitude* in Japanese has gone into three editions in six months! That is more than any book of mine has done over here.

"Why?" I asked them. "What is it that pleases the Japanese about that book?"

I got several answers but all seemed to suggest that the idea itself of solitude and of a woman especially choosing solitude had great appeal to the Japanese. Considering how crowded the Japanese are these days that makes sense.

The Japanese edition is charming and the photographs have reproduced well, such a treasure to hold in my hands! How I wish my father could see this, and my mother! In the night I had planned to make copies on the copy machine of the Japanese poems in *A Private Mythology*. How delightful when Naoko Takeda, the translator, said she had introduced the book to the publisher by quoting from the first one, "A Child's Japan." Here it is shorn of two irrelevant stanzas:

1

Before we could call
America home,
In the days of exile,
My image of holiness

Was Kobo Daïshi,
Young and beautiful,
Sitting on his lotus
In a thin gold circle
Of light.
He is with me still.

My mother
Treated flowers as individuals,
Hated clutter and confusion,
Invented marvelous games—
Paper skaters
Blown across a lacquer tray—
Knew how to make a small room
Open and quiet.

We lived in austere style
Through necessity
And because it suited us,
An artist, a scholar,
And their one child.
How Japanese the rain looked
In Cambridge,
Slanting down in autumn!
How Japanese the heavy snow in lumps
On the black branches!

It is clear to me now
That we were all three
A little in love with Japan.

2

When I flew out into the huge night,
Bearing with me a freight of memory,
My parents were dead.

I was going toward
All they had left behind
In the houses where we had lived,
In the artful measure

And sweet austerity
Of their lives—
That extravagance of work
And flowers,
Of work and music,
Of work and faith.

I was flying home to Japan—
A distant relative,
Familiar, strange,
And full of magic.

I gave Saburo Kawemoto a sheaf of these poems to take with him. What fun if they could be translated! Naoko Takeda not only quoted that first poem but also mentioned two of the short ones that look a little like Haiku. I explained my belief that Haiku must be in Japanese where each word is an image in itself, and that it is too easy to write bad Haiku in English. My guests were in agreement about this. Writing Haiku in English is such an easy game and is even taught here and there. A cultural error.

It was too bad that Pierrot did not make an appearance as Saburo Kawemoto loves cats. Such a charming man—quiet, sensitive, round-faced, like a sensitive teddy bear. As they were leaving, after a fairly tense and interminable photo session, I said to Naoko, "What a charming man he is," and he heard me and turned back at the door and said, "Give me a kiss." So I kissed his cheek and he bowed very low. It was a perfect salute at the end. I was weak in the knees with exhaustion, but very happy.

Saturday, May 16

FOR THE LAST two days this place has looked more beautiful than I have ever seen it, with the still radiantly blue sea at the bottom of the green field and all the daffodils. It takes my breath away every time I look out. Every day now things are happening. There have been several small fritillaria. I have to laugh at the idea of several. There are never more than that, but they are so precious, and they are wonderful in the little small bunches that I make now. Susan brought lily-of-the-valley and that scent was with me all last night. It is so wonderful to have her here. It is like a reprieve because these are certainly hard days. I do not feel better, and things are piling up on me.

Yesterday I had such bad cramps all afternoon that I simply had to stay in bed from one until five when I got up and had a bath and made myself put on a dress to go and meet Charles Feldstein, my adopted brother, who had flown in from Chicago to stay overnight at Stage Neck and take me out to dinner there. I realized I had not worn a dress for two years so I had the problem of finding a slip and stockings and all the rest of it, and trying on a new dress. All my dresses were for someone who weighed fifty pounds more than I do now, and I wanted to try a new dress so that I would know that I could wear it when I get an honorary doctorate next week at Westbrook College. I must have something that looks respectable under my black robe.

I was exhausted and so shaky that driving at night to meet Charles—he no longer drives—was an ordeal. Also, I felt that he did not realize quite how ill I am. He had kindly walked out so that he met me outside and could help me in. But then there was a problem with the menu, somehow we did not get settled into it. We did not really connect completely, I am sorry to say. Charles is very talkative and sometimes does not listen well, but when he does, he listens very well. What I minded was he did not seem aware of how beautiful the sea is as we watched the lace of the waves come in as the tide was rising on that sandy beach at York Harbor, which we looked out on, and, for instance, the beauty of a single figure in a red dress in the middle of all that. Magnificent! I do not know whether he is nearsighted or he does not observe very much, but in a strange way I did not feel that we were doing something together. It may be that he was rather shocked because we have not met for five years and I have become an old woman. There is no getting around that. Charles himself is going to be seventy.

What I truly wanted to do, and we were able to do, was to talk about Janice, his marvelous, brave wife who has multiple sclerosis, and how things are working out, what wonderful inventions there are to help her. She has an electric chair. They live in a wonderfully designed building so that without going out she can go up to a restaurant on the top floor, she can go down to the bottom floor and buy groceries, and their car is parked right outside their door. She does not even have to go downstairs to get into the car, and they have a driver. So altogether everything possible is done. Janice is now a radiant grandmother, her first grandchild. I saw a photograph of the adorable baby. And Charles is infinitely sensitive and attentive. It made me smile when he said how they look forward to the weekends when for one and a half days there is no help and he and Janice manage alone. They both look forward to this as a time of heaven, but it could not be every day, partly because of his work.

Although last night was a little tense, I must say that when he came over today I was touched by how warm and dear he is. We had a good talk. He said that he felt that I was so much better than last night, that he had been very disturbed about me. I am sure he was, but here with Susan to help I revived, although this has been a day of the worst cramps I think I have ever had, which is saying a good deal. I think it may be quite simple. I think it may be that I made myself a fruit shake, which Dr. Khanjani had suggested I do now, of papaya juice, a banana, two or three strawberries, and a pear. It was delicious, but I think it may have given me this diarrhea. It is very annoying. Anyway, Charles' visit was a great birthday event and I am touched that he wanted to come and made the effort himself considering all that he is carrying all the time. By now he must be almost home in Chicago with Janice telling her all about it. I put daffodils in a little vase in his room for him; I asked someone at the Inn to take up the flowers and my books—a book of poems and *Endgame*. He managed to bring back the vase and the daffodils today, which was thoughtful of him. Not only that, he had flowers sent from Foster's to thank me for my flowers and among them are some of those brilliant blue delphinium that lasted two weeks the last time I had them and also some stock which smells luxuriously sweet.

Saturday, May 23

I HAVE ALWAYS been aware that I do not experience anything until I have had time to think about it. The trouble with my life right now, the reason that I am quite depressed, is because so much has been happening, so much that is exciting, so much that is worthy of thought and consideration and of writing down, and I have had no time to think about any of it.

Two days ago Rachel Paulson, who had written to me some time ago, came to have a talk. She is going to do her senior thesis at a Mormon college in Utah on my work. I had felt that I did not have time, but she is going to Switzerland for the summer to work. Interesting. She says she can get a job there; she is going to work in a market, a grocery store I gather, in Lausanne, and she can make about as much as she would here, but she would not be able to get a job in New Hampshire this summer, where her parents live and where there simply are no jobs. So she can combine having the fun of a first trip to Europe and a job.

At last we are having incredible, perfect spring weather, or we were until yesterday, when suddenly it became hot and we jumped from winter into summer. But on the day Rachel came, it was a perfect day at Wild Knoll. The sky and sea were as blue as they were for the Japanese, and the daffodils were still in their glory. They will be gone when I get back on Monday, I am afraid. They are on the way out, but they certainly lasted a long time due to the cold weather.

Rachel Paulson made a good impression and left with me

an essay, an honors essay—she is now a sophomore—that was printed this year about the connection between my life and art. This is a serious, exemplary analysis of why I do not wish to be labeled as a lesbian and do not wish to be labeled as a woman writer but consider myself a universal writer who is writing for human beings and who is primarily a human being. This she has done with tact and excellent quotations. I felt as I talked to her that she knew the material better than many people who have come to talk to me and who think they know it. She recognized so much in the house; that was touching. She said, "I see so many things that I know here." I think she enjoyed it very much. I enjoyed it. It was well worth the energy and the time, though I was tired at the end.

Then Edythe was coming to take me to lunch. We went to the Brickyard—we have not been there lately—and had a superior smoked salmon and light cheese quiche, and I had a glass of ale which I had not indulged in for a long time. It all went well, though I felt pretty tired at the end, and I knew that the next day, yesterday, I would be coming up here to Hallowell. Maggie Vaughan would be coming to fetch me and I would be here for the weekend.

This is a perfectly beautiful place called Twin Elms Farm. When her husband, Bill Vaughan, was alive, it was a dairy farm. They had fifty cows—a real farm, a working farm. Now there are a few cows and calves. There are hens, but the two pigs are gone. There is a resident farmer who takes care of things for Maggie.

The house was built at the end of the eighteenth century, 1798 I think she said. It is remarkable because it has large, spacious rooms. One thinks of a farmhouse like my modest farmhouse in Nelson, which had rather small rooms. But here there is great spaciousness, which creates peace, and it is surrounded by a lovely rolling landscape with a distant view of the Kennebec River. This little bit of blue suddenly reminds

Twin Elms Farm

me, because the house is high up, of certain houses along the Hudson; it has some of that quality of a leisured class high up over a working river because the Kennebec was used all through the nineteenth century for lumbering. Now I think it is not, although it is still a tidal river. Quite amazing, since it is thirty miles from the sea!

There is something I have never seen before. There are weeping apples; you can achieve this by pruning them in a certain way. Two of them are out, and are charming. It is a place full of charms and grace, and it is a joy to be here. I have the happiest memories of Maggie's kitchen, which is the most relaxed kitchen I have ever been in. It has a wall of photographs of her family—she has four children, one son and three daughters, all grown up and with children themselves. There is a semicircular window with a round table at one end and the Agar stove, television, and so on at the other end. It communicates a feeling of space, stability, and peace.

Today I am going to be given an honorary doctorate by Westbrook College where there will be a conference on my work in June. I knew when I accepted this honor, my seventeenth doctorate, that the chances of my feeling well were almost nil. The last three weeks since my birthday have been so crowded with interviews and people that it was inevitable that I have a bad time with indigestion and cramps. Yesterday I wondered if I would make it, but we got to Maggie's by four, I had a rest, she cooked a delicious dinner, and I got to bed early though I did not sleep much because the new drug, Ascendin, Dr. Gilroy has prescribed seems to keep me awake. It is supposed to do something about the muscular spasms; it might make an enormous difference to my general health. I am going to keep at it for a week or so and see whether it will work, because it would be wonderful news if it did.

It is like being at home to be with Maggie in this place where there is no object that is not beautiful and that does not have meaning. It is more than just beautiful. Imagine my delight to find on the wall near my bed, which is usually her bed—she has given up her room to me because it is on the ground floor—a beautiful reproduction of a portrait of a saint by Piero de la Francesca. Also a framed poem of mine, "December Moon," a poem I had totally forgotten.

Maggie escorted me to Westbrook, which is near Portland, a little over an hour from here. There the whole scene was like something from Thornton Wilder's *Our Town*. It is a beautiful campus with an eighteenth-century air—red brick buildings around a quadrangle. There was a delightful brass quartet, rather subdued. Oh, it was just perfect! People were already gathering when we got there at nine, and luckily, because it was a hot day, the people getting degrees and those being given the Deborah Morton Awards, who included a great poet and my dear friend, Constance Hunting, all sat in the shade. We would have been pretty hot in the bright sun today.

Tuesday, May 26

I WANT TO GO back to what a beautiful day it had been for the commencement. I did not get to the most important thing about that commencement because the tape ran out and I did not have a spare with me. The most important thing was Senator Cohen's excellent speech; I have never heard a better commencement address. He had several extremely good, humorous stories, to the point for once, and then ended it with a passionate and convincing plea to the students that the world could be what they make it for their children and that there was an awful lot to be done, but he said it much better than I.

This commencement at Westbrook was moving partly because it is such a small college so it did not go on too long. Then Cohen's speech was exactly right, and the student valedictorian's was almost too short. It ended with something I had forgotten; the rite of throwing the tassel on the cap to the other side. It is not exactly like the throwing of the caps in the air at the Naval Academy, but it is something like that. Charming.

It was wonderful to get it over with. It was also a little

scary to be as weak as I was. Without the wheelchair, which Maggie thoughtfully rented from Hospice and brought in her car, I do not know what I would have done. After the ceremony, what were we to do? We walked over to the church which has now become part of the campus, a delightful, small New England Gothic church, and beautiful auditorium with a ceiling so high that noise gets taken upwards. I sat at President Andrew's table and had an interesting talk with his wife, who is a professor at the University of Delaware and who is bringing two or three of her students to the Conference. The more I hear about the Conference the more exciting it becomes because it is clear that many people are to come. The frightening thing is whether I have enough voice to be able to read. I may have to ask Connie Hunting to read for me if I find that I really cannot.

We gathered in the church and after lunch Maggie and I escaped before the speeches and drove back to Hallowell.

It was wonderful to walk back into that magnificent house, to the peace and elegance of it, and to have a long rest before Brad Daziel and Michael, his friend, came to dinner. The dinner was formal in the great dining room. I have never seen a more beautiful dining room, with its slight oval end that opens out into the garden, and the many, many candles that are lit for any dinner there (there is no electric light). Maggie had cooked a superb meal, and we had good talk. I was so happy to be able to talk a bit with Brad, whom I have not seen for a long time. He and Michael will not be able to come to my party, which is the day after the Conference. He is going to be absolutely exhausted, and it is probably a good thing that they cannot come, but I am going to miss them.

Then Maggie and I fell into our respective beds. I found it hard to sleep. Suddenly there was a loud eruption under my bed; it felt like an earthquake. I was fast asleep by then so I jumped up. It was Maggie's setter dog, Cricket, who usually sleeps under the bed and had somehow crept in. When I realized what it was, I let her out. Presumably she went upstairs to where Maggie was sleeping. Then I did have a good rest, with Sunday opening out the next day as a dream. To be in this house, not to have any pressure, not to have any mail, not to even have the *New York Times,* was a treat. I went back to bed for an hour and we then were due at Brad and Michael's to look at their garden. They have a quite extraordinary garden which Michael, who is a landscape architect, designed. But by then the temperature had dropped from ninety the day before to what felt like forty but was probably about fifty. What made it so cold was an icy northeast wind. So the seeing of the garden was rather limited; we simply could not bear the icy cold. So we went in and had a glass of sherry, talked some more, and then went back to Maggie's for a snack before going to the movies.

What an event for me! I have not been to a movie for over a year. I was very excited to be there with people, to hear the people talking as they came in, all that hush before a performance that you never get on television. It was great fun. It was an Irish movie called *Hear My Song* about a great Irish tenor; it is a plotty movie and not a good one, but it had its moments and we were certainly carried right out of our lives, out of Hallowell into Ireland, and that was lovely for an hour or two. Then we came home and there was time for a regular supper. I actually had a little piece of hamburger; I have not had any meat for more than a year and I do not think I will go back to it, but it was great fun to have it this once.

At Maggie's, by her bed, I had found one of the series of books published by the University of Mississippi in which *Conversations with May Sarton* has just appeared. This one was *Conversations with Eudora Welty.* A fascinating book. It is a collection of interviews. When one heard of the celebrations after she got the Pulitzer Prize it was thrilling. What one envies is what she is in that community, the beloved writer of Jackson, Mississippi, known and adored by the whole community. There is actually a Eudora Welty Day. What I had not realized was how many connections she had made in the literary world through her extensive teaching and through her relation to Diarmuid Russell, her marvelous agent. That was a very good end to the day, to be with Eudora Welty, who is perhaps the most distinguished living American writer and such a dear remarkable woman.

Then came Monday and the inevitable difficult return home, difficult because I hated to leave Hallowell, and I dreaded the pile-up that would greet me, as it did indeed, although it also was thrilling. There were three fan letters from people I do not know who have just gotten *Endgame,* one of them at least as the result of a review in the Sunday *Los Angeles Times,* a review which I found extremely irritating because the writer brushes aside the novels and poems. Never mind. Apparently it is the kind of review that makes people buy the book, and that is all one can ask.

This homecoming was tragic. There were only a few hours when there was no one in the house because Eleanor, who was housesitting for me, left at nine, and I got here at one. When we walked onto the terrace, one of the miniature roses had been cut at the root and the whole branch with its bright, sweet flowers had been thrown onto the terrace. Only a child would do that—or an enemy, and I do not think I have an enemy. So it all landed on me with a hard thud, that sight of violence done to a plant. But now I have picked flowers; I picked the last of the daffodils because there was going to be frost last night. It is bitterly cold, which is very hard to take. Today I have been to Dr. Khanjani who is trying to help me with my voice.

Wednesday, May 27

IT IS NEARLY nine o'clock, and I am in bed after a rip-roaring day which ended when I told myself that I am now not going to hurry. That was after supper, after I had washed the dishes, and I went out in the dusk and picked an exquisite tiny bunch of flowers for my bedside. It has lily-of-the-valley, a lovely piece of vibernum, and a pink hyacinth which is very sweet smelling, and some of the new ground cover that Sister Jean Alice, my Carmelite friend, gave me. What an exquisite feeling to be able to go out and pick such flowers!

Because the deer eat all the tulips, I do not plant them anymore, but there were two surprises, one lavender and one slightly pinkish tulip that I suddenly saw at the side of the fence. I picked them because I was sure the deer would come and eat them, and they are beside me with another dark purple, tipped-with-pink hyacinth and two very pale, almost white, daffodils, the very last of those, too. It is the end of one phase of spring, an opening measure; now come, very soon, the iris, the lilacs, the peonies, and then the roses. Oh, it goes on, an incredible sequence. I picked a branch of apple blossom to put in the front hall yesterday. It is a little droopy now but it will do for tomorrow.

What days these are! Today is spectacular because I had it to myself after Joan left this morning. It was a great blessing to have her this morning because she helped me clear out Susan's cupboard so she has a little more room for her clothes. All mine could be put in the laundry cupboard instead. Joan helped me with that and brought me my breakfast and got the mail. The mail was enormous; I did not think I would ever get through it.

Anyway, I finally did climb the stairs at about quarter of ten and spoke with Cecil Lyon from Norton who gave me the tremendously exciting news that the advance sale for the new journal, *Endgame*, is ten thousand, and that is good. Some of them will come back, but it is good for me; I am not a best-seller. That was heartening, as were a couple of letters from people who are crazy about the book, including a dear one from Dorothy Wallace. Then I began to think of what I ought to be writing and finally did write a letter I have been thinking about for a long time to a photographer friend of mine who has wanted to do a book which would be titled *The Essence of May Sarton,* but we have had a little misunderstanding. I may be wrong in this, but she has been in a way illustrating the metaphors, and the metaphors are only there for the meaning in a poem, so if I talk about the ripple of wind in the field and you photograph that, you are only photographing the metaphor. The meaning of the poem is not there in the photograph. It is rather hard to explain, but I managed to write that letter which was one important letter I wanted to do. I wrote a very short one to Eleanor Blair's friend, the young Wellesley girl who had made her last two years so much happier than they ever could have been without Catherine. I want to see her soon. So I got that off, and a book for Huldah. It is incredible all the people I have *not* sent *Endgame* to, although I send one or two out every day.

By then, because I had the whole day to myself, I dashed out for shopping at eleven and got the acrylic champagne glasses, forty of them, for the party after the Conference at Westbrook. That had been terribly on my mind, for fear I would suddenly not have those glasses and not know where to find them. I got Cranapple juice and a loaf of bread, things that I will not be able to get tomorrow when I hope Edythe will take me to Golden Harvest, an excellent vegetable place in Kittery.

I came home at about twelve and read the paper—an excellent essay by Quindlen on parents of gays and how terribly important it is to be accepting and to make it as easy as possible if you have a gay child. This was a splendid piece of hers; she is a remarkable columnist.

I so often now get little checks from the *New York Times* for the long-ago pieces, one on solitude, that are reprinted all the time. So here comes seventy-five dollars last week, welcome indeed. It more than paid for the champagne glasses.

I did not get up to my rest till about one-thirty, and then I had a call from Carol Houck Smith of Norton, whom I spoke with when I talked to Cecil Lyon. Besides talking about the sales on *Endgame*, we made a plan about next year's books because a great deal is going to happen next year. The plan included publishing the new collected poems, which will be a very big book and will include the last three books of poems which were not in the previous volume of collected poems. That will come out for my eighty-first birthday. Isn't that exciting? Susan's book, *Among the Usual Days*, is due in the fall, and that is going to be a really big thing. Then my own new journal, which may be called *Encore*, would be published, I suggested, in the summer. A journal is a very good thing to take away on a summer holiday. Meanwhile Marilyn Kallet's book of poets on May Sarton's poetry, *The House of Gathering*, will perhaps be out in March next year. It is as if my birthday were going on and on forever. What an extraordinary day! The adrenaline gland is working very hard and I feel extremely well, better than I have for a long time. I think it is because I had a whole day to myself without pressure, which I have not had for months.

Thursday, May 28

IT HAS BEEN a frantic day! It is cold again! It is so miserable! I
hate to look out at the garden and see everything longing for
warm sun, longing to open. The leaves of the big oak are
white from last night's frost, and we will have frost again
tonight. It was a frantic morning because Eleanor Perkins is
here. I had been up since four. When I finally got dressed it
was almost nine, and at that moment the exterminators arrived to take care of the flying ants which had begun to swarm
a week ago. Eleanor was upset because she has asthma and
was afraid of the chemicals they spray, which fortunately they
did not do. I had an interview coming up at eleven and God-
knows-what on my desk that should have been done and was
not because it took me most of the hour to get a new ribbon
into the typewriter, but at last it was done and at last my
hands are clean of all the black I thought I would never get
off.

The interview at eleven was with a charming man from
the Portland *Sunday Telegram.* His name is Greg Gadberry,
and he had found me, interestingly enough, because he studied at the University of Colorado. There he was a student of
Richard Hugo, the poet, who was trying to woo the students
away from Western poets. Strangely enough, the poems that
touched Greg were the ones I wrote about the West, especially "In Texas." I was pleased to have that remembered. He
also had evidently read a lot of my work, including the last
novel and two or three of the journals. So he asked nourishing

questions. By that I mean questions which did not alarm me but gave me a chance to talk openly with him. I liked him so much that I hated it when the hour ended.

After that Edythe and I went to Captain Simeon's and had lunch. I had a chocolate ice cream soda, a tremendous event, very risky, but it does not seem to have had any bad effects. We then went to the best vegetable place where I stocked up on fresh peas and especially dill, which I need badly. I even got some fish, sole, on the way home. But all this takes energy. Now it is a quarter to five. I cannot believe it. The whole day has floated away into nowhere.

I want to talk about two things that have been much on my mind. One was a letter from Betty Lockwood at Star Island for the Unitarian summer series. It is a series of seminars; one week is on the arts, one on religion, and so on. Betty has sold a great many copies of my books over the years and is a tremendously feeling and loving reader of mine. I had a tragic experience at Star Island which I shall tell in a minute because it has been locked up in my heart so long it is poisoning me. In her letter she says, "I've learned to compost hurts and humiliations, to let the trash of life rot away." This wonderful sentence has haunted me ever since I read it in her letter in answer to one of mine where I again referred to this deep hurt.

Lotte Jacobi, the photographer, used to be at Star Island for the arts week. It was great fun and everybody loved her. She persuaded me to go one year and I was tremendously happy and felt that I had at last found my group, my community—that is the word. I have always been such an isolated person. I never found it in Nelson, partly because I did not drink or socialize, and I certainly have never found it in York. But in that week, partly due to Lotte's influence and the fact that she was so loved, I felt at last, "I am at home here," I am accepted, I am loved. I was asked to do a half-hour reading which I was happy to do. When I got home I wrote them and said that I would be happy to offer them a formal poetry reading next summer during the arts week and would give it to them in return for my lodging and food. As I was at that time getting four or five thousand for a reading, I was offering them something fairly valuable. I got back a curt answer informing me that you have to apply long, long before this and also implying that they did not want me and that I had pushed myself on them in an unbecoming way. So that was that.

It was a real rejection, a rejection of a special kind, different from being rejected by a person. I am a Unitarian, I am used in Unitarian churches. I was asked to give the prestigious Ware Lecture and at that General Meeting was given their Ministry to Women award. I suppose some Unitarian minister is quoting me somewhere in America every Sunday, so I had some reason to believe I would be welcome. To not be allowed to belong when you know that you do belong is difficult to handle. I was very upset. I still am.

From the windows of my study I look out, and in the distance there is Star Island. I see it in many lights. Sometimes it seems to be floating on the horizon. Sometimes it is very dark, sometimes it is very light, sometimes it is hidden by fog, but never is it out of my mind that I offered them the best I had to give and was turned down. However, Betty Lockwood is absolutely right, and the image "let the trash of life rot away" is perfect. She went on to say, "Those people don't matter." That is where she is right. I must not feel that I was rejected by the Unitarian community, but I was rejected by the people running the arts week. So now I am going to try to forget it and not wake up at night thinking about it as I have done so many times.

The other thing I would like to tell on this day is a quotation Deborah Straw sent me. She is wonderful at finding things that make me want to buy books. In this case I may not

buy the book, but I am going to read this quotation from
"Friends, Foes and Working Animals" in Gretel Ehrlich's
book *The Solace of Open Spaces.*

> An animal's wordlessness takes on the cleansing quali-
> ties of space: we freefall through the beguiling opera-
> tions of our own minds with which we calculate our mis-
> eries to responses that are immediate. Animals hold us to
> what is present: to who we are at the time, not who
> we've been or how our bank accounts describe us. What
> is obvious to an animal is not the embellishment that
> fattens our emotional resumes but what's bedrock and
> current in us: aggression, fear, insecurity, happiness, or
> equanimity. Because they have the ability to read our
> involuntary tics and scents, we're transparent to them
> and thus exposed—we're finally ourselves.

Saturday, May 30

UNBELIEVABLE! We are almost into June. In some ways we
have not had May because it has been so cold, but now the
lilac is out, that great, exuberant profusion of white and purple and even some shades of bluish lavender that I do not
have. Here I have a tall white lilac that has grown up behind
the house since long before I came here and a lovely purple
bush, in fact two, one on each side of the terrace at the back.
Lilac is one of the few plants that most people have a desire to
plunder, to steal. Susan and I managed to steal a few branches
yesterday feeling extremely guilty. She said, "We have to
write to the owners and explain," and I said never explain, it
might make matters much worse.

It is wonderful having Susan here for a very short forty-eight hours because it shows me what the summer will be like. Pure bliss. We have such a lot to exchange, so much to talk about, and then there is always the pleasure of a video which I never look at alone. This time she brought *Rambling Rose,* which I had suggested when I saw it reviewed last year because it sounded wonderful. It is one of the best movies I have ever seen and one of the few works of art, theater or movie, which gives an accurate idea of the best of the classic South— the romanticism of the men, the strength and vision of the women, even their mysticism one might say, but at least their goodness and strength. It is not in any way sentimental, which was the danger. Rambling Rose herself is a nymphomaniac who comes as a servant into the house where the central characters live and introduces the family's fourteen-year-old son to sex, though she does not mean to. But he is, as he keeps saying, curious. "Let me just feel your nipple." But the movie is so true and so—I cannot say anything but faithfully rendered that it is never shocking, it is only touching and true. She finally has to leave. The father has fallen under her spell and then rejects her. She becomes very ill and has to have an operation which a northern doctor suggests, the removal of her second ovary so that she will not be a nymphomaniac any more. It ends with her getting married, happily married, which somehow one does not expect. Halfway through I said to myself, "She is going to die," and I dreaded it.

One of the moving things in the film was at the end. The young boy has grown up and goes to see his father, who is now an old man, because he has heard that the father had bad news of Rose. When the boy asks, "Is Rose ill?" his father says, "No, Rose is dead." It is a tremendous shock to the son and they talk about it. The last line of the film is when they walk back to the house, the father putting his arm around the shoulders of the boy to whom he has confessed that he loved

Rose too. The father says, "Rose lives. Rose will never die because she was so alive."

One of the things that makes the film magical is the color in which it is all done. It is a film in color, but it is like a painting. There is none of the too-bright Technicolor; it has a gentler tone. Susan suggested sepia, I thought amber; it is somewhere between those two. It was filmed in North Carolina in a real town. One realizes immediately when one sees the cars that it goes back to the 1930s, because the depression was mentioned, but to us now, long ago. Long ago but not far away because it is so true.

Also the music was beautiful. I would like to get a record of it. Unfortunately I missed the composer in the announcements and his name was not given at the end.

So life is going on at a great pace, at a canter, I should say, remembering what Maxine Kumin said in the *festschrift*, "a little canter, a little last canter for May Sarton." It certainly is a canter right now because so much is happening.

One of the things that happened was my revising the journal which will come out next year. Shortly after, the new edition of the *Collected Poems* comes out with the three books that are not in it now. It has been out of print for a long time, so that makes me feel good. Recently I had a letter from somebody who paid eighty dollars for a copy of it, as it has become quite rare. Revising the journal makes me see how rough it is and how much work it needs so that, with a deadline of July 1, I am pushed. At the same time I must get the *Collected Poems* ready with what I need to weed out and what I need to put in.

Carol Houck Smith, who is editing that for me, said on the telephone, "Well, if you are taking poems out it is not 'collected,'" but I think she does not realize that most poets when they present their collected poems have, to some extent, weeded out the less good ones.

Certainly Edwin Muir did that. I am thinking of Edwin

Muir because in this year when so many biographers have
written to me concerning people about whom they are writing
biographies, hoping for information or impressions, I just had
a letter from Patricia Roland Madge, who is doing a biography of Edwin and Willa Muir. She asked whether they really
did come to see Judy and me at Wright Street in Cambridge
on Christmas Eve of 1955. Indeed they did. I went right to the
library and found a book of his inscribed to me in March of
1956. He was giving the Eliot Norton Lectures that year. I do
not know how I met him, but I know we did invite him. He
came first to dinner with us on November eighteenth, Mrs.
Madge says, and at that time we invited them for Christmas
Eve. I had always loved his poetry, but I never knew him or
his delightful wife, Willa. They were a wonderful couple. She
was so vivid, outgoing, the opposite of introspective, and he
was quiet and sensitive, an extraordinary poet. I must quote
on the record here at least one of his poems, while I am talking about him, or shall do so at the end of this day's dictation.

They did come and it brought back all those Christmases
at Wright Street so dearly. Eva LeGallienne had given us
Danish candleholders for the tree so we had small candles,
real ones, lit every Christmas Eve. I certainly would not dare
do that now after I had a bad tree fire here when we were not
even using real candles. It was risky, but we always had water
and extinguishers ready, and I watched like a hawk. We only
lit Eva's candles when there was somebody in our little front
parlor at Wright Street, which had Victorian furniture and
was somehow a perfect Christmas room. We did not use it
very often otherwise, because we did not entertain. It may
have been the Christmas Eve when Barbara and Will Hawthorne, old friends, brought violets because violets are now
associated by me with Christmas Eve. It was so delicious, that
scent, the smell of the pine and the scent of violets. Perhaps I
am now putting together several Christmases. Dorothy Wal-

lace and her children, and once her oldest daughter with a new baby, came to sing carols. We had heard them outside first, singing "Go Tell it on the Mountain." Great days!

Judy and I always planned Christmas to try to give special welcome and pleasure to lonely people. We did not give a party; rather we invited people every night for about ten days, one or two at a time, so they felt cherished and knew that we were really interested in them and not simply writing off a list of partygoing people who never get a chance to tell us their news. I think I should do it here if I had a little more energy.

Before Susan left this morning, I thought I saw an oriole, perhaps a female oriole, at the feeder and got Susan to hang out half an orange. But, as I have not heard the oriole singing this year, I suspect I was wrong. Now that I have looked at that bird again I realize that, of all things, it is a parakeet which must have escaped from its cage. Clearly very hungry, it is eating ravenously at the feeder.

Now I must go back to revising. It is challenging because there is no doubt that dictating does affect my style badly. There are many non-sentences. I am trying to cut out all the "of courses" and the "verys" and change "it's" to "it is" and all this takes time. And there are major problems that have to be gone into too. But while I do it, I shall be playing Mozart, some of the many records my dear cousin, Alan Eastaugh, has been sending me over the years. Since I am only beginning to be able to listen to music again, I have many concerts before me. Perfect bliss.

As promised, the Muir poem. When I first went out to the colleges to read poems I did not read primarily my own because I considered myself a missionary for great poetry, and saved mine for informal meetings with students in class. I built an hour's reading around a theme. Once it was animal poems and naturally this Muir poem was a perfect example. It communicates so powerfully what value silence has in a poem—that troubling silence between the next-to-last line and the last line.

The Animals

They do not live in the world,
Are not in time and space.
From birth to death hurled
No word do they have, not one
To plant a foot upon,
Were never in any place.

For with names the world was called
Out of the empty air,
With names was built and walled,
Line and circle and square,
Dust and emerald;
Snatched from deceiving death
By the articulate breath.

But these have never trod
Twice the familiar track,
Never never turned back
Into the memoried day.
All is new and near
In the unchanging Here
Of the fifth great day of God,
That shall remain the same,
Never shall pass away.

On the sixth day we came.

Monday, June 1

A DISMAL DAY, rain, but we need rain. Luckily there is not much that can be beaten down now except the apple and cherry blossoms, which probably will be blown off. I am recovering from a segment of *60 Minutes* last night which cut me up. I began to write a poem then which I hope I will be able to finish today. The segment was about a small boy who was frightfully tortured by his stepmother into whose foster care he was given although his mother, an alcoholic, had begged when he was taken away from her that they not send him to the stepmother. I shall not go into the extent or the horror of the tortures that he suffered before he was two years old, but finally, I believe due to a neighbor's complaint, he was taken away from the foster mother who had tortured him. He should have been taken away within a month or even a week of being there, but no social worker visited, although by law they were supposed to go once a month and did not go for four or five months. He was then, when it was discovered, in terrible shape; he was dying. He was put into a government hospital for very badly injured children, many of them not normal. There he also did not get the care that he needed as testified by a psychiatrist who said that he was worse and less aware when he left there. We saw him in her arms laughing and obviously able to respond a little but unable to use his arms or legs because he had had no physical therapy. Finally a wonderful woman was found whose life is devoted to helping one very badly disabled child. Everything was set up for him to go there after a short interval at another foster home while her house was being prepared. Then he got double pneumonia and died. I felt as if I had been struck by lightning after that piece, and I felt that I had to do something right away.

I have been haunted ever since World War II by torture, and by what makes people do it. What is it in us that cannot resist hurting the extremely vulnerable? It happens every day all over the world. What shot through my heart last night was the possibility that God is dying in each of us. Another of my preoccupations in this last month of depression caused by the state of the world is that there is too much misery for us to handle. By that I mean we know too much about which we can do very little, so the result is a kind of paralysis of will. That is what the poem is about and I hope I can get it written today.

Tuesday, June 2

IT IS eight o'clock at night now and I am in bed. Again an absolutely stunning day after heavy rain yesterday. The light is so beautiful and everything is rich and profuse now. The lilacs are in their splendor, and I got Nadine this morning to take the ladder and pick some of the white lilac which grows very high. If Susan were here, she could lean over her porch and pick it, but I am afraid to do that. I had not realized how close it was to the roof. Anyway, Nadine picked an armful. It is so beautiful. The purple by the front door is magnificent this year, thanks to Pat's careful pruning in the fall.

For days I've been haunted by a poem of A. E. Housman's, "I to my perils." I want to recite it here:

I to my perils
   Of cheat and charmer
   Come clad in armour
   By stars benign;
Hope lies to mortals
   And most believe her,
   But man's deceiver
   Was never mine.

The thoughts of others
   Were light and fleeting,
   Of lovers' meeting
   Or luck or fame;
Mine were of trouble
   And mine were steady,
   So I was ready
   When trouble came.

Louise Bogan and I each knew it by heart and sometimes when we met we would recite it, but somehow we never quite got to the end. "The thoughts of others" I forgot now and had to look it up. But I remember one special occasion when for some reason we were crossing the George Washington Bridge to the Palisades and we were reciting this poem together. We got stuck, and three times I missed the right exit so we crossed the bridge three times before we got the right words. We were laughing hilariously.

I have said harsh things about Louise and the fact that she could have helped me so much when I was starting out and did not, but I must not forget that we had marvelous times together in the first year or two that I knew her. She was a life-enhancing person as a friend. At that time we were translating Valéry together, which was an interesting experience for me and happened in a curious way. I had translated "Palme," one of my favorite Valéry poems, and sent it to Louise. This is the kind of thing we often did: exchanging work that we were doing. She knew that somebody called Gilbert Maxwell was doing the Valéry translations for Pantheon. She sent my translation to Maxwell and he thought that she had made the translation and wrote her to say, "We have found the translator we have been looking for," and will you do it? So Louise told him that I had done it, and he suggested that we work together and that they would pay us fifty dollars a piece for each poem that we sent. For some months I went to New York every two or three weeks and we worked on Valéry for a couple of nights, from about seven to eleven. I could translate into form and Louise could not, so I worked for eight hours or more on every poem and then brought it to her. She went over it and picked out the weak places, often had good ideas, but did almost nothing of the work, and Sylvie Pasche told me this was true when she and Louise worked on translating Goethe's *Elective Affinities*. Finally, and I think rightly, Pantheon decided not to publish our translations but to publish a prose translation of each poem. It is impossible to translate Valéry, but I am proud of our approximations and they did come out in several magazines.

I am thinking of writing a letter to the reviewer on the *San Francisco Chronicle* who says that my tantrums at bad reviews are famous. I have never had a tantrum about a bad review. Never. Twice I have been made ill by a bad review. Louise used to say, "Pay no attention, it is not important." I took her word for it and tried to pay no attention, but when Karl Shapiro on my *Selected Poems* in the *New York Times* on Christmas Eve said, "May Sarton is a bad poet" and went on like that and ended, "I am sorry to have to do this," it was very hard to take. Anybody would suffer from that! The *Times* has not published a review of my poems since then, and there have been eight books.

The next year, a book of my poems, *In Time Like Air*, was up for the National Book Award. It did not get it, but I was on

The phoenix

what the British call "the short list." Incidentally that year I was also on the short list for the novel *Faithful Are the Wounds*. I wonder whether anybody ever has been considered for two books in two different genres in the same year?

Sylvie Pasche's and Louise's translation of Goethe's *Elective Affinities* was given a damning review in the *New York Review of Books*. Louise went sky high with anger. This was not an important work for Louise; it was not creative work. You would have thought that she had been murdered. So I take it with a grain of salt when writers tell me, "Oh, I never read reviews," or pretend that they do not pay attention and do not care. In the first place, a bad review prevents books from selling and what you want is for your book to sell. It is like being hit over the head and shipped off to a hospital where you cannot speak. As a matter of fact, it is curious that both reviews of *Endgame* in the currently important California papers, the *Los Angeles Times* and the *San Francisco Chronicle,* have been patronizing, but they have been the kind of review that sells books. One of them, I cannot remember which, said it was flat and repetitive and then ends the review, "It is mesmerizing." You cannot win, but it makes me laugh.

I would like to go back to the time Louise and I were crossing the George Washington Bridge three times, reciting Housman.

Friday, June 5

I HAVE FELT centered until today, even as harassed and driven as I am these days by work and all that is entailed in the big conference at Westbrook which will be next weekend. It will begin Thursday and I shall try to read my poems on Saturday and hope that God will help me to have a voice. God and the charming Alex who is a voice specialist whom Karen Kozlowski suggested I try. I think he helped me very much, and he is coming on Tuesday. But today is not centered. Just a little too much happened, too many interruptions.

In the first place I had to return—oh, what a nuisance that is!—two jackets that I had ordered from a place where they were on sale. The trouble is that I cannot get used to being quite so thin, so I ordered a size twelve and it turns out that ten would have been better, so I had to send them back. We will have to see. But that took a lot of energy early in the morning.

I am trying to write a poem about Nadine, one of my helpers, who loves turtles and now has twenty-five in her apartment where she lives with her husband and two of his children by a former marriage. Twenty-five turtles and two children is quite a lot, but Nadine is an extremely capable person. Apparently the turtles are very happy. I am fascinated because I suppose I feel a certain affinity with turtles now that I have become so frail. I sometimes wish I had a shell. But the Nadine poem did not work out; it should have been semi-humorous and somehow I did not quite make it.

Then I wanted to write another poem about seeing a dead hummingbird in the road. The curious and moving thing about it is that I crossed that road three of four times today because I had various errands to do and nobody ran over the corpse. The long, pointed beak remained intact. It must have been hit by a car, and I think that everyone who passed simply avoided running over the hummingbird. It was so sad for such brilliance to die so brutally. It haunts me as the image for a poem. A tragic love affair cannot be brushed aside because it did not last.

Saturday, June 6

LAST NIGHT I dictated for a while but the tape ended, much to my astonishment, as it only had a few days on it. I have now decided to do this last week on the typewriter. It will be easier and quicker for Judy and will keep me from repeating myself as I often do not remember what I have said the day before.

Rain was predicted, so I dashed out to the garden before my supper to pick a few flowers for Maggie's room—she comes today at four for supper and the night. I found an exquisite, pale blue iris. The middle-weight ones I ordered last fall are successful and some of the dwarfs exquisite, one pale yellow with a lavender velvet ribbon on the lip. I picked some bluebells also. They have done well in a shady corner of the perennial border.

Now we are indeed having a rainstorm with a high wind that blows open the doors when they are not locked. Normally I do not lock, except at night. The old, tall, white lilac at the back of the house is bent down but no branch has broken. I think it will recover. I went out on the porch, Susan's porch I call it for it abuts the guest room, and there was the most magnificent sight, a huge river of white lilac, broad and thick, reaching higher than the porch roof. I looked across this to the woods, a most amazing sight, that river of lilac in space. Now it is all beaten down, sad.

The big event yesterday was a letter from Juliette, a rare event now as it is hard for her to write, but always, even in this brief note to thank me for wine and also *Endgame*, she phrases something in such an original way it makes my mind hum with pleasure. In this one she ends a sentence, "wishing I had the miraculous gift of youth myself, to offer you more understanding and support. All that in the hands of the gods—so high up in classical skies that wingless humans like me are ineptly inadequate."

Because I am rereading the *Collected Poems* these days I have been back into the poems I wrote for her after World War II when she and Julian were in Paris for UNESCO. The poems have made me tremble. Now I play Chausson's "Chanson de l'Amour et de la Mer" with Janet Baker's wonderful voice to sing it. Passionate memory is still fresh in my mind after thirty-eight years! I guess memory remembers what is important and chooses to forget what is not.

I hate to go out in the rain and not play the Chausson but I must get the mail and am having lunch with Edythe.

Tuesday, June 9

WHEN NADINE brought my breakfast tray up she asked me if I had the strength to get up for a minute because there was a fledgling great horned owl sitting in a tree behind the house. From halfway up the stairs he was visible, about a foot and a half tall, such a sight! Nadine thinks he is only a few weeks old and cannot yet forage for himself, and I am to call Dr. Beekman at the Wildlife Shelter if the owl is still there by nightfall. He has gone, I trust back to the nest which Susan and I must see, if we can find it. Susan comes tomorrow night for the summer. What a sense of holiday treats, and fun, and dear companionship that gives me!

This morning I had a half-hour lesson for my voice with Alex Davis, the voice teacher who gave me a lesson last week. He is a superb teacher and has given me confidence that I can read my poems on Saturday. My voice still does not obey me always, but most of the time I do say a whole sentence in an even tone. That is a huge advance. It is hard to imagine, I think, if one has not experienced it, how disturbing it is not to be able to control one's voice. It happened to me once in a near disaster when I had to give the commencement address at Clark University and woke in a hotel that morning with such laryngitis it was hard to make a waiter hear when I ordered my breakfast. I called Sue Hilsinger, who had been responsible for my giving the address and getting an honorary doctorate. I hardly knew her then, but she kindly got hold of lemon juice, honey, and scotch for me. I took sips of that, prayed and hoped. I could not believe that I would not be able to control my voice at the eleventh hour. I felt sure it would come back. But when I finally rose to speak, what came out was a whisper, magnified by the mike. I cut the speech in half. The extraordinary thing was the attention my whisper got. Several people told me afterwards it was the best commencement address they had had at Clark! I am sure it was because everyone had to listen so hard! The theme was "The Gentle Revolution."

But I do hope and pray I shall manage on Saturday at Westbrook. The whole conference, three days of it, begins on Thursday, but I shall only go on Saturday when I read the new poems at nine and then introduce my biographer-to-be, Margot Peters. It cannot often happen that the subject of a biography introduces her or his biographer! It is going to be fun.

At last I have, thanks to Tom Barnes who sent it to me, been reading a truly nourishing and inspiring book by Julie Lieblich. It is the story of four nuns, each of whom had to fight the hierarchy to follow a dream and it is passionately interesting. What courage such a course takes! The book is called simply *Sisters*, subtitled *Lives of Devotion and Defiance*. One has been active in the underground to shelter refugees from El Salvador; another is a contemplative, and I think my dear friends at the Carmelite monastery in Indianapolis may have been the inspiration for this one. They are not named.

These are my last days of journal-keeping. I shall miss it but I hope to start on a novella, a change of style.

Thursday, June 11

I AM RIDING a wave of excitement towards Saturday morning at nine when I read the new poems and also introduce Margot Peters at the Westbrook Conference. It is more exciting than almost anything before in my life. What if there is an anti-climax? My voice may crack. Never mind. These three days, the first today, are a peak experience although I can only attend the third. But Susan is my eyes and ears today and will be here tomorrow. I have waited more than half a century to feel confirmed, empowered in this way by peers and friends.

Let me amuse myself while I look down on the green field, so very green now, and the blue, slightly ruffled ocean beyond it, by remembering a few other peak experiences before I close this journal, which may well be my last work in journal form. My next act of creation will be, I hope, a novella I have been thinking about since the trip to London. It simmers and may well die on me, but I simply have to give it a try.

The first peak experience that comes to me is my hanging from a rope waiting for my entrance as the White Queen in LeGallienne's production of *Alice in Wonderland*, music by Richard Addinsell. The White Queen flies onto the stage on a theme played on a bassoon. There I was in LeGallienne's costume, an exact replica of the Tenniel drawing. I had to glue on her semicircular wide chin as she did herself. When I landed, to a ripple of laughter, I felt happy, and the famous line "Jam yesterday and jam tomorrow but never jam today" was met by a solid wall of laughter. The New Amsterdam

Theatre where we were playing both it and Chekhov's *Cherry Orchard,* in which I also played LeGallienne's part of Varya for a week, was much larger than the Civic Repertory so the laughter was far louder than I had ever experienced. Thrilling!

The second peak that comes to mind was one autumn day when I got up and looked out and saw an enormous moose (every moose is enormous) standing in the field right up against the wall. Rene Morgan was here and we marveled. Luckily Tamas was inside, too low to see out, so no barking took place, and in a short time the moose nonchalantly sauntered away.

The third peak is a whole week I spent alone on the magic island of Sark. No cars are allowed. One stands on a clear round of high cliffs, seagulls flying around below. There I sat in a field of primroses and bluebells and had a picnic, as happy as I have ever been. It was a mistake to go back later with someone I hoped would love it as I do but who treated me so badly it almost destroyed the memory of when I was there by myself, writing poems.

The fourth must be the night in May when Grace Dudley and I heard six nightingales singing in the little wood for which her adorable house, once a hunting lodge, was named. I had come right off the boat to *Le Petit Bois* where all the fruit trees were in flower and Grace's moving voice filled the house. She was not a professional singer but she told me that often when she sang people began to cry, as I did alone in my room looking down on the small formal garden. The power of a voice can be overwhelming, haunting one for years.

The fifth peak is one I have mentioned recently, Raymond Philbrook welcoming me to Wild Knoll with a bunch of wood anemones, the start of our gardening friendship. How much he taught me!

The sixth goes back exactly sixty-six years to the magical

summer I spent with my parents exploring the French side of the Pyrenees from west to east. I was making a collection of wildflowers and found the walks intoxicating. One day we watched a shearing, an old-fashioned one, done by hand with clippers and the wool coat of the sheep turned over to look like pure gold as the shepherd clipped. That summer I fell in love with the Basques and when I got back to the Shady Hill school gave an impassioned speech about them at assembly—my first impassioned public speech, but not my last! One of the things we learned at that wonderful school was to be able to speak well and naturally to an audience.

The seventh peak is a walk through the lion and tiger house at the London Zoo with Alan Cameron, Elizabeth Bowen's husband. He adored her, and so did I. I was staying with them in the house on Clarence Terrace in Regent's Park. Alan and I stopped and looked deeply at every lion, panther, or tiger and always Alan whispered as he looked, "Elizabeth." She did look like one of the great cats; there was something both dreamy and a little abstract in her glance. She seemed absorbed in her own inner world, although she could also laugh in long sustained ripples of response, especially to David Cecil.

I shall end with a more recent unforgettable image. Maggie, Pat Keen, and I watched a superb performance of Shaw's *Heartbreak House* in London this spring. Such a haunting play, with more silence in it and more between the lines than any other Shaw play I know.

I have to add the rich day when I saw the first white tree peony open in my garden.

Some of these I have written about in this journal or an earlier one, but such wonders are repeatable, inexhaustible sources of comfort and joy.

Monday, June 15

I AM RECOVERING from the three, peak-experience days of the Westbrook Conference, where papers about my work were read on the first two days. I felt it would be too much for me to go as I had to hoard my energy for my own poetry reading on Saturday. Susan went and heard all that she could. She told me about Vicki Runnion's tremendously moving essay on "Themes of Death and Grief in the Work of May Sarton: A Hospice Perspective." I am so touched that she says in it that she found her vocation with Hospice partly due to reading what I have said on those subjects. I feel honored, for Vicki is a radiant person who communicates sensitive goodness totally unselfconsciously. Constance Hunting gave one of the four keynote addresses, hers on May Sarton as editor, and this too Susan reported was excellent. It was tantalizing to know such things were in progress while I was not present, but it is possible that some of the presenters felt a kind of freedom because I was absent, and at least some of the papers will be published by the Puckerbrush Press.

Brad Daziel, who has spent this whole year orchestrating the conference and who is not well, was triumphant, as Susan described his keynote address. Unfortunately Carol Heilbrun on "The May Sarton I Have Known" was scheduled at night so Susan did not hear that but all the reports were glowing and all spoke of the constant delighted laughter. It is twenty years almost exactly since Carol came to Nelson for a weekend, the first critic in the United States to pay attention. How

marvelous that was and still is! I can never be grateful enough
for her insight and the power she has used so willingly on my
behalf, not least in persuading Lola Sladitz at the Berg Collection of the New York Public Library to buy my archive while I
was in Nelson.

At last, early Saturday morning on a rather warm sunny
June day, we set out for Portland, Susan and I, and arrived at
the charming old New England church Westbrook College
uses as its main auditorium. Already before half past eight
people were gathering. I was to read at nine. We were early
on purpose so I could try the mike and as soon as possible I
climbed the four steps to the stage and tried out my always
now disappointing voice. It will never be what it was even five
years ago, but Alex Davis did help me place it a little lower for
greater clarity. Apparently the voice is apt to get lower with
age, either that or go very high. The only trouble was that,
once up on the stage, I did not have the courage to go down
again and by now the audience was arriving in full force. I
should have made the effort because what happened was
hard to handle. Since I was sitting in an armchair on the stage,
people with cameras swarmed up below me and took endless
photographs, some with a flash. How could I have said no?
But after a time, a very long time, it seemed to me, I suddenly
felt very nervous and close to tears. Finally President Andrew
came and sat beside me and that was a help.

When he had introduced me and I finally got to my feet, I
began by saying that I was writing poems again and would
read from new poems, except for a very few. I began in fear
and trembling, and without a very clear voice, with "Mozart
Again" because I had told them that recently for the first time
since the stroke I have been able to listen to music. Until now
I could not because especially a Mozart record brought on
floods of tears, touching, as it does, the source of poetry for
me—and until now I have not written poetry in any concen-

CREDIT: SUSAN SHERMAN

May and President Andrew at Westbrook College

trated way since the stroke made chaos of my mind.

As I went on into the new poems I felt better and I think sounded a lot better by the end. The audience listened marvelously and I was not even thrown by a few late arrivals who went up to the balcony. I have not read poems for an audience for two years and it was thrilling to be back in harness, even though the old horse could not summon the old verve. It is a strange experience not to be in full control of one's voice. But I felt a few of the poems got across as well as anything I have written. And the audience was so with me that in some mysterious way I could not fail, and I did not. I ended the reading with "On a Winter Night." The last verse is

> Nor old, nor young,
> The burning sprite
> Of my delight,
> A salamander
> In fires of wonder,
> Gives tongue, gives tongue!

At that point the audience that filled the church stood and applauded for several minutes.

I realized then what a perilous dare to myself it had been to read poems without my real voice and I was trembling with joy and relief.

Tuesday, June 16

ANOTHER OF THESE clear perfect days with just an edge of ice and the ocean like a satin scarf laid along the emerald field, no wind. I have in the last hour and a half written ten more little notes of thanks to the friends who have so generously praised me in the *festschrift*. I have just ended with Buzz Meredith, who calls me "Dearest May," and such a flood of memories came back when I read that that tears pricked my eyes. Back then when he and I were both apprentices at the Civic Repertory Theatre it was quite clear that he would be a star almost immediately, and indeed he was taken into the company after that single year.

Now I cannot find the three pages I wrote yesterday about the conference at Westbrook, that apotheosis—how can they be lost? It seems almost impossible to re-create them, but they ended with my reading, so there is a lot more to be said.

It was now my turn to introduce Margot Peters. I suggested that it must be rare for a biographer to be introduced by her subject, and I described my own crisis after we had begun to talk because I felt I was being forced back into the past, so often painful, when all I want now is time to watch the sun rise, and to listen to the birds. I even begged Margot to leave me alone for three months. She did that, and then, when we met again, the wall came down. We had two important talks, and I was suddenly at ease. What I felt was that with her humor and good toughness as well as her perception and depth of understanding, she was becoming what is usually thought of as a definition of lovers, my "significant other."

It is a pity that I had to stay in my penitential chair on stage because I could not hear all she said, the mike directing her voice toward the audience. I did hear her introduce Victoria Wilson, the chief editor at Knopf, who will publish the biography, a nice touch. She also said I had told her I did not want to read the manuscript. "A classy attitude," she thought, but the fact is I do not remember saying anything of the sort. I shall be very curious if she has completed it before I die, with a proviso I think only fair, that I would suggest no changes unless there is an error of fact.

After Margot's reading we walked slowly across the campus to the May Sarton Room in the Maine Women's Collection in the library where Susan was to read from the book of excerpts from my letters and early journals which will come out in the fall under the title *Among the Usual Days*. The room was full of people eager to be invited into some of my unpublished work, intimate as it is. The whole atmosphere was one of joyful and loving appreciation even before she uttered a word.

I found a place near the front. Everything farther back, where I should have liked to be, was already occupied. I have never heard Susan read and I did not know what she had chosen to give that day out of the rich volume of her book. It was a remarkable performance. Susan has an unerring sense of the phrase, the pause. She took her time. The material was fascinating, especially the final section on death at a time when so many of my dearest friends, such as Koteliansky and Lugné Poë, were dying, or had died. I was aware of a very intent silence. Many people told me they had tears in their eyes, and I myself was moved to tears. After all, I have no memory of a letter written thirty or forty years ago; Susan's reading flooded my mind with memory.

We were coming close to the end of these extraordinary days and the climax of the conference, a presentation by Sandra M. Gilbert, the illustrious critic and co-author with Susan Gubar of *The Madwoman in the Attic*. I felt a twinge of anxiety. Would I be buried in faint praise or attacked once more for using form? Or for that matter, for using free verse? I need not have worried. Gilbert launched into an intricate analysis of what the woman poet following on the era of H.D. and Millay could bring to literature and this was, she told us, a merging of Walt Whitman and Emily Dickinson, the *Einseit* of Rilke plus the bardic quality of Whitman, and she suggested that I am a leader in this transition. She talked wonderfully about both Yeats' and Rilke's influence on me and how I have used it, especially in "At Muzot," a poem no one has quoted until now. It was a thrilling, complex, respectful reading of my poems, the first I have had at such depth since Basil de Selincourt reviewed my first book of poems, *Encounter in April*, in the *Manchester Guardian*. It was the accolade I have longed to be given before I die. What a strange sense of arrival after a long journey it gave me!

I wished I could be two people and once could have heard Marilyn Mumford talking about sound in my poems. I am slightly amused that three or four contributors chose to talk about silence in the poems, but only Marilyn about sound. I think sound is not looked for these days, a part of thrashing old-fashioned form. But I am happy that four or five composers have chosen lyrics of mine to set to music.

Was the fervent applause at the end of her twenty-minute segment the end of the conference? For many of the ticket holders it was, although they still had a chance to see Karen Saum's film on me, *She Knew a Phoenix,* and Stephen Robitaille's film, *Creativity in the Upward Years,* if they had missed them the day before.

For me there was still to come a very exciting luncheon. I had ordered a limousine to pick up Carol Heilbrun, Sandra Gilbert, Margot Peters, Susan, and me to take us to a restaurant for lunch. We were all five slightly intoxicated by being in a limo, not a thing any of us is accustomed to. I had hoped to take them to Roma, a distinguished Italian restaurant in a Victorian house where I met Berenice Abbott, the great photographer, when she was over ninety. "Beautiful and brave warrior" she calls me in the *festschrift,* and that single line moves me very much. Dorothy Healey, with whom Berenice often stayed, arranged that meeting, and I think we each fell a little in love. For months after that Berenice called me occasionally and wanted me to go and stay with her and her friend overnight, but it would have been more than a five-hour drive and I was much too ill. Oh how I regret it! Such a warm flame after a single meeting!

Roma was closed on Saturday so we were whisked off to a comfortable, rather ordinary lobster place on the water in South Portland, a nice airy room, so it was all right. I think we all five felt like kids let out of school, and the table buzzed with good talk and laughter as we devoured excellent lobster salad. It is so rare for me to sit down and talk with fellow writers, I found it intoxicating, and drank Sandra's generous praise with the wine.

Tuesday, June 23

SO MUCH HAPPENS every day these days of peak experiences, it is hard to go back and remember. For instance last night I looked out at about nine, before going to bed, to see the magical flashing points of the fireflies for the first time this year. And last week we watched the strawberry moon rise every night, in a clear sky, a most amazing deep rose. We have had one bright, cool day and night after another. The garden is full of wafts of the sweet scent of peony and iris and several of the de Rothschild azaleas are very sweet and spicy. I picked a bunch last evening for Susan's mother, who is blind now at ninety, a bunch of scents. The most fragrant is probably the pink rugosa rose. Susan drove off this morning to spend the day with her parents in Connecticut, a good driving day.

Our festive luncheon was not the last of the extraordinary happenings. On Monday I heard that the Women's Press in London will, at my suggestion, publish in March in one volume my last three books of poems under the title *Halfway to Silence*. All those poems were written after I was sixty and the Press agrees with me that a lyric poet who goes on into her eightieth year is rare. They will promote it accordingly. I shall go over in the spring. It is the first time the poems have been published in England since—yes!—1939, when the Cresset

Press brought out *Inner Landscape*. So it is for me a hope realized after years and years of frustration because publishers wanted only what would sell: the novels.

On the Sunday following the conference I invited those contributors whom I knew personally and a few friends attending to come here for champagne and sandwiches from eleven A.M. to one. My idea was that many people would be glad to stop over on their way home and many would not have seen this place or had a chance to meet me at Westbrook. It turned out to be another of these perfect June days. The peonies in the garden and the miniature roses inside the terrace wall looked wonderful. Pat has done a splendid job of making it cared for again, as a formal garden must be.

Judy had found a caterer for me and brought trays full of elegant small sandwiches of crabmeat and cream cheese and small lobster rolls. Mary-Leigh and Beverley had given me eight bottles of French champagne for my birthday so they were cooling in the refrigerator. It all could not have been easier, with Judy, Susan, Nancy, and Edythe helping in any way that was needed. I did feel rather shaky, so simply sat in a low chair in the library where people came and sat down by me to talk for a half hour or so and then play musical chairs. Many chose to stay on the terrace with its ravishing view that day down the green field and its tempting grassy, clipped walk to the very blue sea. It was such a casual, relaxed affair that I felt happy and at ease, and managed to have some real talk, especially with Duffy, who brought some of the photographs she has made to suggest the spirit of my work, which she calls "From May Sarton's Well." They are stunning. Martha Wheelock and I had a good exchange about *As We Are Now*, which her Ishtar Film Company is in the process of trying to sell to a TV or motion picture company. Joanne Woodward has agreed to play Caro. And Martha left me with a video she had made of a poetry reading of mine in Los

Angeles in April five years ago when I still had my voice.

I suppose that seeing the video with Susan at the end of the day was the most poignant happening of all. There were six hundred that night in the attentive audience in Los Angeles. They only burst into laughter now and then but were otherwise perfectly still. Five years ago I was not yet the rather bent-over old lady I have become since. It was terribly moving for me to think this performance will be there long after I am dead, for it is one of the best I have ever given. I had on the most beautiful dress I have ever had, and read a few of the poems as well as I ever have. It made me feel happy but also sad for it showed clearly what I have lost. When I showed it to Maggie, who came for the weekend, she agreed but added that in the reading at Westbrook, in spite of the damaged voice, there was a new "softness," gentleness. I am glad there could be some redeeming grace.

I HAVE been thinking about Eric Swenson all day. At seventy-four he is skippering his boat in the Bermuda race. I hope he has the right wind and that all goes well. He has taken that boat through some pretty angry seas and always survived. God be with him, best of editors, dear friend.

Wednesday, June 24

IT IS STRANGE to imagine that this may be the last entry in a journal by me. I shall miss very much what it does to make me aware of what is really happening, the novella I dream of starting as soon as this book goes off to Norton with the photographs, and all of it revised. It will be late August before I am ready, and shall I try to use the machine for that? Or settle once more for bumbling typing on my Olivetti? I shall have to try both ways.

People often think that I give myself away in these journals written for publication. They do not realize apparently that large areas of my life are never mentioned. I have never gone deeply into a love affair. For that important side of my life, intimate relationships, deep friendships, readers have to go to the novels, and not only *Mrs. Stevens*.

I heard two days ago that Barbara Hawthorne (Lady Hawthorne) had died. She was much in my mind when I was writing *A Reckoning*. In that novel about a woman dying of cancer, Laura's greatest wish is that her old friend, her "best friend," Ella, would come before she died, and in the book Ella did come. A mean woman reviewer in the *New York Times* accused me of fudging on what was (to her) clearly a lesbian relationship. But I think I might say categorically that one does not usually fall in love with the "best friend" who goes back to the fourth and fifth grade in school. The reviewer's view also suggests that the idea of a close friendship between two women is suspect. Nonsense!

There is something else I would like to clear up about a journal written for publication. More than once an opinion has been expressed that there is something suspect about it, that a journal must be private and written for the eyes of the writer alone. But poems are also highly personal, yet every good poet hopes a good poem will be published someday. A paradox? Perhaps. The journal written for publication is a genre in its own right. Great French writers have used it well. The Pléiade edition of André Gide's published journals is over one thousand pages. Both Julien Green and Mauriac kept journals and published them. And in England Frances Partridge, the most lovable of the Bloomsberries, did also. She has been a mentor for me for her unselfconscious natural style, which is more artful, I am sure, than it seems. Style in this kind of journal should never show off but rather do as Montaigne adjures us: "I want things to dominate, so filling the thoughts of the hearer that he does not even remember the words. I like the kind of speech which is simple and natural, the same on paper as on the lip; speech which is rich in matter, sinewy, brief and short."

Knowing my journals would be read has provided a certain discipline for me. It has forced me to try to be honest with myself and thus with my readers, not to pretend that things are better than they are, but learn to evaluate without self-pity or self-glorification what has been happening to me.

I write poems, have always written them, to transcend the painfully personal and reach the universal. I think possibly the poem, if it is a good one, may be like a goal, to which I try to climb, and reach if I *think* hard enough about what I have been *feeling*. "My poems teach me where I have to go," is a line from a famous poem of Theodore Roethke's. The journal tells me where I have been.

And where have I been in this journal? Through a thicket of ill health into an extraordinary time of happiness and fulfillment, more than I ever dreamed possible, and here it is. In my old age, the recognition I longed for, a rare kind of love shared with Susan, and even enough money to be able to give a lot away! But far more reason for happiness even than these, the sovereign reason is that I am writing a poem almost every day.

It is hard to say goodbye to journals and if I live to be eighty-five I might resume one for the joy of it. Meanwhile let me end with a poem by dear George Herbert, a poet of the early seventeenth century whom I have read and reread for the last forty years. Three stanzas from his poem, "The Flower":

Who would have thought my shrivel'd heart
Could have recover'd greenesse? It was gone
    Quite Under ground; as flowers depart
To see their mother-root, when they have blown;
        Where they together
        All the hard weather,
    Dead to the world, keep house unknown.

These are thy wonders, Lord of power,
Killing and quickning, bringing down to hell
    And up to heaven in an houre;
Making a chiming of a passing-bell.
        We say amisse,
        This or that is:
    Thy word is all, if we could spell.

And now in age I bud again,
After so many deaths I live and write;
    I once more smell the dew and rain,
And relish versing: O my onely light,
        It cannot be
        That I am he
    On whom thy tempests fell all night.